CRUELTY OR HUMANITY

CRUELTY OR HUMANITY

Challenges, Opportunities, Responsibilities

Stuart Rees

First published in Great Britain in 2020 by

Policy Press, an imprint of
Bristol University Press
University of Bristol
1-9 Old Park Hill
Bristol
BS2 8BB
UK
t: +44 (0)117 954 5940
e: bup-info@bristol.ac.uk

Details of international sales and distribution partners are available at
policy.bristoluniversitypress.co.uk

© Bristol University Press 2020

British Library Cataloguing in Publication Data
A catalogue record for this book is available from the British Library

ISBN 978-1-4473-5697-4 hardcover
ISBN 978-1-4473-5698-1 paperback
ISBN 978-1-4473-5448-2 ePub
ISBN 978-1-4473-5699-8 ePdf

Front cover design by Steve Harris and Alex Penny, who crafted the cover from the artistry of
sculptor Ben Hammond and photographer James Porto

Bristol University Press and Policy Press use environmentally responsible
print partners.

Printed in Great Britain by CMP, Poole

To those with the courage
to campaign for peace with justice,
for those who have never
experienced peace with justice.

Contents

List of poets and poems   ix
Acknowledgements   xi
Foreword by Richard Falk   xiv

Introduction: towards a theory   1

1   Perpetrators and victims   11

2   Values, attitudes, behaviour   23

3   Explaining causes   49

4   Cruelty as policy   81

5   Humanitarian alternatives   109

6   Cruel or compassionate world?   129

7   Humanity on a bonfire   151

8   Language for humanity   161

References   173
Select bibliography   197
Index   205

List of poets and poems

Mandelshtam, Osip	*The people need poetry*	1
Paz, Octavio	*Remembrance*	11
Akhtmatova, Anna	*Requiem*	15
Auden, W.H.	*Epitaph on a tyrant*	16
Fenton, James	*Tiananmen*	19
Rees, Stuart	*Thanks to Stéphane*	21
Johnson, Eva	*A letter to my mother*	25
Khlebnikov, Velimir	*Suppose I make a timepiece of humanity*	30
Darwish, Mahmoud	*Psalm*	33
Sabawi, Abdul	*Gaza sea and sky*	33
Hernández, Miguel	*Waltz poem of those in love and inseparable for ever*	37
Brecht, Bertolt	*When evil-doing comes like falling rain*	38
Brecht, Bertolt	*To those born later*	39
Vasefi, Saba	*Asylum*	44
Wordsworth, William	*Humanity*	49
Wright, Judith	*Two dreamtimes*	49
Éluard, Paul	*Dawn dissolves the monsters*	51
MacNeice, Louis	*Prayer before birth*	59
Neruda, Pablo	*The dictators*	74
Levertov, Denise	*Thai Binh (Peace) Province*	76
Levertov, Denise	*Weeping woman*	76
Owen, Wilfred	*Anthem for doomed youth*	81
Brecht, Bertolt	*Violence*	82
Nunucaal, Oodgeroo	*The protectors*	90
James, Clive	*Statement from The Secretary of Defense*	94
Rees, Stuart	*Tell me the truth about war*	100
Wordsworth, William	*Humanity*	110
Stafford, William	*Poetry*	111
Brecht, Bertolt	*The bread of the people*	111
Donne, John	*No man is an island*	112
Nunucaal, Oodgeroo	*All one race*	113
Angelou, Maya	*Human family*	113
Shelley, Percy Bysshe	*The mask of anarchy*	115
Waters, Roger	*Each small candle*	116
Seeger, Pete	*If I had a hammer*	117
Murray, Les	*Equanimity*	120
Stafford, William	*You reading this stop*	120
Krieger, David	*True to himself*	124

Rendra, Willibrordus	*I write this pamphlet*	125
Rees, Stuart	*The empty chair*	126
Wright, Judith	*The flame tree*	127
Milosz, Czeslaw	*This world*	128
Yeats, W.B.	*To a friend whose work has come to nothing*	144
Yeats, W.B.	*Meditations in a time of civil war*	144
Angelou, Maya	*A brave and startling truth*	145
Sabawi, Samah	*Cultivating hope*	145
Levertov, Denise	*What it could be*	147
Levertov, Denise	*About political action*	148
Levi, Primo	*Almanac*	151
Yeats, W.B.	*The second coming*	163
Darwish, Mahmoud	*If we want to*	164
Lichtenstein, Alfred	*Prophecy*	171
Auden, W.H.	*September 1, 1939*	172
Rees, Stuart	*Ninety plus campaigner*	172

Acknowledgements

Motives to start this book came from several sources. I needed to react to states' cruelties and to their disregard for human rights. Accounts of cruelties were difficult to ignore. Conversations with friends who championed human rights gave clues to pursue. Richard Hil, Jennifer Granger, Cathy Peters, Peter Slezak, Hannah Middleton, Dennis Doherty, Juliet Bennett, Mary Kostakidis, Karen Collier, Erik Paul, Frank Stilwell, Peggy Craddock and Evan Jones might be surprised that their coffee-time conversations contributed to this book. May such face-to-face exchanges continue.

Invaluable commentary on early drafts confirmed the direction of a journey and identified ideas and evidence that I needed to collect. Insightful academic colleagues Ken Macnab, Joe Camilleri and Jim Ife were selfless in reading completed drafts. I benefitted from their ideas and encouragement. Alec Pemberton and Adam Courtenay gave generous feedback on early chapters.

It is appropriate to acknowledge the referees whom my publishers asked to evaluate the book proposal and manuscript. Former Professor of Peace Studies at Coventry University Andrew Rigby, and Richard Falk, Professor of International Law at Princeton and the University of California, Santa Barbara, gave positive evaluations of the timing, relevance and content of the proposed book. I owe a particular debt to Richard. A highly regarded jurist, wonderful international citizen and amazingly busy person, he nevertheless responds quickly to ideas and requests and does so with a generosity which underlines a key dimension of humanity.

Characteristic patience and support from Ragnhild has as usual been indispensable, even though, at the beginning, she commented, 'You're not going to write another book are you?' Ragnhild nevertheless knew the significance of this project. On the vexed problem of my limited understanding of computers, my eldest granddaughter, Isabella Celata, has been the always available, skilful, humorous problem solver. I have benefitted from the consistent support and research inquiries of Susan Moy and am also very grateful to my generous, research-experienced and literary astute friend Alison Wallace, who proof-read the final manuscript.

The cover of this book was crafted by a distinguished artist, Steve Harris, and a skilled website designer, Alex Penny. They worked from the *Son of Odin* image given by the brilliant sculptor Ben Hammond and from the *Phoenix Rising* image provided by the international photographer James Porto. I acknowledge their skills and generosity.

Obtaining permission to quote lines from poetry and from songs has been the final trek on this journey. Lines from *If I Had A Hammer*, words and music by Peter Seeger and Lee Hays, are used by permission of Ludlow Music, Inc./Essex Music Australia Pty. Ltd. Roger Waters, singer-songwriter and campaigner for justice, was generous and unhesitating in agreeing to my request to quote lines from his songs. The poets David Krieger, Saba Vasefi and Samah Sabawi were enthusiastic about my using examples of their work. Samah also spoke on behalf of her father, the significant Palestinian poet Abdul Sabawi.

The publishers New Directions agreed to my quoting lines from Denise Levertov poems, *Thai Binh (Peace) Province*, *Weeping Woman*, *What It Could Be* and *Political Action*. David Higham Associates agreed to my quoting lines from *Prayer Before Birth* from a Louis MacNeice anthology. Fred Courtwright from Confluence Press gave permission to quote from William Stafford poems, *Poetry* and *You Reading this Stop*. Lyn Coffin gave copyright permission to use Anna Akhmatova's *Requiem* and Emma Raddatz from Archipelago publishers gave permission to quote lines from Mahmoud Darwish, including *A River Dies of Thirst*. Lines from Les Murray's *Equanimity* are reproduced by permission of the Estate of Les Murray, c/o Margaret Connolly & Associates Pty Ltd and from Carcanet Press. *Epitaph on a Tyrant*, copyright renewed 1968, by W.H. Auden from *Collected Poems by W.H. Auden*, edited by Edward Mendelson, is used by permission of Random House, an imprint and division of Penguin Random House LLC. *September 1 1939*, copyright renewed 1968, from *Selected Poems by W.H. Auden* is used by permission of Vintage Books, an imprint of Knopf Doubleday Publishing Group, a division of Penguin Random House LLC. *A Brave and Startling Truth* from *A Brave and Startling Truth* by Maya Angelou, copyright©1995 by Maya Angelou is used by permission of Random House, an imprint and division of Penguin Random House LLC. *Human Family* from *I Shall Not Be Moved* by Maya Angelou, copyright©1990 by Maya Angelou is used by permission of Random House, an imprint and division of Penguin Random House LLC. Petrina Walker, beneficiary of the literary estate of Kath Walker, granted permission to republish excerpts from *All One Race* and *The Protectors*, each poem credited to Oodgeroo Nunucaal. Monica Tavazzani, from Garzanti, represented authorization for Primo Levi's works and gave permission to quote from that poet's *Almanac*. Harper Collins Publishers Australia Pty Ltd gave permission to quote lines from Judith Wright's *Two Dreamtimes* and *The Flame Tree*, taken from Judith Wright's *Collected Poems*.

Under the 'fair usage' criteria, Seren Adams from United Agents supported my quoting from James Fenton's poem *Tiananmen*. Bertolt Brecht Heirs, publishers Suhrkamp Verlag, granted permission to quote from Brecht's *When Evil-Doing Comes Like Falling Rain*, *Violence*, *To Those Born Later* and *The Bread of the People*. Carcanet Press of Manchester did the same with extracts from an anthology by Octavio Paz. Professor Harry Aveling, translator of poems by Willibrordus Rendra, gave permission to quote from his work. The Rights Executive of Pan Macmillan agreed to my quoting lines from Clive James' *Statement from the Secretary of Defense*. Robert Bly, translator of Pablo Neruda's poems for Beacon Press, granted permission to use lines from Neruda's *The Dictators*.

Throughout the crafting of the manuscript, I have benefitted from the interest, advice and support of all the editorial and publicity staff at Bristol University Press. I am grateful for their professionalism: their constructive observations, their responses coming usually by return and with enthusiasm.

I have undertaken to obtain permission to use copyright material reproduced in this book. Information from copyright holders that will enable me to rectify any error or omission would be welcomed. The sources of all poems and songs are given in chapter references listed at the end of the book.

Stuart Rees
Hyams Beach, NSW, Australia

Foreword

We are living in an anguishing historical period. From one direction come dire warnings about humans' future if the challenges posed by climate change and ecological instability are not addressed within a rather tiny window of less than twelve years. From another direction come depressing indications that peoples around the world are choosing by their own free will, extremist autocrats, even demagogues, who are extinguishing fires of freedom, building walls to keep the unwanted out and stigmatizing the stranger. In such an atmosphere, human rights are in retreat, empathy for the suffering of others is repudiated, international law is all but forgotten in the annals of diplomacy and the United Nations is often reduced to the bickering of irresponsible governments seeking nothing grander than maximum national advantage, and in the process, let the common public good of humanity be damned. Facing such reality with eyes wide open is a challenge that few acknowledge, and even fewer have the stamina, insight, compassion, wisdom and imagination needed to discern a brighter alternative future for humanity.

Stuart Rees is such an exception. His *Cruelty or Humanity* has the courage to portray reality in all its degrading ugliness without taking refuge in some specious bromide. His book addresses the range of cruelties that befall those most vulnerable among us in myriad specific circumstances. With an astonishing command over the global and historical landscapes of cruelty, Rees leads us through the wilderness of the most evil happenings, which have been enacted individually and collectively. And yet, through it all he manages to guide us toward the light of hope without indulging sentimentality or embracing false optimism.

What gives this perilous journey its defining originality is the degree to which Rees brings to bear the knowledge and timeless wisdom of poets both to depict the intensities of the darkness but also to instruct readers that the disciplined and lyrical insight of a poet can better than the rest of us find shafts of light that illuminate paths leading to empowerment, transcendence and liberation. Rees has actually written two parallel interacting texts, brought together in a single, fully coherent book: on one side, a fearless and comprehensive reportage of the facts and figures of human cruelty in many distinct settings of place and circumstance, stressing the plight of those most victimized, ranging from asylum seekers to Indigenous peoples tortured in their homelands and extending to the horrifying torments endured by animals and a variety of thoughtless encroachments on our natural surroundings; on the other side, this depressing litany of cruelties inflicted on masses of people is simultaneously refracted through prisms of light offered by a multitude of poets who share the agony while intoning the most vital truth of all, that hope is not futile, that human society has dreams, aspirations and untested anthropological potentialities. Rees shares with readers extracts from dozens of world-famous and relatively unknown poets, in this parallel form of narrative that interacts with the gory reportage of cruelty to offer a creative tension between entrenched evil and its transcendence.

Rees's undisguised autobiographical engagement with this inquiry gives *Cruelty or Humanity* a quality of urgency and sincerity that it would not possess if confined to the scholarly canons of ethical and political detachment. The fact that Rees cares so deeply about choosing humanity over cruelty is evident on almost every page. He conveys his concerns without ever diluting the profound difficulties of overcoming the evil being done by humans, mainly men, to others stigmatized and rendered inferior, punitively instrumentalized to serve ambitions, manipulate fears and satisfy sadistic urges of those in power.

In personalizing his immersion in this difficult subject matter Rees's residence in Australia becomes evident in the manner that he treats the severe cruelties over centuries inflicted on the original natives of the land, and currently reproduced in the manner that Australian asylum-seekers have been sequestered in an isolated island and often driven to suicidal desperation, a horror show that is mostly hidden from the world, but shocking when disclosed in all its ferocity. It casts doubt on the ritualized apologies that some liberal Australian politicians offer to the aboriginal people and their forebears for past wrongdoing. The cruelties of Israel toward the Palestinian people receive deserved attention from Rees, as a leader of Palestinian solidarity efforts in Australia, in depicting the cartography of cruelty.

Rees advances a strong case for the positive side of the human condition, resting on the rock of shared humanity. He quotes these arresting lines from Maya Angelou, which really captures the essence of his ethical message:

> In minor ways we differ
> In major ways we're the same.

The political implication of this affirmation is a strong embrace of the spirit and substance of equality, which implies a rejection of hierarchy, as well as making positive use of the interplay between the unity of humanity and the many differences evident in the way individuals and communities choose to live. Another poet, William Stafford, is quoted approvingly in words intended to repudiate hierarchy and its companion, stigmatization of 'the other' deemed inferior:

I can't eat that bread.

In the end, Rees manages to nurture hope, which he rests on what might be best identified as 'the transformation-to-come'. This radical departure from the present will be recognizable only when political leaders begin to articulate their programmes and policies in what Rees calls 'the language of common humanity'. Of course, a humanistic worldview naturally follows such a linguistic trope. It draws its normative direction from existing traditions of international human rights, international law and a rising respect for nature. Whether such an axial moment, if and when it comes, can be operationalized in the form of humane patterns of governance will be the ultimate test of whether equality can become a way of life for the human species as well as an uplifting slogan.

In the end, we should be thankful to Stuart Rees for providing us with such an inspiring reading experience, which contains within it a roadmap that could help humanity escape from the species' eco-ethical slide toward extinction. This will happen only if enough of us are sufficiently responsive to Rees's damning diagnosis of the present and then heed his liberating prescriptions for the future.

Richard Falk
Santa Barbara, California

Introduction: towards a theory

The people need poetry that will be their own secret
To keep then awake forever
And bathe them in the bright-haired wave of its breathing.[1]
Osip Mandelshtam

Mankind cannot live by logic alone but also needs poetry.[2]
Mahatma Gandhi

In commentators' evaluations of social and foreign policies, cruelty as an intended, or as an unanticipated consequence of policies, has received little attention. In policy appraisals, the notion 'cruelty' seldom appears, not even in an index, and has not been acknowledged to be a purpose of policies even if the cruel consequences have been obvious. It was as though an alleged rational process should be cleansed of any consideration of irrational actions such as causing serious harm to citizens or to animals.

The absence of regular commentary on the business of inflicting cruelty prompts this book's aim, to show cruelty in the play of politics, in the design and implementation of state policies and in non-state responses. If truths about worldwide cruelties become evident, the elimination of such practices should become a key consideration in any future crafting of policies and in the advocacy of values which influence political cultures. Advocacy of humanitarian alternatives to cruelty would depend on the spirit of universal human rights, challenges to oppressive uses of power and the promotion of policies to address social and economic inequalities.

The behaviour of nation-states, their governments, institutions and the cohorts of politicians, public servants and media acolytes who contribute to cruelty needs to be exposed. Identifying the cruelties of citizens who act as individuals, or as loyal members of well-organized groups, prompts questions: do they look in a mirror, do they pretend all is well, nothing unusual has happened?

Cruelty refers to a wanton and unnecessary infliction of suffering on body and mind. The adjective 'wanton' describes conduct without regard to what is right, just or humane. That could include discrimination, torture or murder by individuals or by a state, as in the mass famine in China from 1956 to 1976 (the Great Leap Forward) which killed tens of millions of people.

In Western parlance, cruelty also warrants definitions according to specific contexts. In marriage relationships, cruelty includes mental and physical harm occurring over a period of time. Cruelty to children encompasses physical and mental battering and abuse. Regarding responsibilities for animals, it includes the infliction of physical and mental pain or death.

Distinctions need to be made. One cruelty should be distinguished from another. An act of torture would be particularly conscious. With abiding poverty, it may be unconscious. Subsequent analysis in Chapter 4 addresses this continuum, from direct to indirect, and from conscious to possibly unconscious acts. Along that continuum persist cruel policies which may be deliberate, or conducted by enabling the acts of others. Cruel policies may be carried out by deception, or could involve collusion with cruel allies.

Cruel acts and policies are worldwide, though the United Nations has set prohibitions on cruelty which represent global standards. Article 5 of the 1948 UN *Declaration of Universal Human Rights* says, 'No-one shall be subjected to torture or to cruel, inhuman or degrading treatment or punishment.'

Article 3 of the 1953 *European Convention on Human Rights* prohibits 'inhuman or degrading treatment or punishment'. The European Court of Human Rights holds that this provision forbids the extradition of a person to a foreign state if they are likely to be subjected to torture, which has been interpreted as referring to the death penalty.

In the International Covenant on Civil and Political Rights, adopted by the UN General Assembly in December 1966, Article Seven says, 'No-one shall be subjected to cruel, inhuman or degrading treatment or punishment. In particular, no-one shall be subjected without his free consent to medical or scientific experimentation.' Article Eight says, 'No-one shall be held in slavery; slavery and the slave trade in all their forms shall be prohibited.'

The UN's Convention against Torture and other Cruel, Inhuman or Degrading Treatment or Punishment was passed by the General Assembly in December 1984 and came into force in June 1987.

The Convention on the Rights of the Child was ratified by the UN General Assembly on 20 November 1989. Article Three of that Convention states, 'In all actions concerning children, whether undertaken by public or private social welfare institutions, courts of law or legislative bodies, the best interest of the child shall be a primary consideration.' Article Six says, 'States Parties recognize that every child has the inherent right to life.'

These charters, covenants and conventions have provided standards of human decency to which most of the world's nations said they would adhere. Through the machinations of politics, by badly crafted, thoughtless policies, or in atrocities committed by those who oppose states and their institutions, these significant UN aspirations and rules are being derided, or ignored. Like a malignant disease, cruelties persist, even though anyone with a belief in the importance of human rights and the rule of law could recognize and oppose them.

I scanned records of familiar cruelties, of discriminatory and brutal responses to Indigenous people, asylum seekers and refugees. I felt confronted by the inhumanities, swamped by records of human rights abuses from several continents, by news of the latest ethnic cleansing, of torture and killings so routinely explained and so automatically justified.

My research addressed questions, how to gain insight into cruelties, how to portray human dimensions without departing from the formal responsibility to marshal and record diverse sources of information. Overwhelming evidence of atrocities to human beings, to animals, plus disregard for a precious environment, posed the conundrum: how to handle feelings of dismay and disbelief?

In response to that last question, poetry provides ideas and insights. Extracts from poems illuminate those insights which can remain elusive in prose. The English poet Shelley said that poets were the unacknowledged legislators of the world. He implied that lessons could be learned from poetry which unmasked the past, undressed the present and forecast a more socially just future. Images and messages in poetry contribute vision and understanding. Without the insights, irony and softness of poetry, accounts of cruelty could seem relentlessly macabre.

With the help of poets, this book appeals for truths to be told about governments' oppressive ways to implement domestic and foreign policies, and extremist groups' ways to wreak vengeance on people they deride or hate.

The cruelty as policy question began with random examples of cruelty practised by any state, any group or individual. Learning came with exploration which revealed ideas about the motives for cruelty, the political, cultural and psychological forces which influenced those motives. As that delving came to an end, though such head-scratching reflections never really end, clarity emerged, but with a caution: don't expect a psychological treatise. The psychological dimension exists, but is wrapped in the contexts of other forces. Addressing the causes question coincided with clues as to the ways in which foreign and domestic policies have been formed and fuelled by cruelty. Advocating humanitarian alternatives is a work in progress for every writer and reader, for every social scientist and journalist, every student, bureaucrat and politician. That part of this book was the easiest to write because it was moved by an educational, political and moral imperative: without humanitarian alternatives, we are all lost.

The value of theory

Understanding cruelty can be made easier by theory about patterns which persist irrespective of differences between countries and cultures. Such theorizing confronts possible criticism of detail, 'There are so many examples, we can't distinguish one from another', or, more specifically, 'How is one individual incident of cruelty linked to extreme events such as state torture, murderous wars and genocide?'

A brief theoretical guide addresses those questions and begins by highlighting two concepts. The first concerns a state, its actions, responsibility and accountability. State includes government, whether democracy or dictatorship, elected coalition or one-party rule. It includes state organizations: religious agencies, educational institutions, non-governmental organizations (NGOs), corporations subsidized by governments, militant groups which claim official authority, even individuals who wear uniforms, such as security personnel, or who may operate in plain clothes.

Reference to culture gives the second clue. An assembly of beliefs, rules about male/female conduct, plus time-honoured means of discrimination contribute to cultures. Beneath the visible, tourist-popular features of cultures lie values about order, normality, rewards, punishments and the exercise of power.

As insightful observers on the effects of cultures on life chances, poets have warned of harmful effects. Irish poet Louis MacNeice pleaded, 'I am not yet born, O fill me with strength against those who would freeze my humanity, would dragoon me into a lethal automaton'.[3] The national poet of Palestine, Mahmoud Darwish, wrote, 'We travel like other people, but we return to nowhere. As if travelling is the way of the clouds'.[4] The English poet Housman protested the persecution of anyone who might be considered abnormal, 'The laws of God, the laws of man, He may keep that will and can, Not I: let God and man decree Laws for themselves and not for me'.[5]

A first step in theorizing concerns the common ground between degrees of cruelty. A continuum stretches from modest cruelty (if that's not an oxymoron) to what might be termed middle-range offensive acts, to easily recognized extreme cruelty. In spite of apparent differences, each act derives from values operating within a state. Here is the thin-end-of-the-wedge argument. Bullying by individuals at home, in a playground or workplace has ripple effects and reappears in national policies and in the conduct of international relations. In every context, cruel acts are influenced by a concern with order and control, with disparagement and punishment.

Another pattern emerges. Slides of cruelty examined through a microscope show signs of superiority and inferiority. A need to maintain the superiority of one group at the expense of another looks like the catalyst for cruelty. Embedded in state rules and cultural beliefs, assumptions about superiority give an entitlement to act against the supposed inferior beings, human or animal. The functionaries who represent states and cultures can assume permission to be cruel. The Myanmar military expel and murder the Rohingya. In response to a powerless woman's alleged blasphemy, Pakistani mobs howl for blood. Indigenous people in the Americas and in Australia can be eliminated by supposed superior races.

Not just by murder and mayhem, dominant people have been desperate to assert their superiority. Aboriginal children removed from their parents, the babies of unmarried mothers transferred to adoptive parents, asylum seekers detained indefinitely irrespective of the rules of international law, fences and walls built and guards employed to maintain border controls and keep inferior people out.

Policies which maintain inequality appear as a corollary of assumptions about superiority. Unequal opportunities are bolstered by state powers and by beliefs nourished by ethnic traditions and by carefully maintained religious customs. Machiavelli taught that inequality helped to sustain order, that cruelty to someone regarded as an equal never happened. Victims of cruelty are the unequals, Dalits victimized by upper castes, Afro-Americans by white superiors, Roma people by powerful states, people living with disabilities by those considered 'normal', refugees of every colour and creed by operatives who do not want them. Such inequalities are sustained by a top-down exercise of power which is often violent and from the perspectives of victims, almost always cruel.

Inequalities may continue without evidence of cruelty. Experience of inequality is not a cruelty in itself. It is the persistent experience of social, economic and other status-bound inequalities which creates vulnerability to cruelty, directly and indirectly.

In policy circles, efforts to maintain inequalities are clouded in claims about efficiency. It is inefficient to reward people who do not work hard, even if job opportunities do not exist. It hardly matters if the victims of such policies are hungry, poor or homeless. An efficient system has to be maintained and cruelty never acknowledged.

The economist J.K. Galbraith argued that free-market economic policies could be explained more by morality than economy. Efforts to achieve efficient productivity and vigorous economic growth were state priorities and should be pursued irrespective of cruel consequences. As part of their ideology, 'you deserve what you get and get what you deserve', political elites, such as members of the Republican Party in the US, punish the poor by denying them resources yet also claim that such polices would save people by motivating them to work harder. Inequality begets further inequality. Conspicuously wealthy people urge the character-building value of abolishing public services and instead claim that policies of deregulation and privatization will help the poor. Galbraith judged that one of man's oldest exercises in moral philosophy was the search for superior moral justification for selfishness.

Governments' and state institutions' concern to be efficient derives partly from 'economic' concerns, as in charges about cost-effectiveness, about not wasting taxpayers' money, protecting individual and corporate interests. Advocacy of efficiency is also evident in moralizing by religious powers which want vicious punishments for alleged abnormal sexual behaviour. In personal relations and in international affairs a status quo is protected, and to defeat supposed enemies, efficient yet horrendous military goals are permitted, as in the obliteration of Dresden, Hiroshima, Nagasaki and, more recently, the Iraqi city of Fallujah.[6] Efficiency becomes taken for granted, uses violence whatever the human cost and not just in military operations.

Geological strata of cruelties reveal prominent layers, superiority, inequality and efficiency. Fear also appears. A commander takes the Machiavelli cues that engendering fear, not seeking love, is the way to rule, a lesson followed by African and South American dictators, President Duterte in the Philippines, Hun Sen in Cambodia and by Prince Mohammad Bin Salman of Saudi Arabia. Fear is also experienced by inferiors who expect admonishment or punishment if they do not comply with the orders of a perceived superior, a theme explored so significantly by Stanley Milgram.[7] In both instances, concern with morality has been jettisoned and the fear inherent in experiences of authoritarianism usually ensures compliance.

Another layer appears to be present in each of the others. It is difficult to see. Called concealment, it refers to lying and denial that a cruel act occurred, or if it did it was someone else's responsibility. Bureaucratic formalities, supposedly conducted for public interest, are invisible, the decision makers unknown and the rationale for their decisions seldom tested.

From victims' perspectives, the concealment of cruelties may be exposed only when a Truth Commission investigates or when state leaders offer official apologies, albeit decades after the hurtful actions had occurred.

Somewhat ironically, an understanding of humanity derives from observing cruelty, and provides the rationale for 'humanitarian alternatives', the second half of this book. The philosopher of the French Renaissance, Michel de Montaigne, said 'The horror of cruelty impels me more to clemency than any model of clemency could draw me on', and when opposing state and religious justification of cruelty he insisted there were no naturally inferior or superior people.[8] He might have said that goals of justice and humanity derive from the realization of the interdependence of peoples and of all living things. That thesis ranges from a 16th-century English poet who envisioned that no man is an island to current environmentalists advocating the importance of preserving a unique and precious planet.

That brief theorizing is introduced to help navigate the evidence in the following chapters.

Outline and themes

Chapter 1, 'Perpetrators and victims', lists individual cases of cruelty which illustrate the character of perpetrators, whether governments, state institutions or individuals, and the awfulness experienced by the victims. Speculation whether one form of cruelty is worse than another, whether state-sanctioned brutalities should be taken more seriously than violence perpetrated by the representatives of institutions or by extremist religious and political groups, is avoided.

Chapter 2, 'Values, attitudes and behaviour', identifies the social, religious, political, economic and cultural forces which facilitate cruelties. In those accounts, the platitude 'it's part of human nature' is not helpful. Even where notorious killers and torturers could be identified, the moral and cultural contexts of their acts require an examination, which includes cruelty to animals and violence to the environment. The evils of violent cultures, such as the security politics of Israel, Iran's authoritarian theocracy, America's love of imprisonment and entrenched discrimination in the Indian caste system, will also be discussed.

Chapter 3, 'Explaining cruelty', addresses causes. It covers a continuum of explanations from the banality of evil to automaton-like behaviour in bureaucracies, from pleasures derived from sadism to the cruelties fostered by selfishness. There's also a postscript about cruelty driven by managerial demands for efficiency, a powerfully addictive notion which is not value neutral.

Chapter 4, 'Cruelty as policy', moves from cruelty as a *deliberate* motive to situations where it looks as though the architects of policies *enabled* cruelties to take place but did not direct them. Then come the *denials* and *deception*: who could possibly think that countries such as the US, Russia, Israel, Syria, Saudi Arabia, Indonesia, Iran or Myanmar would indulge in human rights abuses such as collective punishments, ethnic cleansing, floggings, torture, arbitrary imprisonment, targeted killings and executions? Finally, there's *collusion*. Alliances are made with countries which commit cruelties but their allies behave as though this is nothing to do with them. When the US ignores Israeli cruelty to Palestinian children, that's *collusion*. The European Union (EU) and the UN may also collude by silence which encourages perpetrators.

An impression may have been given that the story of cruelty concerns only direct violence, as in torture, bombings, executions and other acts of war. That would be a wrong conclusion. Cruelty is also promoted by policies which promote inequality and maintain poverty.

Chapter 5, 'Humanitarian alternatives', explores the opposite to cruelties, as in diverse forms of advocacy for a common humanity through literacy about non-violence and for the health-promoting values of creative, non-destructive uses of power. In commentary about the vision required to build an economy not based on inequalities and injustices, the place of technology, whether it is help or hindrance, is also assessed.

Chapter 6, 'Cruel or compassionate world?' highlights the responsibilities of corporations and the cruelty involved in the threat and possible use of nuclear weapons. A final drumroll for humanity returns to the need to recover respect for human rights, for humanitarian law and for the ideals written into the UN Charter.

Chapter 7, 'Humanity on a bonfire', argues that in analyses of cruelty, if the rules and niceties of social commentary and academic rigour are removed, the chequered picture of subtle and not-so-subtle differences in cruelty is lost. Instead there emerges a stark, almost universal picture of human rights being derided and any respect for a common humanity thrown on a bonfire, literally in some cases. That trend shows the danger of not paying serious attention to cruelty as policy.

Chapter 8, 'A language for humanity', carries a final message. Seizing the opportunities to remove cruelties depends on enthusiasm for a revived democratic politics, plus facility in language to reinterpret human rights, advocate UN peace-keeping responsibilities and promote the principles of humane governance.

Perpetrators and victims

The men in power are convinced that it is only violence that moves and guides men, and they do so boldly use violence for the maintenance of the present order of things. But the existing order is not maintained through violence but through public opinion, the effect of which is impaired by violence. Thus, the activity of violence weakens and impairs precisely what it intends to maintain. (Leo Tolstoy)[1]

> *This century is possessed*
> *In its forehead, nail and sign,*
> *A fixed idea burns: each day it serves us*
> *The same platter of blood.*
> *On some corner he waits*
> *– Pious, omniscient, and armed –*
> *The dogmatist with no face, no name.*
>
> (Octavio Paz)[2]

A malignancy

Joy Gardner was born in 1963 in Jamaica to a 15-year-old mother. She never knew her father. When she was seven, her mother moved to the UK to work. Joy would not follow her mother until 1987, by which time she had a grown-up daughter of her own and was pregnant with her son. She had the boy, Graham, while in Britain and sought leave to remain to be with her mother but was refused. Although her mother was British, rule changes meant her adult offspring had no right to remain. A team of police and immigration officers arrived at her north London home on 28 July 1993 with instructions to deport her and her son to Jamaica. She was bound, gagged and restrained with a body belt. She collapsed, fell into a coma and died of asphyxiation.[3]

In October 2005, Otto Ondawame from West Papua knocked on my office door. He was on the run from the Indonesian army's special forces unit Kopassus. Otto had protested the 1969 'Act of Free Choice' when 1,026 West Papuans were held at gunpoint and ordered to vote for integration with Indonesia.[4] Ondawame had committed a serious crime by raising the flag of his country and in 2001 had protested when the West Papuan leader Theys Eluay was found with his throat cut. Together with colleagues, I protected Otto during his years of exile and study in Australia. The Australian Department of Immigration eventually deported him to Vanuatu, where he died in 2014.

Around the globe, cruelty seems endemic. In common with others the sadism of Saudi Arabia's rulers astounded me when, in 2012, their courts sentenced Raif Badawi, a brave blogger for free speech, to 1,000 lashes and 10 years in jail. In October 2018, in the Saudi Arabian Embassy in Istanbul, a 15-member Saudi hit team allegedly strangled the Saudi/American journalist Jamal Khashoggi, dismembered his body and disposed of it. Khashoggi's columns for the *Washington Post* had been critical of human rights abuses in Saudi Arabia.[5]

On 27 August 2017 in Gaza City, 53-year-old Howayda lay on a sofa in extreme pain. The medication to relieve her suffering was not available. She lived in a city which had been under siege for 10 years, where clean water was in short supply, electricity only available for two hours per day. On 7 September the mother of five died. Her eldest daughter, Sameeha, told me, 'I am at comfort that my mother is no longer in pain and that she won't be stopped at a checkpoint or won't be asked for permits anymore.'

For over four years, from 2013 to 2017, the Australian government contained 1,500 asylum seekers, men, women and children, in detention centres on remote Nauru and Manus Island in Papua New Guinea. They were kept there at immense humanitarian cost.[6] Against the rules of international law, left with no hope of freedom, in the short term the asylum seekers were offered the choice of accepting their fate or returning to the countries from which they had fled.

By February 2018, 700,000 Rohingya people had been driven from their homes in Myanmar in a military operation which the UN described as textbook ethnic cleansing. On muddy, almost treeless hillsides, with little shelter, neither ample food nor clean water, the newly arrived refugees found temporary refuge in Bangladesh.

In October 2017, a young Rohingya refugee fleeing Myanmar told a *New York Times* journalist, Jeffrey Gettleman, that after she was raped by government soldiers, her baby son was snatched from her arms and thrown screaming into a fire, burning to his death. Gettleman recorded that other eyewitnesses confirmed what happened.[7]

Between 5 May and 9 June 2018, US Customs and Immigration officials stationed at the US Mexican border separated over 2,300 children from parents who had been arrested for alleged illegal entry into the US. Mostly from Guatemala, Honduras and El Salvador, the children were sent to one of more than 100 US government-contracted detention facilities spread over 17 states. Pictures of bewildered, traumatized children torn from their parents, and statements from families saying they had no idea where their children were, provoked public outrage at President Trump's 'zero tolerance' policies. The President insisted that he was protecting Americans from undocumented migrants whom Democrats wanted 'to pour into and infest our country'. Pope Francis said the order to separate children from parents was immoral. Confronted by overwhelming opposition, even from previously supportive Republicans, on 20 June the President reversed the order.

Acts of gratuitous cruelty by individuals may not appear to be in the same league as the abuses just described, but even passing cruelties merit attention. They can be the thin end of a wedge. One act becomes a potential habit, subsequently justified.

In September 2014, Australian Prime Minister Julia Gillard's father died. During her prime ministership Gillard had been derided by an influential radio journalist, Alan Jones. The broadcaster seldom missed an opportunity to ridicule Gillard, her gender and her policies. He said she was a liar, that it would be beneficial if she was dumped at sea in a chaff bag. On the death of Gillard's father, Jones commented, 'the old man died of shame'.

In April 2017, 1,200 Palestinian prisoners in Israeli jails began a hunger strike to protest degrading conditions and to seek an easing of restrictions on visiting rights. Soon after the strike began, Israeli settlers set up barbeques outside the jail. They aimed to ridicule the prisoners. Reporters said that the settlers wanted the smell of meat to waft into the prison.

In each of these events, in the first seven examples and the last two, individuals lived in contexts of discrimination and violence. Political forces, government policies and cultural influences prepared the stage and built the contexts. For example, behind successive British governments' image of adherence to due process in the administration of justice, conduct hidden from public view now reveals powerless people treated cruelly.

In relation to the plight of Indigenous West Papuans, influential politicians in Britain and Indonesia had promoted the idea that such people were primitive and did not deserve to be independent.

Gaza under siege imprisons almost two million people. Howayda's painful death is one example of a policy of denying basic healthcare to stigmatized people.

Under the guise of a policy called border protection, Australian governments had for years stifled the rights of asylum seekers who had attempted to escape to Australia by boat.

By the end of 2017, reports continued of atrocities committed by Myanmar forces against Rohingya refugees.

In Saudi Arabia's response to dissidents, vicious punishments are an apparent cultural and policy norm.

Policies influenced and reinforced by cultural norms are not confined to Saudi Arabia. That country's close ally, the 'make America great again' Trump White House, had US culture in mind when the President boasted about sovereignty, protecting borders and showing zero tolerance to the unwanted and vulnerable. In the Mexican border controversy, many of the victims were toddlers, small children and teenagers.

In relation to the two incidents of cruelty by individuals, cultures which encouraged stigmatizing had sent a message: the stage is set, if you have a grievance against those you don't like or even hate, now's your chance, play your roles, act out your script. A Sydney radio station had fed listeners a diet of derision, yet still obtained popular ratings. In response to Israel's oppression of Palestinians, the international community had refused to oppose decades of serious human rights abuses.

Twentieth-century genocides and mass murders

A reminder about the mass murders of the 20th century, several of which are counted as genocides, illustrates precedents to current cruelties. Despite the 'never again' motives of those who crafted the Charter of the United Nations, the Universal Declaration of Human Rights and the small print of the Geneva Conventions, those genocides gave momentum to cruelty which has not been easy to stop.

Between the Northern spring of 1915 and the autumn of 1916, with a view to solidifying Muslim dominance, Ottoman-Turkish authorities, including military forces and civilians, engaged in mass shootings and mass deportations of ethnic Christian Armenians. Survivors of the shootings, elderly men, women and children, were marched in convoys to holding camps, but on the way hundreds of thousands died as a result of dehydration, exposure, disease and attacks from local officials, nomadic and criminal gangs. The violence included robbery, rape, abduction of young women and girls, extortion, torture and murder. As many as 1.2 million people died.[8] The US Ambassador, Henry Morgenthau Snr, wrote in his memoirs, 'When the Turkish authorities gave the orders for these deportations, they were merely giving the death warrant to a whole race, they understood this well.'[9]

Between 1932 and 1933, Russian dictator Joseph Stalin's forced famines are calculated to have killed over seven million Ukrainians.

In the late 1930s, during the time of The Terror, Stalin ordered the mass execution of millions of his own citizens whom he considered 'socially harmful elements' and 'enemies of the people'.

In relation to that terror, in her poem *Requiem*, crafted over three decades, 1935–61, the Russian poet Anna Akhmatova wrote,

> *No, it wasn't under a foreign heaven,*
> *It wasn't under the wing of a foreign power, –*
> *I was there among my countrymen*
> *I was where my people, unfortunately, were.*[10]

In the years immediately preceding the Second World War and despite a 1925 Geneva protocol banning 'bacteriological methods of warfare', the US and Japan generously funded the scientific investigation of the possibilities of biological warfare. Such investigations soon realized not just a potential weapon but a lethal form of cruelty. Michael Pembroke reports that by the end of the Korean war, in one secret biological warfare site the US employed over 3,800 personnel. Another classified site was nicknamed 'Fort Doom'.[11] But it was Japanese enthusiasm for biological weapons that showed sadism without limits, a promotion of evils which probably surpassed in cruelty even Joseph Mengele's experiments in Auschwitz. In Manchuria, a Japanese unit called 731 developed macabre trials to expose human beings, mostly Chinese prisoners, to lethal bacteria. Pembroke's analysis merits rereading and repeating. In one of his most disturbing passages he writes, 'The process was unfathomable – a phantasmagorical nightmare in which Japanese medical scientists infected helpless prisoners with anthrax, plague, cholera, typhus, dysentery, botulism, brucellosis, tularaemia, meningitis and smallpox while monitoring and meticulously recording the effects on their vital organs as they slowly expired.'[12] In these experiments, over 10,000 prisoners are estimated to have died.

In the Holocaust, 1941–45, Nazi Germany murdered six million European Jews, as many as 20 million victims in total, including Romanies, people with disabilities, ethnic Poles, Soviet prisoners of war, homosexuals and individuals labelled communist or socialist. Based on racist beliefs that Germans were superior people and that others, in particular Jews, were racially, biologically and socially unfit, extermination of the inferior by gassing in concentration camps became the brutal 'final solution'.[13]

The administration of extermination needed cruel leaders in a society conditioned to accept that state bureaucracies should operate in the service of a politics of militarism and racial purification. With the wisdom of hindsight, that fascist culture gives clues about the persistence of cruelty: a banality of evil, faceless compliance in bureaucracies and the sadistic character of those who gave and carried out orders.

Almost in anticipation of the Holocaust, in 1939 the English poet W.H. Auden wrote *Epitaph on a Tyrant*.

> *Perfection of a kind was what he was after,*
> *And the poetry he invented was easy to understand;*
> *He knew human folly like the back of his hand,*
> *And was greatly impressed in armies and fleets;*
> *When he laughed, respectable senators burst with laughter*
> *And when he cried the little children died in the streets.*[14]

While the Holocaust was under way in Europe over three million Bengalis were starving to death, a result not just of a poor rice harvest but because British Prime Minister Winston Churchill had ordered the diversion of food from starving Indians to the already well-supplied British soldiers and stockpiles in Britain, in Europe, including Greece and Yugoslavia.

Shashi Tharoor reveals how Australian ships laden with wheat were docking in Calcutta but were instructed not to unload their cargo but to sail on to Europe.[15] In a forensic analysis of the Bengali famine, in what she titles *Churchill's Secret War*, Madhusree Mukerjee documents the racism inherent in classifying some people as worthy and others of no consequence. Bread rationing in wartime Britain was regarded as an intolerable deprivation, but famine in India could be tolerated. Regarding those policies, Lord Wavell, the Viceroy of India, commented that the British government treated Indians with neglect, even sometimes with hostility and contempt. Mukerjee quotes Churchill, 'I hate Indians. They are a beastly people with a beastly religion. The famine was their own fault for breeding like rabbits.'[16]

The greatest mass murderer in history is considered to have been Mao Zedong, founder of the People's Republic of China. From 1958 to 1962, during a policy named The Great Leap Forward, designed as an effort to catch up with Western economies, 45 million people were worked, starved or beaten to death.[17] That period of mass killings had been preceded, in the 1940s and 1950s, by the elimination of landlords, peasants and anyone who dared to challenge the social and economic transformation ordered by Mao.

There's an irony in these killings. Records were carefully kept by China's Public Security Bureau, but were secret. Keeping the records of cruelty secret enabled subsequent denials that such action occurred. That's a process we'll see again and again.

British 1950s governments' administration of their disappearing colonial empires, as in their response to the Mau Mau rebellions in Kenya, included officially sanctioned cruelties, 'a tale of systematic cruelties and high-level cover ups', as in the use of concentration camps comparable to those used by Nazi Germany and in Stalin's gulags.[18] The Mau Mau who rebelled against British settlers and colonial rule are estimated to have murdered as many as 50 settlers, but thousands of their own Kikuyu people. In response the British are reported to have crammed up to one million people into heavily guarded camps, killed unknown numbers by beatings, starvation and torture and hanged up to 800, a majority for offences other than murder. At the height of the emergency as many as 50 hangings took place each month.[19] Details of British fascination with violence as the means of governance are discussed in the next chapter, 'Values, attitudes, behaviour'.

Less than 10 years after the British brutalities in Kenya, between October 1965 and March 1966, anyone suspected of being a member of the Indonesian Communist Party was hunted down and murdered. Published estimates indicate that between 500,000 and one million Indonesians were killed by the Indonesian Army, who were aided by civilian militias mostly from Islamic groups.[20]

The record of this mass murder and incarceration of Indonesians displays a couple of issues. For decades, information about the massacres, and about the roles played by the US, Britain and other major powers, was suppressed. Detailed analyses are now coming to light.[21]

Between 1975 and 1979 in Cambodia, with the objective of establishing the Khmer Rouge version of agrarian socialism under the leadership of Pol Pot, 3,314,768 people died, an estimated 25% of the population. The deaths were caused by several factors: forced relocation from urban centres, torture, mass executions, forced labour and malnutrition.[22]

In 1975, with the connivance of Western powers such as Australia and the US, Indonesian forces invaded East Timor and occupied the country for the following 24 years. In 2002, the Timorese Commission for Reception, Truth and Reconciliation estimated that during the years of occupation, and in excess of normal rates of mortality, well over 100,000 Timorese died from starvation and deprivation, five times higher than the number of targeted killings and disappearances, estimated to be at least 18,000. The Truth Commission found that by formulating policies to cause mass starvation and death, members of the Indonesian armed forces and government officials committed war crimes and crimes against humanity.[23] The Department of Demography and Sociology at the University of California, Berkeley, concluded that even with the most conservative assumptions, the total number of excess deaths in East Timor during the entire Indonesian occupation ranged from 150,000 to 200,000. Those estimates included the 1991 Santa Cruz massacre of 271 protesting civilians. In 1999, after the Timorese voted overwhelmingly for independence from Indonesia, pro-Indonesian militia killed an estimated 1,000 supporters of independence. One quarter of a million East Timorese fled to West Timor, and in their final scorched earth policy the Indonesians destroyed more than 70% of East Timorese housing.

In 1988, the supreme leader of Iran, Ayatollah Khomeini, issued a fatwah for the killing of prisoners identified as intellectuals, students, left wingers, members of the People's Mojahedin of Iran, of ethnic and religious minorities, many of whom had been sentenced for non-violent offences, such as taking part in demonstrations and collecting funds for prisoners.[24] The people charged appeared before summary Islamic courts to answer questions 'Are you a Muslim?', 'Do you pray?', 'Do you recant your beliefs and political activities?' If the answers were judged insufficient, they were sent for execution. In June 2012, a London Tribunal estimated that as many as 5,000 prisoners were executed. The prisoners, including women and teenagers, 'were loaded onto forklift trucks and at half hour intervals were hanged from cranes and beams in groups of five or six'.

In 2011, barrister Geoffrey Robertson reported on 'The Massacre of Political Prisoners in Iran, 1988'. Following a detailed inquiry, he concluded that the state of Iran had broken the rules of international law, and had committed war crimes and crimes against humanity. His account of breath-taking brutality in the name of a religion reveals an unrelenting sadism, an issue explored in Chapter 3. Robertson's conclusions exposed Iran's 'policy of systematic denial, historical falsification and destruction of evidence of the mass executions'.[25]

A year after the mass graves of Iranian victims had been covered and concealed, in June 1989, thousands of young Chinese democracy protesters set up camp in Beijing's Tiananmen Square. As many as 10,000 Chinese troops moved in and massacred large numbers of protesters. The exact number of deaths is unknown. Since that time, Chinese authorities have censored information about the massacre. Such suppression links cruelty to denial. In his poem *Tiananmen*, written less than two weeks after the massacre, James Fenton conveys the suppression of a story.

Tiananmen
Is broad and clean
and you can't tell
where the dead have been
and you can't tell
what happened then
and you can't speak
of Tiananmen.

You must not speak.
You must not think.
You must not dip
your brush in ink.
You must not say
what happened then,
what happened there
in Tiananmen.[26]

Between April and July 1994 in Rwanda, mass slaughter occurred in 100 days. The violence emerged from a century or more of injustice and brutality from both the Hutu majority and the minority Tutsis. Following the shooting down of a Hutu President, and with a view to hanging on to power, extremist Hutus acted to wipe out the Tutsi completely. The genocidal slaughter of the Tutsi people by members of the Hutu majority claimed up to one million victims, including moderate Hutus.[27]

In 1995, in the Bosnian town of Srebrenica, over 8,000 Bosnian men and boys were murdered by forces under the command of Serb General Ratko Mladic. Despite overwhelming evidence about the victims and the perpetrators, the atrocities have been denied by Serbian leaders. A group of 200 'Srebrenica Mothers' continue to fight the official silence and denials.

In a resolution passed by the General Assembly of the UN, these killings were judged to be a genocide, part of an ethnic cleansing which targeted Bosnian Muslims and Croats. The 'cleansing' included murder, rape, torture, beatings and other inhumane treatment of civilians.[28]

In 2003, in Darfur, the western region of Sudan, government armed and funded Arab militias, the Janjaweed, 'devils on horseback', burned villages, polluted water supplies, murdered, raped and tortured civilians. An estimated 500,000 were killed and up to 2.8 million people displaced.

In March 2009, as a result of the Darfur atrocities, the International Criminal Court issued an arrest warrant for Sudanese President Omar al-Bashir for crimes against humanity. A year later Bashir was charged with genocide. His oppressive rule continued. In 2019, in response to protests about the cost of living, corruption and mismanagement of the economy, protesters demanded Bashir's resignation. In response the President quoted verses from the Quran to justify the killing of protesters, dissolved the government and appointed military and security officials to run Sudan's 18 states.[29] In May 2019, following massive public protests seeking democracy, Bashir was overthrown, his regime replaced by a Military Council but not by civilian rule.

In all these slaughters, the perpetrators were leaders of governments, politicians, military and religious personnel, self-appointed vigilantes and diverse groups usually referred to as rebels or terrorists. This gruesome list does not return to the days of the Inquisition, to the enslavement of 20 million Africans, to the slaughter of Indigenous peoples in the Americas, in Australia and the Indian sub-continent, a consequence of violent colonial invasions and economic domination of a black and brown world, but there has to be a time limit to the examples. Hereafter, with a few dips into earlier decades, examples will come mostly from events in the last part of the 20th century and from 2000 to 2020.

Silence and denial

From 2000, participants in cruelty could include media personnel poised with their microphones or sitting upright at their keyboards. They may say or write nothing about inhumanities presented to them. They can enable the public to remain ignorant or indifferent to suffering.

Citizens who stay silent about cruelty may be as responsible as the leaders of governments, as responsible as the members of police forces and military who obey politicians' orders. Influential citizens represent an establishment, the taken-for-granted opinion makers, such as public servants, university managers, journalists, academics, business executives, the leaders of NGOs or even the organizers of writers' festivals. Despite publicity about cruelties, their silence can be deafening.

This may sound like charges against those who act cruelly and those who stay passive because they want to get on with their lives. The charges should be made. This is also advocacy for humanitarianism to become centre stage in citizens' thinking and actions, a humanitarianism characterized by creative, non-destructive exercise of power. Such conduct would include kindness, generosity, love and hospitality plus creativity in others' interests, respect for all living things and for every individual's dignity, as illustrated in all 30 clauses of the Universal Declaration of Human Rights. That last example emphasizes the universality of humanitarianism, across countries and cultures, even within the policies of diverse governments. That is the optimistic side of the argument, a healing story.

Such a story has been told by the late Stéphane Hessel, French resistance fighter, survivor of the Buchenwald concentration camp, a contributor to the committee which drafted the Universal Declaration of Human Rights and author of *Time For Outrage* (2010). In gratitude to Hessel, the first verse of *Thanks to Stéphane* says,

> *Thank you for your courage*
> *in insisting on equality*
> *by speaking as an ageless sage*
> *on human needs for dignity:*
> *'Please never sit upon a fence,*
> *your outrage makes a difference.'*[30]

Outrage is never sufficient to end cruelties. The UN's September 2017 condemnation of Aung San Suu Kyi's silence over the killings and expulsion of Rohingyas had no effect on the Myanmar military's attitudes and policies. UN resolutions condemning Israeli settlements as illegal appear to have been an incentive to build more settlements and to boast the irrelevance of international law.

Hessel insisted that if people were not outraged by injustice, they would lose touch with their own humanity.[31] He appealed specifically to the younger generations to be outraged and involved, to challenge official denials of inhumanities.

Two names, Potemkin and Katyn, each related to Russian politics and policies, convey the significance of pretence and denial by governments. In 1787, in the government of the Empress Catherine, Minister Grigory Potemkin created fake villages in order to fool Catherine about a growing population. Whether or not the story is a myth, the point is that 'Potemkin pretence' appears to have grown as a principle of government.

In 1940, in the Polish Katyn Forest and surrounding areas, Soviet secret police, the NKVD, under Stalin's orders, murdered 22,000 Polish nationals, mostly military officers and lower ranks. Until 1989, when President Gorbachev admitted Soviet responsibility for the atrocities, the Soviets had attributed the blame to the Nazis.

Pretence that all is well is a Potemkin phenomenon. Denial of atrocities is the Katyn practice that enables cruelties to proceed unhindered. As an elaboration of Potemkin/Katyn practices, George Orwell, in his depiction of 'Newspeak', reminded readers of the infinite capacity of powerful people to deceive even themselves.

In the March/April 2018 'March of Return' protests staged by thousands of Gazans at the Israel/Gaza border, Israeli snipers killed over 100, many shot in the back. By December 2018, up to 200 had been killed, an estimated 20,000 were maimed, many made cripples for life.[32]

As part of an exercise in justifying virtues despite evidence to the contrary, an Israeli Defence Force (IDF) spokesperson said that his soldiers knew where their bullets went and he repeated the well-rehearsed claim that Israel had the most moral, the most humane army in the world.[33]

To highlight states' reliance on duplicity and denial as a means of government, it is necessary to recall not only the claims of IDF personnel, those made by the regime of a Russian Empress or a Nazi dictatorship. Justification for the 2003 invasion of Iraq depended on US, British and Australian governments' careful and vigorously presented deceit and denial. Referring to risks to London, British Prime Minister Tony Blair said that Iraq possessed and could dispatch weapons of mass destruction in 45 minutes. On both sides of the Atlantic, that claim was supported by dossiers riddled with lies, and with assertions about the benefits of regime change. The cruelties of the invading allies competed with the sadism of Saddam. A 'Coalition of the Willing', the US and its allies, invaded Iraq, destroyed the country, killed up to one million Iraqis and spawned the extremist Islamic force ISIS.

Official denials, often bare-faced lying, are just one of the dominant themes in accounts of cruelties. Individuals are stigmatized by being labelled unworthy or faceless, of little consequence, barely human. Asylum seekers are called illegals and potential terrorists. Reliance on force in domestic policies, in times of war and as a cue for state and non-state terrorists, gives rise to a chemistry of cruelty, each act as inventive and gruesome as the next.

Life-enhancing, health-promoting, non-violent alternatives to cruelty are cherished by citizens and can be promoted by politicians. Ideals for a common humanity can be formulated in the minds of politicians, civil servants, journalists and in states' policies. Such ideals already occur in the visions of poets, in challenges from classical composers and through appeals by singers of songs of protest.

2

Values, attitudes, behaviour

There are very few people who are going to look into the mirror and say, 'That person is a savage monster.' Instead they make up some construction that justifies what they do. (Noam Chomsky)[1]

No civilized society can thrive upon victims whose humanity has been permanently mutilated. (Rabindranath Tagore)[2]

Instead of listing cruelties under the names of countries, rebel or terrorist groups, it is revealing to identify patterns of values, attitudes and behaviour, beginning with the age-old stigmatizing of victims. Such negative labelling is implemented in policies of national inclusiveness: whom to regard as normal and worthy, as compared to policies of exclusiveness which designate whom to see as abnormal and unworthy.

Under various jurisdictions and in different periods of history, the stigmatized have included people with a disability, those suffering mental illness, Indigenous peoples, Indian untouchables, Hazaras in Afghanistan, Tamils in Sri Lanka, homosexuals, Jews, Christians, gypsies, non-believers, apostates, asylums seekers, refugees, mixed-blood Aboriginals and unmarried mothers.

In many countries and cultures, cruelties are sustained by an automatic acceptance of religious and moral justification for the manner of conducting relationships. Under the rule of inflexible monarchies and theocracies, as in Saudi Arabia and Iran, stigmatizing also seems motivated by efforts to appear masculine and to degrade women. Such practices have persisted for centuries but have achieved new support under the influence of conservative Islam, or by extremist beliefs and intolerance fuelled by any religion. With the imposition of religious rules comes a ghoulish pleasure in observing pain being inflicted on others.

Sadism is not practised only by religious extremists. Military regimes display a dependence on violence as though they can think of no other way to exercise control. Addiction to violence is aided by the international arms trade and by the availability of the latest weapons as well as by cinema, video games and the media.

These patterns overlap. Reference to terrorism has become the cue to justify torture and other forms of cruelty, and to say that such behaviour is permitted by law. The terrorism labelling overlaps with the demonization of individuals, with sexual motives for violence and with religious justification for such practices, even if such conduct is denied.

Denial aids cruelty in the following ways. Human rights abuses exist but allegedly do not. Cruelty can be observed yet can be said to have been only imagined. To ensure that cruelty continues, reports of cruelty are claimed to be fake news.

Stigmatizing

Stigmatizing the other has been the ages-old means of demonstrating the normality and superiority of a dominant group. Fuelled by racism and a taken-for-granted assumption that violence was the way to promote powerful people's economic, political and religious interests, notions of rights and justice have not occurred to the stigmatizers. The stigmatized, whose identity and languages were derided, eroded and even forbidden, endured centuries of powerlessness.

Roma people, for example, are one of Europe's most marginalized groups. Traditionally a travelling people, many came to the UK in the 1990s to escape persecution in Eastern Europe. About 300,000 live in the UK, but by mid-summer 2018, many were at risk of deportation if they could not provide the necessary documents to be given settled status. In the wake of the 2016 UK Brexit decision to leave the EU, Roma and other EU nationals would be asked questions about identity, proof that they had no convictions and that they had a permanent address in the UK, those questions to be answered in an online form. This insistence on computerized responses from people who have no computers or smartphones, many of whom are illiterate, shows the automaton-like source of cruelty which I'll elaborate in Chapter 3.

At least in Britain there has been an attempt to welcome Roma and to improve their lives after experiences in European countries, mostly but not entirely in the East, of being attacked and their homes burned down. In contrast to the UK's response to Roma who had faced persecution, in July 2018, Italy's far right Interior Minister Matteo Salvini threatened to expel thousands of Roma. In an upsurge of nationalism in Italy, the vulnerable Roma were caught in the waves of hatred being whipped up against other migrants, in particular from Africa.[3]

In October 2017, Australia became a member of the UN's Human Rights Council, even though the country's human rights record was unimpressive, not least regarding the treatment of Indigenous people.

Between 1905 and 1969 in Australia, up to 10,000 children are estimated to have been removed from their parents.[4] These were identified as mixed-race children who could be trained to work in white society, eventually marry whites and be assimilated into mainstream society. Historian Henry Reynolds observed, 'The greatest advantage of young Aboriginal servants was that they came cheap and were never paid beyond the provision of variable quantities of food and clothing.'[5]

The report on the experiences of stolen Aboriginal children, titled *Bringing Them Home* (1997), concluded that, unlike white children who came into the state's control, far greater care was taken to ensure that Aboriginal children never saw their parents or family again. Sociologist Robert van Krieken concluded that children were often given new names and the greater distances involved in rural areas made it easier to prevent parents and children from tracing each other.[6]

Cruelty guaranteeing a painful sadness became the lot of the Stolen Generation. In the first verse of her poem *A Letter to My Mother*, written in 1985, Aboriginal poet Eva Johnson reveals this sadness.

> *I not see you long time now, I not see you long time now*
> *White fella bin take me from you, I don't know why*
> *Give me to Missionary to be God's child.*
> *Give me new language, give me new name*
> *All time I cry, they say 'that shame'*
> *I go to city down south, real cold*
> *I forget all them stories, my Mother you told*
> *Gone is my spirit, my dreaming my name*
> *Gone to these people, our country to claim*
> *They gave me white mother, she give me new name*
> *All time I cry, she say − 'that shame'*
> *I not see you long time now, I not see you long time now.*[7]

Widespread incidence of chronic illness, such as diabetes, plus a 10-year difference in life expectancy exposes a huge gap between the life chances of Indigenous and non-Indigenous Australians. Disproportionate numbers of Aboriginal citizens in prisons, many dying in custody, have been a lasting consequence for members of the Stolen Generation. The April 1991 Royal Commission into *Aboriginal Deaths in Custody* reported on 99 deaths[8] but, since then, incarceration rates of Aboriginal citizens have increased; so too have suicide rates among younger Aboriginal and Torres Strait Islander people.

Acknowledgement of past cruelties came in belated but highly valued official apologies. On 13 February 2008, Australian

Prime Minister Kevin Rudd apologized for centuries of mistreatment of Indigenous Australians.

> We apologize for the laws and policies of successive Parliaments and governments that have inflicted profound grief, suffering and loss on these our fellow Australians.
>
> We apologize especially for the removal of Aboriginal and Torres Strait Islander children from their families, their communities and their country.
>
> For the pain, suffering and hurt of these Stolen Generations, their descendants and for their families left behind, we say sorry.

In a hint of cruelty to come, Peter Dutton, a future Minister of Immigration, boycotted the apology ceremony.

Rudd promised that the injustices of the past would not be repeated. He envisioned a future of equal opportunities for all citizens and an equal stake in shaping the country's future.

Since those hopeful days, the gap in the differences between Indigenous and non-Indigenous Australians' life chances has continued and shows Prime Minister Rudd's hopes not being fulfilled.

The experience of the Aboriginal stolen generations was matched by the cruelty experienced by children sent from Britain to Australia and other Commonwealth countries after the First World War. Estimates show that between the 1920s and 1960s, over 150,000 young children were dispatched to institutions and foster homes abroad so that they might have happier lives in underpopulated Commonwealth countries.[9] The National Archives of Australia record that between 1947 and 1953, over 3,200 children migrated to Australia. Commonwealth and state governments contributed to the running costs of the voluntary and religious organizations which housed the children.

The child migrant policy was motivated by the supposed need to make available good, white stock to rejuvenate the colonies and to give children a better life than in post-war Britain. Separated from their parents, on arrival in Australia, the children were housed in religious and philanthropic institutions. Often parted from their siblings, sent to work on farms, thrashed for small indiscretions, hounded by police if they ran away, many children were treated as slave labour. One of the child migrants, John Hennessy, recalled being sent to Bindoon Boys Town in Western Australia. He explained, 'Life at Bindoon, run by the Catholic Church's Christian Brothers, was a catalogue of cruelty where beatings and sexual assaults were daily events.'[10]

In November 2009, Australian Prime Minister Kevin Rudd and Opposition leader Malcolm Turnbull gave a national apology to the Forgotten Australians, who had left Britain as children, lived in institutions, orphanages and foster care and had survived a brutalized childhood.

In February 2010, British Prime Minister Gordon Brown told the House of Commons he was 'truly sorry that the voices of these children were not always heard, their cries for help not always heeded'. He acknowledged that the policy represented a 'shameful ... deportation of the innocents'.

Another acknowledgement of the cruel consequences of stigmatizing the unworthy also appeared, in Australia's case, in the 2013 *National Apology for Forced Adoptions*.[11] Unmarried mothers had been regarded as sinful and emotionally incapable. Alleged illegitimate children could be deemed bastards. Estimates indicate that over 800 mothers and children were affected by such adoptions.

In her national apology of 21 March 2013, Prime Minister Julia Gillard said,

> We say sorry to you the mothers, who were denied knowledge of your rights. You were given false assurances. You were forced to endure the coercion and brutality of practices that were unethical, dishonest and in many cases, illegal.
>
> Sometimes consent was achieved by forgery or fraud. Sometimes women signed adoption papers whilst under the influence of medication ... Most common of all was the bullying arrogance of a society that presumed to know what was best.

The notion of illegitimacy had such a hold on the dominant morality of cultures, that forced adoptions were common in many countries. In 1960s Britain, more than 160,000 babies were adopted, many against the will of the birth mothers. The UK report *Half a Million Women*,[12] published in 1992 for the Post Adoption Centre, shows how mothers were seen not as victims of bad luck but were pathologized as emotionally disturbed or as a discredited person.

In respective *Observer* and London *Guardian* reports, mothers who were forced to give up their babies gave their accounts of efforts to seek justice. Jill Killington, 68, said, 'I was never asked whether I wanted to go ahead with the adoption. It was a *fait accompli* ... Nobody ever gave me any information about support or benefits, even though these would have been available at the time.' Veronica Smith, 71, explained, 'I was a perfectly healthy, capable adult. I'm still angry that my child was taken away ... I was sent to the Catholic Crusade of Rescue ... we were made to scrub the floors as a penance for our sins. I held my daughter for a week. And then she was gone. I never had any more news of her ... It's a big injustice. The churches and the authorities have a lot to answer for.'[13]

Unworthy asylum seekers

More than 50 years after the arrival of the migrant children, immigration policies repeated the fears generated over attitudes to Chinese migrants in 19th-century Australia and regarding alleged red peril threats during the Vietnam war. Twenty-first-century fears referred to prospective terrorists and a need to protect borders. In Australia, in defiance of international law, the apparatus of government included mandatory detention, offshore processing, bridging and temporary protection visas. Deterrence through a guarantee of punishment became central to governments' policies.

Between 2013 and 2017, up to AUS$5 billion were spent to contain asylum seekers on Papua New Guinea's Manus Island and on Nauru.[14] By the end of 2016, over 1,500 men, women and children were contained in those centres.

In the 2014 Australian Coalition government, Peter Dutton became Minister for Immigration and Border Control. Outwardly incapable of showing compassion, he would complain that even asylum seekers officially recognized as refugees were trying to exploit Australia's supposed reputation as a safe refuge. The dog-whistling was never-ending and effective.

In such utterances, Dutton and his colleagues aligned themselves with Pauline Hanson and the One Nation Party, which appealed to citizens who claimed they had most to lose if people of the wrong colour and religion arrived and seemed likely to take jobs intended for locals. Dutton presented as strong in defence of his country's sovereignty. He defined hard workers as desirable citizens but had no respect for asylum seekers, and was always antagonistic to those he called people smugglers.

New Matilda of July 2017 included an analysis of ways to rescue refugees with policies influenced by a touch of humanity.[15] The article provoked vitriol from contributors to the comment columns. They appeared to be the audience to whom Dutton played. Being cruel required permission from a powerful other, someone perceived as higher up in any chain of command. The Minister had given that permission.

A contributor described as 'Has Been' wrote, 'The refugees are trying to play the Australian people as is the author. Give refugees residency and safety and the first thing they do is to fly back "home", to the place they fled in fear of their lives. Just to marry or set stuff up but not enough to affect Centrelink payments.'

In another post, someone called Moonshine wrote, 'So here we have another of these totally useless, worthless academics, happy to sit on their fattening arse, sucking their sustenance from the taxpayer teat. … What a pity we can't find another island somewhere to banish these ingrates to, where they would have to fend for themselves or starve. The same thing we should be doing with gate crashers, masquerading as refugees.'

Then came a contribution from 'X factor', 'If they take a boat and drown, let them drown. It's their own doing. If they cause trouble, harassing Australians and/or their property, shoot them, that's legitimate self-defence, but make their deaths as unpainful as possible.'

Although these comments were made by individuals, such viciousness had been encouraged by right-wing groups and by xenophobic governments. Anti-immigrant, anti-refugee and anti-Muslim fervour has also spread fear in the US and across European countries, such as Holland, Denmark and France, and is said to threaten the survival of liberal democracies.[16]

Cruelty under the Trump Presidency is apparent in the operation of ICE officers. This is not a reference to policies to control drugs but to Immigration, Customs Enforcement. Trevor Timm of the *Guardian* has perceived ICE agents as a growing threat to civil rights. He described a contest between agents to test who could be the most cruel. 'An ICE detainee was even removed forcefully against her will from a hospital where she was receiving treatment for a brain tumour.'[17]

President Trump's promise to his constituents to build a wall on the Mexican border legitimized the behaviour of ICE personnel. Trump tweets. The agents follow. Fear is fomented. In addition to the Trump administration using executive orders to strip away immigrants' due process protections, the US Justice Department attempted to cut off legal representation for immigrants.

In *Immigrants in Our Own Land*, Native American poet Jimmy Santiago Baca captured the persecution experienced by citizens dubbed migrants, even in their own country. He wrote that he hoped for better days but discovered that he needed to escape from officials who broke down doors, 'swinging clubs and shooting guns as they pleased' and 'arrested us when they felt like it'. From such oppression he learned nothing of value, except the fatalism that nothing could be done.[18]

Mexican Americans say they feel persecuted in the US. In April 2010, Arizona passed laws to arrest undocumented migrants without warrant, banned unauthorized immigrants from seeking work and made their presence a state crime. The US Supreme Court struck down those provisions but many migrants said that to protect their mental sanity, they left their lives behind and got out of the US. One migrant explained that he and his family endured years of fear. 'We would feel persecuted and harassed … It was nerve wracking, especially when we had to go outside for work.'[19]

President Trump is skilled at scaring people. Central Americans have been said to 'prefer to seek asylum in Mexico, which (officially) grants asylum to people persecuted for their race, religion, nationality, gender, membership of a social group or political views'.[20]

Cruelty as a lubricant for administering justice flourishes not only in the US penal and immigration system. Homeless people as well as migrants are the targets of punitive policies. More and more homeless people have been arrested, prosecuted and killed for actions related to their poverty.[21] The UN has condemned the US for criminalizing homelessness and has called US practices 'cruel, inhuman and degrading'.

Fascination with violence

Violence displayed in policies on immigration becomes even more direct and routinely justified in times of political purges and war. Russian futurist poet Velimir Khlebnikov, who knew oppression, advocated more humane futures, as in the first seven lines of *Suppose I Make a Timepiece of Humanity*, written early in the 20th century.

> *Suppose I make a timepiece of humanity,*
> *Demonstrate the movement of the century hand –*
> *Will war not wither like an unused letter, drop*
> *From your alphabet, vanish from our little gap*
> *Of time? Humanity has piles, got by rocking*
> *In armchairs forever and ever, compressing*
> *The mainspring of war.*[22]

When listing the mass murders and genocides which occurred from the beginning of the 20th century, details of British governments' detention of up to one million Kenyans, the torture of thousands and the execution of many (including hundreds for crimes other than murder) were omitted. The British colonial administration's fascination with violence produced brutal policies to repel the rebellion, for which the supposed trigger was the Mau Mau slaughter of 32 white settlers and African chiefs loyal to the British crown.

This brief appraisal of British governance in Kenya in the 1950s covers three issues: (i) the stigmatizing of Africans, (ii) the extent of brutality and (iii) a hierarchy of responsibility.

In Britain the Mau Mau rebels were portrayed as representing the re-emergence of a primitive bloodlust that the twin benefits of colonisation – Christianity and civilization – were intended to eradicate. British perception of Kenyans as inferior peoples was expressed by a veteran of detention camps, Njero Mugo who observed, 'from the first day the missionaries arrived, we never believed that the British stood for the rule of law. They stole our land. They treated us as though they had more right to be in our country than we did. Did you know that if you were walking down the street and you met a white person you had to remove your hat?'[23]

Stigmatizing Kenyans as inferior became excuse and justification for an administration which operated floggings, starvation, working people to death, plus the rape and sexual abuse of women. In October 2016, 10 survivors of the British response to the Mau Mau rebellion came to London, suing the government for what they said was officially sanctioned torture and other human rights abuses. Espon Makanga described life in the Kandongu camp in 1957 as a routine of tortures, beatings and typhoid that claimed hundreds if not thousands of lives. On arrival in Manyani camp, Makanga recalled, the prisoners were thrown into a pit of disinfectant. 'The guards surrounded us and beat us to force us in as if we were cattle.' A British colonial district officer justified beatings and other brutality as 'enlightened humane and Christian-based', but an assistant police commissioner, Duncan McPherson, said it was impossible to intervene to prosecute camp officials. 'I would say that the conditions were worse, far worse, than anything I experienced in my four and a half years as a prisoner of the Japanese.'[24]

Front-line staff, such as a notorious and feared torturer, district officer Terry Gavaghan, said that the brutalities were carried out with the approval of the Attorney General, an indication that cruelty was an all-of-government policy. From the Colonial Secretary Alan Lennox Boyd, to the Kenyan Governor Sir Evelyn Baring, to the Attorney General Eric Griffith Jones, to the likes of Terry Gavaghan, the banality of evil, though often denied or ignored, was widespread. Top officials' denial or indifference could be interpreted as official approval. A new Colonial Secretary, Iain Macleod, said that a veil should be drawn over the whole business. In 2005, British Chancellor of the Exchequer Gordon Brown said Britain should stop apologizing for colonialism. Given 'British values' such as liberty, tolerance and civic virtue, the country should be proud of its history in Africa.[25]

As an accompaniment to cruelty to individuals, the Saudi/ US coalition's intervention in the Yemeni civil war has oppressed a whole people.[26] The blockade of the main Yemeni port by the Saudi/US forces resulted in seven million people facing starvation and 17 million people experiencing food insecurity. In March 2017, UNICEF reported, 'At least one child dies every ten minutes because of malnutrition, diarrhoea and respiratory tract infections.'[27]

About the war in Yemen, *New Matilda*'s investigative journalist Michael Brull concluded that the famine in that country was not the result of some strange confluence of factors or an act of God. It was a conscious war policy adopted by the Saudi/US-led coalition.[28] Robert Naiman of *Just Foreign Policy* argued, 'It is beyond reasonable doubt that Saudi Arabia's war and blockade in Yemen would not be possible without US approval.'[29] In an international cruelty duet, the US is Saudi Arabia's enthusiastic partner.

From their torture of prisoners in Iraq's Abu Ghraib prison to the maintenance of Gulag Guantanamo, from botched executions in US prisons to the imprisonment of over two million citizens, the highest proportion per capita in the world, US government policies seem unduly influenced by cruelty.

The violence of US government policies has ranged from the persecution of migrants and homeless people to the use of the death penalty, and has witnessed political support for the idea that the torture of prisoners could be in a nation's interests. Former President George W. Bush secretly ordered the torture of terrorism suspects, then he and his Vice President, Cheney, openly approved of the torture and encouraged the US public to think in the same way. They denied using torture, speaking instead of 'enhanced interrogation techniques'.

Encouraging the public to applaud cruelty shows how any commitment to compassion can be easily ignored. Reporting on the debate in the 2011 US Presidential election, Jonathan Schell noted the applause which greeted the Texas governor's boasts about the number of executions in his state. Schell wrote, 'Enthusiasm for killing is an unmistakable symptom of cruelty. It also appeared after the killing of Osama bin Laden, which touched off raucous celebrations around the country.'[30]

In New York at the time of the announcement of Bin Laden's death, applause for a killing was lauded in the supposed land of the free which prided itself on due process in the administration of justice.[31]

US governments cooperate closely with countries willing to buy their weapons with a view to punishing any person or country who might oppose them. The indispensable US/Israel alliance illustrates an enthusiastic cruelty collective.

Palestinian national poet and significant voice of resistance, Mahmoud Darwish has referred to the decades-long disregard of his people's lives and rights. In lines from *Psalm 2*, he identifies a country acknowledged secretly and in death.

> *Country, turning up in songs and massacres,*
> *Show me the source of death;*
> *Is it the dagger or the lie?*
> *Country, turning up in songs and massacres,*
> *Why do I smuggle you from airport to airport*
> *Like opium,*
> *Invisible ink,*
> *A radio transmitter?*[32]

To address the cruelties in Israel's oppression of Palestinians, an endless list of atrocities would serve little purpose. The task can be simplified by identifying specific issues: the cruelty to almost two million people living in the Gaza Strip, the 1982 massacres in the Sabra and Shatila refugee camps and the abuses of power by the Gazan government of Hamas.

Israel's 50 years of occupation of the West Bank and a siege of Gaza 14 years old in 2020 is inhumanity writ large. My last visit to Gaza, in August 2016, showed a resolute people who survived among piles of rubble with drinking water in short supply, electricity available for only a couple of hours a day, raw sewage pumped into the ocean and bathroom showers only available from sea water.

Gazan poet Abdul Sabawi remembered the home from which he was driven and to which he could not return.

> *Sea and sky, what is there of Gaza?*
> *Only sea and sky and lives foregone*
> *Pledged for the homeland*
> *Eyes hiding tears*
> *Lighting up the candles*
> *Despite the deep wound*
> *They manage to smile.*[33]

Over a Gaza dinner one evening with a school teacher and his family, we sat around the dining room table. In less than an hour the lights went out. The mother retreated to the kitchen for candles. In the gloom, the father asked, 'What have we done to deserve this? Being punished for being citizens of Gaza? This punishment has been going on for ten years. Why?'

The siege of Gaza illustrates the key ingredient in cruelty: where human beings are used as a means to an end, a bargaining chip for political gain. The cruelty practitioners who show no remorse over Gaza include the Palestinian Authority, the governing party Hamas, Israeli, Egyptian, US governments and a compliant EU.

Even if the international community, represented by members of the UN and the EU, are aware of cruel policies, compassion for long-suffering Gazans receives little consideration. Gazans are caught in political conflicts. They are walled in. The air, the land, the sea are blocked by Israeli forces. The people are trapped. The so-called international community looks on.

Lives of powerlessness in Gaza have been replicated in numerous refugee camps since 1948. Sixty-year-old Hosni Abo Taha is the chairman of the popular committee of the Bourj el-Barajneh refugee camp in the southern suburbs of Beirut. This is a slum of improvised dwellings held together by cement likely to crumble because made with salty water. Beneath a spaghetti-like maze of electric cables slung over sewers which are often flooded, one- to two-metres wide alleyways meander between the buildings. In 2015, it was home to 37,000 people, an influx of 15,000 over the previous 18 months due mainly to the influx of Syrian refugees. Although refuge is given to people who have fled a siege, famine or violence in the Syrian Yarmouk refugee camp, safety is an illusion. The crumbling buildings have been erected without foundation and 800 homes have been condemned as likely to collapse. Hanan, a social worker, paraphrased the despair felt by camp residents, 'We are dying every minute of our lives, so why does it matter to take a risk to leave here, to nothing?' Hosni told me that he respected the ideals of democracy but thinks that elected governments 'only pay lip-service to human rights, they only pretend being democratic'. Hosni made a final appeal, 'We love life. We want to live our lives in freedom, as we did before 1948. We deserve the chance to prove we are human beings.'[34]

When atrocities have been committed against people who are stigmatized and not considered important, it has been easy to forget their fates.[35] The neighbouring camps to Bourj-el-Barajneh, Sabra and

Shatila, should be remembered for a savagery which is part of history but could so easily be forgotten.

September 16th, 1982 started a 36-hour holocaust without mercy. After Palestinian leader Yasser Arafat and his men surrendered their weapons and evacuated from Beirut, with guarantees that the civilians left behind in refugee camps would be protected by a multinational peace-keeping force, Israeli Defence Minister Ariel Sharon surrounded Sabra and Shatila. He claimed that 2,000 terrorists were hiding there and he would root them out. He left that task to the right-wing Christian militia the Phalangists. The Palestinian Red Crescent Society estimated that at least 2,000 women, children, men and infants lay dead after 36 hours of killing.

A subsequent UN inquiry said that the killings in Sabra and Shatila were a criminal massacre, an act of genocide. Sharon was judged directly responsible but no one was prosecuted. Subsequent analysis in *The Nation* by Rashid Khalidi showed the US role in the massacre. It supplied lethal weapons. It gave guarantees of safety which meant nothing.[36]

Characteristics of this slaughter survive the test of time. Humans as powerless pawns. Violence with no regard for the human costs. Lies about respect for human rights. Abuses justified by perceiving victims as of little consequence.

Such use of force is also a technique favoured by Hamas, the Palestinian party which has ruled the Gaza Strip since 2007.

Interviews with Hamas leaders give first impressions of strong convictions, sophisticated in their political analysis, yet allowing little or no dissent. To control their population and to oppose Israel, fear has been maintained by arbitrary arrests, torture and summary executions of those suspected of betrayal for cooperating with Israel. Hamas' promotion of fear to ensure others' compliance has guaranteed abuse of others Gazan citizens' rights and, in policy deliberation terms, allows no room for doubt.

Human Rights Watch reports that Hamas authorities had sentenced 88 people to death between 2007 and 2015 since taking control of Gaza. They have executed at least 46 people, most without any judicial process. In common with Israeli forces killing Palestinians, no one is held accountable. Killers act with impunity.

In May 2015, the *Washington Post* reported that under cover of the 2014 Israeli invasion, six men were paraded in front of a mosque in Gaza city and executed.[37] An Amnesty International Report said that security forces from Hamas' Interior Ministry used an outpatient clinic at the Shifa hospital 'to detain, interrogate, torture and otherwise ill-treat subjects, even as other parts of the hospital continued to function as a medical centre'.

War and denial

Under shadows of war, a state of anomie gives free rein to protagonists in uniform and in plain clothes to carry out horrific abuses against people in custody, or against anyone defined as an enemy. Wars of independence and civil wars have an unenviable record of savagery.

The years 1954–62 in Algeria witnessed a French occupation regime which fought an equally cruel and determined Algerian resistance. In order to justify torture, imprisonment and slaughter, each side demonized the other. Negative labelling via well-organized public relations campaigns were crucial ingredients to provoke fear and initiate revenge. The French said they were fighting terrorism. Algerian independence forces (the FLN) said they were fighting a brutal Gaullist regime.

Colonization of Algeria had generated a 'them and us' polarization between allegedly worthy rulers and an underclass of less-than-worthy citizens whose powerlessness was compounded by their being Muslims not Christians. Into this messianic mix came a frightening masculine militarism and sadism which derided ideas about peace but promoted violence as the only way to win some kind of victory. In that war, an estimated 1.5 million Algerians were killed.

A distinguished French journalist, Henri Alleg, who as editor of *Alger Republicain* had been publishing diverse views on the dispute, was arrested and tortured. He survived and gave a personal testimony of the sense of endless time in torture, each day of cruelty blurring into another, the pleasure in watching his agony becoming routine for his French paratrooper interrogators. Alleg concluded that serving in that French army of occupation had become 'a school of perversion for young Frenchmen'.[38]

Decades later, the *Independent*'s Beirut-stationed journalist Robert Fisk confirmed Alleg's verdict. He described a culture of violence and cruelty which infected every party. 'French officers indulged in an orgy of torture while their Algerian opposite numbers slaughtered each other, as well as the French, in a Stalinist purge of thousands of their own followers suspected of collaborating with the French occupation'.[39] Even in 1959, after President Charles de Gaulle had recognized Algerian independence, revenge and slaughter continued, in particular against those Algerians, known by the derogatory expression 'Harkis', who had been allies to the French.

An approximate 150,000 Harkis and their dependants were estimated to have been killed.

In a tradition of sadism, atrocities continued in the Algerian civil war of 1992–98 and in the slaughters, from 2011, committed by protagonists in the Syrian civil war and by Daesh, ISIS. Previous protests against such traditions have not been heard and have not stemmed the brutalities. In his 1930s work, *Waltz Poem of Those in Love and Inseparable Forever*, and in the last verse, Spanish poet Miguel Hernández lamented vicious practices towards those who had been counted as nothing.

> *Hunted down, crushed,*
> *left alone and abandoned*
> *by moons and memories,*
> *Marches and Novembers,*
> *they saw themselves whirled*
> *like dust that counts for nothing:*
> *they saw themselves whirled,*
> *but they have each other's arms forever.*[40]

UN and Arab League envoys to Syria estimated over 500,000 deaths; the majority of fatalities included non-combatant civilians, men, women and children. Controversy persists as to the number of militia men killed – Syrian, Iranian, Afghans, Iraqis, Pakistanis, Palestinians, Serb volunteers and Russian contractors, some of the many thousand pieces in a jihadist jigsaw.

Tens of thousands of refugees are also casualties of a vicious conflict. The UN estimates that within Syria, six million people have been internally displaced. Beyond Syrian borders, five million have become refugees. From a collection published in 1993, in *Elegy for the Time at Hand*, Syrian poet Adonis foreshadowed the savagery of the civil war which began in 2011. He predicted the savagery of militarism. Even after suffering destruction from cyclones, everyone's souls would be at the mercy of swords, the salt of autumn would settle on wounds, thereafter there would be no spring and no tree could bud.[41]

The misery of refugees, the loss and grief of families are a consequence of forces preoccupied with trade in arms and violence. The Syrian government, US, Russian, Iranian, Turkish and diverse rebel groups representing one side or another have participated in Dresden-like destruction and fights to the death. To retake (liberate) the previously ISIS-dominated Raqqa, US forces reduced the town to rubble. Russian and Syrian forces had done the same to Aleppo, and by March 2018 had also pulverized the citizens and the buildings of a previous rebel stronghold in the Damascus suburb of Eastern Ghouta.

Regarding the bombing and shelling of Raqqa to battle defenders into submission, Patrick Cockburn showed governments lying about the costs of such assaults. He reported that air forces were in denial or deliberately misleading, pretending that modern, high-precision targeting had transformed the nature of bombing. 'But the ruins of East Aleppo, Raqqa, Mosul and Eastern Ghouta look very much like the pictures of Hue in 1968 or Hamburg in 1945.'[42]

In mid-July 2018, 14 civilians were killed in US bombing raids in the Kanduz province of Afghanistan. Official responses followed a familiar pattern of lying and denial followed by reluctant admission. Immediate US and Afghan responses said that no civilians were killed because only Taliban terrorists were targeted. Subsequent explanations claimed that if there were civilians in the building, they were being used as human shields by the Taliban. Then came regrets about the unnecessary loss of life of civilians and statements that if it could be proved, US forces would apologize. *New York Times* reporters commented that denials by the US military and by officers from Afghan government forces followed a pattern displayed in 2015 when American bombing of a Doctors Without Borders hospital in Kunduz killed 42. The US military initially denied its actions and Afghan officials falsely claimed that the Taliban had been fighting from inside the hospital. A few days later, President Obama apologized for the attack.[43]

Denial of responsibility has been inherent in cruelties. Much of the violence has been visible. Some of the most offensive acts have occurred behind locked doors and in far-away places. Denial accompanies arrests. Denial facilitates torture and ethnic cleansing.

German dramatist and poet Bertolt Brecht warned of the silence and invisibility that facilitates unending violence. In *When Evil-Doing Comes Like Falling Rain*, he wrote,

> *When evil-doing comes like falling rain, nobody calls out 'stop!'*
> *When crimes begin to pile up they become invisible. When sufferings*
> *become unendurable the cries are no longer heard. The cries too,*
> *fall like rain in summer.*[44]

In the Syrian civil war, torture began in 2011 when a 14-year-old in the Syrian town of Daraa was arrested for his graffiti, 'It's your turn Dr Bashar al-Assad', a suggestion that in the Arab Spring uprisings, the Syrian dictatorship would be the next to fall.[45] In consequence, the 14-year-old was tortured for weeks, then released and fled into exile.

His arrest and torture became one of the fuses that led to explosions of protest and the civil war.

On 24 April 2017, the Australian Broadcasting Company's (ABC) *Four Corners* investigative team exposed Syrian government use of torture as a routine of war, recorded yet denied. The investigators' revelations were made possible because Syrian police, soldiers and bureaucrats were so enamoured of order that they kept a record of photographs and documents which depicted their brutality. The programme displayed the paradox of torturers who kept records yet denied what had been shown. A young man spoke of having his ribs broken, being hung from a ceiling by his wrists. A clamp was attached to his penis and a broom handle thrust up his anus. Following this harrowing account, President Assad was filmed denying that anything like that ever happened, even though the detention centre where torture took place was only 1.5 kilometres from the Syrian dictator's palace.

A caveat about the reliability of any sources depicting cruelty should be made. In relation to violence in the Syrian conflict, Western journalists have been accused of distorting information to comply with a preconceived stereotype of President Assad being such a bastard that he would use chemical weapons against his people, despite evidence that such attacks could have been made by Al-Qaeda or other militants.[46]

However, illusions of civility are maintained by lying. Cruelty is fostered by denial. The Syrian dictator's, 'How could anyone think this of me?' is only one example.

Bertolt Brecht's comments about the depravity associated with the Nazi dictatorship foreshadowed the horrors in Syria. Here is the first verse of Brecht's *To Those Born Later.*

> *Truly, I live in dark times!*
> *The guileless word is folly. A smooth forehead*
> *Suggests insensitivity. The man who laughs*
> *Has simply not yet had*
> *The terrible news.*[47]

In regard to Rohingya Muslims fleeing Myanmar, by late September 2017 the Myanmar Ambassador to the UN was insisting, 'No ethnic cleansing, or genocide against Muslims'.[48] By early October 2017, over half a million Rohingya people had been driven from their homes by the Myanmar military and had crossed into Bangladesh. Amnesty International released videos and satellite photographs showing at least 80 sites being torched. The Amnesty records included eyewitness accounts of murder and rape by the military.

In the *New York Times* of 19 October 2017, Jeffrey Gettleman wrote, 'Rajuma's story stopped me. She told me (and everything she said was consistent with dozens of other witness accounts), that Myanmar government soldiers stormed into her village in August and burned down each house. They separated men from the women and summarily executed the men. Then they raped the women.'[49] As documented in Chapter 1, 'the women' included Rajuma, whose baby son was thrown to death in a fire.

In response to these reports and to an incredulous audience at the UN, the Myanmar Ambassador said, 'The leaders of Myanmar, who have long striven for freedom and humanity, will not espouse such policies. We will do everything possible to prevent ethnic cleansing and genocide.'

By October 2017, the war in Yemen had reportedly killed over 10,000 people, displaced millions, led to famine and a widespread cholera outbreak. In early October 2017, the UN blacklisted the Saudi Arabia-led military coalition for offensives in 2016 which led to the deaths and injuries of 683 children and which involved attacks on dozens of schools and hospitals. The UN also named the Houthi rebel group, Yemeni government forces and Al-Qaeda for violations against children.[50]

Riyadh immediately rejected the UN Report.[51] The Saudi spokesman said that the figures of child deaths were 'inaccurate and misleading'. Then followed Orwellian-like slavery is freedom claims, 'We exercise the maximum degree of care and precaution to avoid civilian harm.'

ISIS or Daesh atrocities, many recorded in gruesome beheadings of tied and bowed prisoners, used fear of cruelty as the way to discipline supporters and potential opponents of their Caliphate. The cruelties included burning a Jordanian pilot alive, mass executions of Iraqi soldiers, beheading or throwing gay men to their death and blowing up prisoners. The ISIS depravity had seemed endless.

In an atmosphere of revenge, Iraqi forces rivalled the ISIS atrocities. Photo journalist for the *Toronto Star*, Ali Arkady, recorded the physical abuse, torture and murder of Sunni Arabs by units of American-trained, Coalition-equipped Iraqi commandos. He documented how knives, guns and live electric cables were held to detainees' heads, fingers pressed deep into eye sockets. He showed video clips of suspects suspended and beaten, screaming their innocence.[52]

An impression of good guys versus bad guys, compassionate personnel versus abusive thugs, would be a false representation of events. Despite Arkady's photographs, the torture and extrajudicial killings in the battle for Mosul have been officially denied. Iraqi Brigadier-General Yahya Rasool said that these video records could have been fabricated. 'There might have been some misbehaviour or inappropriate conduct.'[53]

In communist North Korea, human rights abuses are concealed and denied. Under the leadership of Australian Justice of the High Court Michael Kirby, the UN established an inquiry to investigate crimes against humanity perpetrated by the highest level of that State. The report of UN's *Commission of Inquiry into Human Rights in ... North Korea* was published in 2013.[54]

Justice Michael Kirby records the regime's denial that political prison camps existed, despite strong testimony from survivors and corroboration from internationally available satellite images. Justice Kirby concluded, 'North Korea is a land of ceaseless propaganda, of torture and inhuman treatment, of arbitrary arrest and detention, of public executions to which children are brought to look and learn what happens to State enemies'.[55]

Militaristic and religious motives

Under the rule of South American military dictatorships, techniques for dealing with critics included a mix of militarism, sex and religion. The unbending dogmatism of the military looks like a religion. The sexual motivation and pleasure in torturing opponents is easy to identify.

Under Brazilian dictatorships, from 1964 to 1985, militarism and politics merged. Military ministers took pleasure in humiliating and torturing women. Survivors spoke of being paraded naked, having their nipples repeatedly pinched, being genitally violated with bits of wood and being made to work naked while being subjected to a barrage of obscenities and jokes.[56]

Between September 1973 and March 1990, under the military dictator General Augusto Pinochet, over 30,000 Chilean citizens suspected of being leftist sympathizers were imprisoned, tortured or killed. Torture techniques included electric shocks, water-boarding, beatings and sexual abuse. The Chilean National Commission on Political Imprisonment and Torture, November 2004, reported that under Pinochet, 27,255 people were tortured, 2,279 were executed, 200,000 suffered exile and 3,200 disappeared. In an effort to suppress all political dissidence, making people disappear became a specific part of the regime's torture repertoire.

Several techniques characterized the conduct of the Pinochet regime: instilling fear, stigmatizing 'leftists', ensuring that government was invisible, inaccessible and non-accountable. From the earliest days of the 11 September 1973 overthrow of his predecessor, Salvador Allende, Pinochet used an army death squad, 'The Caravan of Death', to suppress any hint of opposition. He justified that army unit's work as being in the interests of national security.[57] Claims about 'security' became a blanket to cover acts of cruelty and to justify suppression of human rights. In other countries too, coupled to the word 'terrorism', the 'security, security' chorus boomed.

In the 'dirty war' ruled by Argentinian military dictators from 1976 to 1983, captured leftist opponents were also tortured and summarily executed. There was no legal process.[58] In his account of torture and imprisonment by the Argentinian military, Jacobo Timerman identified links between stigmatizing, humiliation and subsequent atrocities. He recorded how his Argentinian torturers made prisoners run naked, shouting such things as, 'My mother's a whore ... The whore who gave birth to me ... I masturbate ... I respect the corporal on guard ... The police love me.'[59]

Explicit religious arguments are also used to strip citizens of their humanity. Religious beliefs provide a rationale for punishing critics, non-believers, apostates and blasphemers. The identity of a mob can be cemented. Culturally sanctioned religious values can be implemented by violence and justified by references to the divine. In explaining President Trump's May 2018 policy (subsequently reversed after public outcry) of separating children from their parents at the border with Mexico, US Attorney General Jeff Sessions defended the policy with a verse from the Bible. He said, 'I would cite to you the apostle Paul and his clear and wise command in Romans 13 to obey the laws of the government because God has ordained the government for his purposes.' Sessions apparently believed that the government was not accountable if it was merely doing God's will. Journalist Nesrine Malik commented, 'The words Sessions quoted were used in the 1840s and 1850s to justify slavery.'[60]

A dominant religious or nationalist culture can amputate and eliminate the non-compliant. Religious and nationalist rationale is also bolstered by a morality concerned to judge alleged abnormal sexual conduct. Lovers who are not married, adulterers, homosexuals and even those who merely display their affections in public can be pursued, prosecuted and even executed. A staunch Western ally like Saudi Arabia tortures, imprisons and beheads gay people. In other countries, from Nigeria to Qatar, being gay is a crime punishable by death.

In the Russian province of Chechnya, beatings, mass arrests and even confinement in concentration camps are being used to stamp out homosexuality.[61] To explain such homophobia, a British journalist explored two streams of thought. That the country's leaders wanted to police what it is to be a man, and they enjoyed maintaining the subjugation of women. The two streams are linked.

Defining morality in terms of sexual conduct shows a pleasure in witnessing cruelty. The *Guardian* of 27 May 2017, reported that, in readiness to view the public flogging of two gay men in the Indonesian province of Banda Aceh, girls and boys arrived early on motor cycles and on foot from nearby boarding schools and two universities. They climbed trees to obtain the best possible views.[62]

A few months later four women were flogged for adultery, punishments demanded by a conservative Islamism. In October 2016, the *Independent* reported that an Indonesian young woman was caned in front of a jeering crowd for standing too close to her boyfriend. On Western Sumatra, 13 people were flogged for touching, hugging and kissing between unmarried people. One woman was given a reprieve because she was pregnant, but the Deputy Mayor, Zainal Arifin, said she would still be caned after she had given birth to the baby.[63]

Violence against women is also legitimate in Iran. Shala Lahiji, a defender of women's rights, says that in many cases, abuse of women is normal. Mehrangiz Kar, a human rights campaigner says, 'In very traditional and religious settings in which many in Iran live, their understanding of religion and the interpretation given to them throughout the centuries is that a man can beat his wife.'[64]

Taking violence towards women for granted looks like an inevitable consequence of an unforgiving penal code. Under Iranian law, many non-violent crimes such as insulting the Prophet, apostasy, same-sex relations, adultery and drug-related offences have been punishable by death. *Al Arabiya English* reported that Iranian intelligence services tortured Sunni Kurdish prisoners before executing them. Iranian intelligence said they would arrest family members of the executed men if they spoke to the media about the torture.[65]

Even children are not accorded special protections or rights. In March 2016, the UN Children's Human Rights Committee reported that in Iran the age of marriage for girls is 13, that sexual intercourse with girls as young as nine was not criminalized and judges had discretion to release some perpetrators of so-called honour killings without any punishment.

In 2016, Iran continued to sentence children to death. At least 49 inmates on death row were convicted of crimes when they were under 18.[66] On 25 May 2016, Iranian authorities reported the flogging of 17 children in western Azerbaijan province, after their employer sued them for protesting the firing of fellow workers.[67]

In the first verse of *Asylum*, Iranian poet Saba Vasefi tells of experiences which drove her and others to flee their country. She left Iran in 2010 after being sacked from her university for opposing capital punishment.

> *This pen splatters the page*
> *With my blood,*
> *My words download*
> *Anxiety. My memories clack down,*
> *My childhood lies, its forehead broken,*
> *Before me on the page, and voices leak*
> *From it, voices from fig roots*
> *Near the school yard, from bullets lodged*
>
> *In the blackboard's throat; voices from*
> *A lacerated blood bag; voices*
> *From a veiled girlhood, bruised by*
> *Boot soles and batons. Even the deaf*
> *Dolls dare not cry among the rubble, under*
> *Bombardment.*[68]

Saudi Arabia's litany of cruel punishments sits in its penal code. All public gatherings, including demonstrations, are prohibited. Women are discriminated against. Access to human rights organizations is not allowed. Entrenched religious discrimination against Shia citizens is as routine as are decisions to deport migrant workers as a way of managing an economy. Arbitrary arrests and detention are as commonplace as torture in prisons.

In 2012, Saudi blogger Raif Badawi was arrested for 'insulting Islam through electronic channels'. For arguing for democracy, rationalism and freedom of speech, he was sentenced to 1,000 lashes and 10 years in prison. Three years later he received 50 lashes, after which doctors have discussed whether Badawi would be strong enough to be flogged again.[69]

Badawi was supposed to have broken Saudi Arabia's technological laws and to have insulted Islam. It is difficult to fathom the values which could justify such brutality, or to identify what satisfaction could be gained by the officials who order such a sentence, or by those who carry it out, or by those who look on.

An appraisal of the licence for cruelty given by religious beliefs should include some consideration of responses to blasphemy, those utterances which question, criticize or repudiate God, Muhammad or Islam.

If robot-like repetition of hate-filled slogans gives millions of people a way of illustrating their beliefs and demonstrating their identity, it becomes highly dangerous for anyone to stand against them. Like tanks rolling relentlessly across an open plain, no human can hinder their momentum because the tank drivers' only purpose is to crush any individual who gets in the way. Not even the leaders responsible for assembling the tanks dare counter-command the onslaught which they have set in motion. Even viewed from a safe armchair in a democratic nation, it sends a shudder to think that mob hatred leads to on-the-spot cruelties, savage punishments and murder, the consequences of several countries' blasphemy laws.

A mind-boggling, mob-like cruelty flourishes in responses to alleged blasphemy. In relation to the eight years of solitary confinement meted out in Pakistan to Asia Bibi, a Christian farm labourer, Harriet Sherwood, the *Guardian's* religious affairs correspondent, refers to a 'Tolerance of hate'.[70] That there could exist a Pakistani political party – Afzal Qadri of Tehreek-e-Labbaik (TLP) – whose purpose and preoccupation is to punish blasphemy seems incredulous. The mobs who chanted for the death of Asia Bibi seemed intent on demonstrating they were better believers than other apparently more liberal parties. Whatever the explanation, here is another example of actions and punishments which have been documented in previous illustrations of torture and cruelty. Incredulity about blasphemy laws asks why this licence for hate? In the blasphemy-fired anger towards the powerless Asia Bibi, the characteristics of other cruelties reappear but with religious credentials.

Those characteristics include the exercise of one-dimensional power in which only obedience is demanded. They show individuals content to escape from the freedom to reflect and to think for themselves. They include disdain for any idea of religious freedom, let alone freedom of thought and speech. In anticipating subsequent appraisal of causes of cruelty, this has the appearance of a banality of evil. Such responses may derive from edicts that flow from bureaucracies, but the pleasure from being sadistic looks like the most plausible explanation. That sadism is legitimised by religious, political and cultural licence as formidable as those tanks rolling across an open plain. These frightening events, including the murder of Christians and of officials who dare to try to lessen the sadism inherent in the blasphemy laws, will be explored in the following chapter.

Beliefs derived from religious extremism, such as Wahhabism, are not confined to countries where Islam is the dominant faith. Fundamentalist Christians have fostered their own extremism, subjected their children to accusations of being infinite sinners unless they displayed unquestioning belief in God, followed a literal interpretation of the Bible and accepted that as the end was nigh, they'd be unlikely to grow up to be adults. Survivors of this extremism have reported that such teachings amounted to psychological torture.[71]

After his arrest and imprisonment by the Nigerian government in 1967, Nobel Prize recipient the poet Wole Soyinka wrote in *Harvest of Hate* that by mid-morning even the sun had died, that palm fronds had been savaged to bristle, and with no sanctuary left, all living things were falling 'to the tribute of fire'.[72]

In northern Uganda in the late 1980s Joseph Kony, the founder of the Lord's Resistance Army (LRA), claimed to be possessed by spirits. He said he would fight to implement the Ten Commandments, would purify the Acholi people and turn Uganda into a theocracy. To that end, between 60,000 and 70,000 children were abducted to become soldiers and sex slaves. An estimated two million people were displaced. Kony and his followers became notorious killers. Willingly or unwittingly, governments and the international community have also participated.[73]

Attention given to the Kony cruelties deflected attention from the Ugandan government's oppression of the Acholi, Teso and Langi people. Following the brutal dictatorship of Idi Amin, governments led by President Museveni herded an estimated 95% of Acholi and others into 200 concentration camps. Thousands of children died each week in what a former Ugandan Foreign Minister, Olara Otunnu, called a 'secret genocide'. These atrocities remained secret because powerful governments, UN agencies, NGOs and human rights organizations had decided that President Museveni was a new breed of African leader. Commitment to that stereotype view enabled Museveni to enjoy international patronage and to do as he pleased.

In 2003, Kony was indicted by the International Criminal Court (ICC). He has never been captured. In evidence to the ICC, witnesses said that a former LRA leader, Dominic Ongwen, instructed his escorts to administer dreadful beatings and even, on at least one occasion, to kill, cook and eat civilians who had been abducted in attacks.[74]

Following the indictment of Kony, and after 20 years of confinement in camps, Acholi and Langi people were forced back to their villages, to places which had been mined, where there were neither roads, schools nor healthcare.

A record of cruelties has a capacity for repetition. The US government contended that the November 2013 abduction of 200 Nigerian schoolgirls by the terrorist group Boko Haram was inspired by Joseph Kony's cruel tactics.[75]

In late 2017, the experiences of the Ugandan Acholi people have been repeated in the experiences of Rohingya people of Myanmar. They have been ethnically cleansed from their home country and are trying to survive in makeshift camps on the Bangladesh border. They have been told to go home but have no homes to return to.

Policy pointers

Conditions which foster cruelty are not to be understood by a catalogue of atrocities and not by psychologizing the supposed traits of perpetrators or victims. Rather, the influence of cruelty on policy and on the motives of those who oppose states' governance is the product of political, religious and militaristic forces which have stigmatized as unworthy or dangerous groups such as Roma people, asylum seekers, 'leftists' and religious non-believers. They have been victimized by political, military and religious leaders' fascination with violence, practised on the assumption that excessive force is the way to squash conflicts and solve problems. As that pattern continues, strenuous efforts are made to deny that such violence occurs. Questioning powerful actors' commitment to lying is a major task for anyone wanting to analyse and evaluate policies.

From this chapter's range of examples, it is apparent that cruelty has been justified by motives in which religious and sexual gratification merge, in which ethical considerations are absent and humanitarian law is regarded as irrelevant. The following exploration of the causes of cruelty will show a mingling and convergence of these forces.

3

Explaining causes

What a fair world were ours for verse to paint
If Power could live at ease with self-restraint!
                                (William Wordsworth)[1]

I am born of the conquerors,
You of the persecuted
Raped by rum and an alien law,
Progress and economics,
Are you and I and a once loved land
Peopled by tribes and trees;
Doomed by traders and stock exchanges,
Bought by faceless strangers.

                                (Judith Wright)[2]

The concept of inherent rights is fundamental and that everybody possess them, whether they are rich or poor, men or women, black or white. Until we establish that principle, we shall have made no progress, whoever holds political office. (Tony Benn)[3]

Psychological, social, political, religious, cultural forces? How to explain cruelty?

To respond to those questions, I'll explore three overlapping theses: the banality of evil; conditioned, automaton-like behaviour; the attraction of sadism. Following that exploration, and with a feeling of travelling up a tributary of the main arguments, I'll also ponder the force of ideas about efficiency as a fuel for cruelty, though I'll only be pursuing that line of inquiry with regard to the civil war between Colombian government forces and Revolutionary Armed Forces of Colombia (FARC) rebels in Colombia. That exploration comes at the end of this chapter.

The banality thesis identifies widespread acceptance of cruelties if legitimized by states, their governments, their policies and/or by other powerful institutions. Analysis of conditioned behaviour refers largely to operators of state and non-state organizations who keep the wheels of cruelty turning, yet such personnel usually remain invisible, inaccessible and non-accountable. Completing the cruelty puzzles requires accounts of sadistic behaviour, which is embedded as much in cultures of violence as in the pathology of any one person.

The explanations overlap but have distinct characteristics.

The banality of evil

Conversations about cruelty usually prompt references to Hannah Arendt's concept 'the banality of evil'. At the 1961 trial of Adolf Eichmann, charged with the murder of millions of Jews during the Second World War, philosopher Arendt observed an apparent conventional individual who appeared to be blind to the evil he had committed.[4] Supposedly bereft of any capacity to ponder the immorality of his actions, Eichmann could remain obedient to his Nazi masters and carry out his murderous tasks unhindered by ethical considerations. His cruelty was evil, yet seemed commonplace. In Arendt's view, Eichmann considered himself not in charge of his actions and therefore unable to change anything. He showed none of the shame or guilt usually associated with behaving immorally.

Revelations from the Eichmann trial did not mean that this man was a cruel exception. The responsibilities of a wider public can't be dismissed with the claim that this was the once-in-a-lifetime extreme anti-Semitism which contributed to the Holocaust. On the contrary, there's a case for saying that Arendt's banality of evil argument could also be called the evil of banality, so widespread are cruelties, so often ignored because so constantly denied.

In democratic societies, governments insist that they respect international law and human rights, though they may ignore both, hence the persistence of cruelties. A politics of cruelty can affect everyone's minds and actions, even as citizens might claim to be disinterested in politics. In her poem *Children of Our Age*, Polish poet Wislawa Szymborska highlighted the effects of political cultures in which participants were not just politicians. She insists that everyone's daily and nightly affairs are political, that we are all a product of politics and it would be foolish to deny that. What we say and do not say is also politically significant. All day long, all through the night, all affairs, yours, ours, theirs, are political affairs. It's in your genes, your political past and cast, so whatever you say reverberates and you are talking politics.[5]

Claims about the banality of evil suggest that perpetrators of cruelty are blind to the implications of their actions, or do not pause to reflect. If incapable of reflection, they will not trespass from the mindset which allows cruelty to continue.

Massacres in Sabra and Shatila refugee camps occurred while the Israeli defence forces looked on and the US government colluded. The slaughter of thousands was explained away because a proportion of the camp residents were defined as terrorists, only valuable if dead. Savagery could be swept under a carpet as though nothing of consequence had happened.

Syrian President Assad knows of the violence he promotes, yet in media interviews he dons his psychopathic mask, pretends that civility reigns and that chemical weapons would never be used. How could interviewers think otherwise? In his memoirs, the significant American journalist Seymour Hersh records how powerful leaders facilitate mass murder, do so with impunity and love to lie about their policies. A compliant media, says Hersh, enables cruelties to continue.[6] In the following chapter, 'Cruelty as policy', Hersh's conclusions are elaborated.

Confronted with evidence of the massacres in Srebrenica, Serbian leaders denied that such killings occurred. They could see, but pretended they were blind. A banality coursed their minds and influenced the attitudes of the populations they represented.

Poet and French resistance fighter Paul Éluard (1895–1952) opposed the banality of repressive regimes. He wondered why humanitarian perspectives were replaced by abuses of power. He advocated avant-garde interpretations of freedom. Here are the first and fourth verses of *Dawn Dissolves the Monsters*.

> *They did not know*
> *That the beauty of man is greater than man*
>
> *They gnawed away the flowers and smiles*
> *They found a heart only at the end of their rifles.*[7]

The evils of life imposed on residents in Lebanese refugee camps, in the slaughters in Bosnia and in the Syrian civil war, may appear to be examples of extremism. Commonplace actions of politicians and their followers display similar patterns, as witnessed in political and religious cultures in which powerful men have administered cruel policies. To support the argument about banality rather than any thesis that cruel actions derived from the warped traits of individuals, let's consider how a US Attorney General and Australian Ministers of Immigration came to their positions in cultures which made discrimination and other inhumanities appear normal.

President Trump's choice as Attorney General was the former Alabama Senator Jeff Sessions. In the US Senate, prior to his appointment to the Trump White House, Sessions had for two decades opposed every Immigration Bill that should have enabled immigrants to obtain citizenship. Sessions liked to promote his self-image as a foreign-policy tough man, evidenced by his opposition to an amendment that would have banned 'cruel, inhuman or degrading treatment of prisoners'.[8] In regard to questions of race, he is alleged to have supported the Ku Klux Klan until he discovered that they smoked marihuana. Evidence of Sessions' racist attitudes prompted the Alabama-based Southern Poverty Law Centre to say that Sessions' presence in Trump's inner circle was 'a tragedy for American politics'.

The Southern culture which Sessions breathed, and that apparently influenced his beliefs, derived from the 19th-century Jim Crow laws which established different rules for white and black Americans, sanctioned racial segregation and contributed to 4,000 lynchings across 12 states, and was usually justified by religious beliefs.[9] Sessions, a deeply committed Christian, held convictions which look like a leftover from the Jim Crow days. In an analysis titled *Christian Soldiers*, Jamelle Bouie said that the lynchings of black Americans were not just vigilante punishment or acts of racial control and domination, they were also rituals of Southern evangelism and a dogma of purity, literalism and white supremacy.[10] Bouie concluded that religion permeated communal lynchings, that these murders occurred within the context of a sacred order designed to sanction holiness. The 'sacred order' was white supremacy and the 'holiness' was white virtue, symbolized by white womanhood.

Jeff Sessions did not repudiate a religious culture in which the brutality of segregation and lynchings was justified by the Christianity of the day, in which politics demanded acts of terror and control. Through his religiosity, similar traditions continued and, once in government, he appears to have become banal about such practices. In July 2017, he announced that the US Department of Justice would create a 'religious liberty task force' to 'help the department fully implement our religious guidance'. He said he wanted to ensure that staff in the Department of Justice would know their duties to accommodate people of faith. A few months later, in May 2018, he quoted from the Bible to justify why migrant children who entered the US illegally should be separated from their parents.

Within another culture in which racist attitudes had been cultivated for years, successive Australian Ministers of Immigration such as Philip Ruddock and Peter Dutton managed to behave cruelly by turning the immoral into something honourable. They did so without appearing to be disturbed by the nature of their actions and on occasions seemed able to discard the usual moral codes.

The longest-serving member of the Australian Parliament, Mr Ruddock officiated as Minister for Immigration between 1996 and 2003. In that role he disguised his indifference to the rights of refugees with membership of Amnesty International and gave the impression he would welcome people seeking refuge from persecution. In late August 2001, Ruddock played a significant role in preventing asylum seekers aboard the Norwegian cargo vessel the MV *Tampa* from entering Australian waters. In the subsequent challenge to Ruddock, to Prime Minister Howard and Defence Minister Reith, the Victorian Council of Civil Liberties mounted a case in the Federal Court to have the asylum seekers released.

In October 2001, just prior to a Federal election, Ruddock announced that asylum seekers on 'a suspected' Illegal Entry Vessel (SIEV 4) had threatened to throw their children overboard. Subsequently, a Senate select committee of inquiry found that the event did not happen, that the evidence did not support the 'children overboard' claim.

By wearing an Amnesty International badge in his jacket lapel, Ruddock tried to augment his claims to be a supporter of human rights. The human rights organization asked him to remove this badge when performing ministerial duties. Ruddock's daughter left the country in disgust over the absence of compassion in her father's policies, but on retiring from Parliament, Ruddock became Australia's envoy for human rights.

Even though he was known for consistently opposing the death penalty, Ruddock's decades of thumbing his nose at supporters of refugees seemed tantamount to saying, 'It's my career that is important. I respect human rights when it suits.' Interviewed following his retirement from Parliament, Ruddock said he had no regrets about his strong stands against asylum seekers. He blamed the 400 asylum seekers on the *Tampa* for standing over Australia. A powerful politician blamed the victims, a process we'll witness in many other countries.

This portrayal of a politician whose policies contributed to human rights abuses does not place him in the same historical bracket as authoritarian monsters who ordered mass murder. The Ruddock record suggests a potential for cruelty in almost everyone, but such potential is not realized if individuals are able to ask themselves, is this policy consistent with the notion of human rights, with respect for the dignity of every person?

There is evidence that on occasions, in the eyes of refugees and following a detailed evaluation of immigration policies, Philip

Ruddock was perceived as humane and 'an energetic advocate of the migration programme'.[11] This suggests Jekyll and Hyde traits in the perpetrators of cruel acts, blind to cruelty in some roles, repudiating it in others. That caveat is important lest it appear that the cruelty-as-policy thesis lumps together every cruel act and does not discriminate between them.

In another conservative administration, Minister Dutton appeared at first sight to follow Ruddock's example, but Dutton would not be seen dead wearing an Amnesty International badge and in his decisions about refugee issues he showed an arrogant certainty, never the ambivalence displayed by his predecessor. In early 2016, an asylum seeker imprisoned in offshore detention on Nauru set himself on fire and died. Dutton responded by arguing that people self-immolated merely in order to get to Australia. The politics of the time seemed to allow and even encourage such behaviour. About this incident, Professor Robert Manne commented, 'Australians somehow did not notice how truly remarkable was the Minister's brutality.'[12]

It is tempting to blame the cruelty of one powerful individual, but the Minister's statement was preceded by a long period of cultural preparation. Years of defining asylum seekers as a threatening other, as illegals, even as potential terrorists, made it easy to abuse powerless people. The stage was set, the culture ready, stereotype assumptions decorated conversations. Aided by a prejudging media, listeners and readers could endorse the Minister's explanation.

In his elaboration of the banality of evil, Robert Manne wrote that an eventual moral history of Australia's asylum-seeker policy would reveal 'the process whereby the arteries of the nation gradually hardened; how as a nation we gradually lost the capacity to see the horror of what it was that we were willing to do to innocent fellow human beings who had fled in fear and sought our help'.[13]

Questioning the psychopathology of asylum seekers and refugees acts like a convenient diversion from a cruel policy. Probation officers in the courts and prison systems in Britain and in Canada were familiar with the need to look out for offenders who showed few moral restraints, or who showed none. The latter could be defined as amoral. They were also regarded as alert, intelligent, charming and at first sight completely plausible. They might also be pathologically cruel. Their amoral traits needed to be recognized, yet apportioning the attribute 'a banality of evil' only to alleged psychopaths misses the point. If acceptance of cruelty becomes built into a culture, even the psychopath could be considered little different from any other citizen. He or she could disappear into the crowd.

In the killing fields of Cambodia after the Pol Pot genocide of an estimated 25% of the population, I interviewed survivors who lived alongside individuals who had participated in the massacres. They reported that they could not forget and could not be friends with their new neighbours. These neighbours had been killers, but in a return to post-conflict life, they showed no obvious remorse. The families of victims recalled that the participants in murder had explained their behaviour as a part of history and therefore inevitable.

The interviewees said they protected themselves by trying not to think. They thought their neighbours did the same. An out-of-sight, out-of-mind perspective enabled living to start again. Such neighbours could present themselves as normal. The families whose members had been victims felt powerless, with little alternative but to try to forget.

A banality of evil prevails when a large public approves of torture and killings determined by their political rulers. Since Rodrigo Duterte took office as President of the Philippines in June 2016, as a consequence of his war on drugs, an estimated 7,000–8,000 Filipinos have been killed. A Human Rights Watch report submitted to the International Criminal Court (ICC) in 2017 produced evidence that since his election as Mayor of Davao in the Philippines in 1988, Duterte had been responsible for three decades of extrajudicial killings and mass murder.

Nevertheless, Duterte and his policies remained popular. The killings were said to be actions which people would have wanted to do by themselves but now they had someone doing it for them.[14]

Police, military and judicial institutions closed ranks in support of Duterte's policies. This also helps to explain public attitudes. Even if people wanted to complain, there was nowhere for them to go. The police were involved in the killings. The Department of Justice said there was no such thing as extrajudicial killing. The Philippines House of Representatives covered up for the President.[15]

A blanket banality also puts human rights organizations at risk. Abandonment of rules of law produces a state of anomie where any official violence can be regarded as normal. On 16 August 2017, Duterte instructed Philippines National Police personnel to shoot those who opposed his policies, such as members of human rights organizations.[16]

In the war on drugs atmosphere in the Philippines, it appears impossible for rules of international law to be respected, let alone implemented. On being informed that his policy represented crimes against humanity, and that he would be referred to the ICC, Duterte responded, 'the international court is "bullshit", "hypocritical" and "useless"'.[17]

Similar ridiculing and rejection of humanitarian law has characterized the policies of successive Israeli governments towards Palestinians, including Arab citizens of Israel, West Bank residents and inhabitants of the Gaza Strip.

Dr Vacy Vlazna, of *Palestine Matters*, argues that in relation to Israeli governments' treatment of Palestinians, moral disengagement has become part of Israeli national culture, that once pathological cruelty was seen as normal, it could be ignored.[18] If Palestinians could be regarded as less than human, it was not necessary to feel any shame when treating them cruelly. A political–military system permitted violations of human rights.

In his comprehensive analysis of the Israeli occupation of Palestinian lands, which he subtitled *Life and Loathing in Greater Israel*, Pulitzer Prize-winning author Max Blumenthal recorded incidents in the 2009 Operation Cast Lead invasion of Gaza.

> Unarmed civilians were torn to pieces with flechette darts sprayed from tank shells; several other children covered in burns from white phosphorous chemical weapon rounds were taken to hospitals; a few were found dead with bizarre wounds after being hit with experimental Dense Inert Metal Explosive (DIME) bombs designed to dissolve into the body and rapidly erode internal soft tissue. A group of women were shot to death while waving a white flag; another family was destroyed by a missile while eating lunch; and Israeli soldiers killed Ibrahim Awajah, an eight-year-old child. His mother, Wafaa, told the documentary film maker Jen Marlowe that soldiers used his corpse for target practice. Numerous crimes like these were documented across the Gaza Strip.[19]

To explain how such cruelty had become regarded as commonplace, Blumenthal paraphrased the judgements of a revered Israeli intellectual, Yeshayahu Leibowitz. This professor of neurophysiology concluded that a tide of messianism and jingoistic euphoria which included a veneration of military commanders as demi-gods would produce a culture of racism. Such a culture, he said, would consume society.[20]

Evil has become banal in many countries. Political elites have coupled derision of human rights to claims about the moral superiority of their supporters and have thereby promoted macabre means of suppressing opposition. In such an atmosphere, pleasure could be derived from cruelty.

Automaton behaviour

Sociologist Max Weber warned that if bureaucracies were left unchallenged, they would threaten individual freedom. Conformity would be demanded, punishment dished out for non-compliance and people would end up in an 'iron cage'.

The Czech novelist Franz Kafka described nightmares resulting from cruel bureaucracies because avenues of appeal, let alone efforts to gain an audience with bureaucratic chiefs, would be blocked. He described unaccountable procedures, inaccessible documents and encounters with faceless, humourless officials.

Bureaucracies can operate efficiently if applicants conform and play by the rules, even if the rules are perceived as technological online nightmares which are difficult to understand and follow. Policies of free-market economic rationalism have been behaviourist in their carrot-and-stick attitudes to the means of making societies operate efficiently, a view which insists that the economically successful should be rewarded and unsuccessful competitors hounded and punished. Individuals such as migrants, refugees, people with a disability, ex-prisoners, the homeless and the unemployed are deemed economically unsuccessful because they can't compete and won't conform.

There's a sinister paradox in operation: to keep the wheels of governance turning, bureaucratic inertia must be maintained. Within the bureaucracies, staff may be encouraged to avoid using discretion, to discard emotions, operate like efficient robots and thereby become almost as powerless as the people they are supposed to help. In this way, policies to influence everyday events lose touch with reality.

Poet, playwright and former President of Czechoslovakia Václav Havel identified automatic, inflexible behaviour from the representatives of state institutions – invisible bureaucrats who administered cruel policies automatically.[21] In Czechoslovakia's communist years, such officials may have privately reflected on their tasks, but the system required no disturbance to the continuity which governed their actions. Their work required routines which should be maintained and seldom questioned. In this way, said Havel, an entire population could be manipulated.

Forty years after the publication of Havel's work, but this time in a democracy not a communist state, another bureaucracy, the Home Office in Britain, was treating large numbers of people who had lived in the country for decades as individuals with no rights and of no consequence. Suddenly, in early 2018, long-standing citizens who could not produce the paperwork issued on arrival in Britain from Commonwealth countries when they were kids were being sent to homeless shelters, detention centres or were deported. A deliberate government policy to create a hostile environment for supposed illegal migrants had been the brain child of Prime Minister Theresa May when she was Home Secretary. The bureaucracy became brutal and incompetent, their actions supported by legislation which had dismantled the means by which migrants could challenge Home Office decisions. One commentator concluded that this was cruelty by design, 'Incredibly, this is not a glitch in the system. It is the system.'[22]

A woman whose appeals for citizenship were initially rejected by this British bureaucracy and who had been threatened with deportation described the trauma she experienced and the creation of a culture which encouraged cruelty to migrants. Nesrine Malik wrote,

> It is hard to describe what it feels like to confront the possibility of leaving a country in which you are settled. I had by then been living, working and paying taxes in the UK for nine years and enjoyed all the natural extensions of that investment – a career, close friends, a deep attachment to the place, a whole life. It is almost as if the laws of nature change, like gravity disappears and all things that root you to your existence lose their shape and float away.[23]

Automaton-like behaviour bereft of humanity occurs in a political culture which allows discrimination and cruelty to flourish. In Britain, that culture had been fostered by a Tory right wing aided by newspapers which were breathless in reporting threats from migrants who might be terrorists. Campaigners to leave the EU via voting in the Brexit referendum fostered an angry populism which claimed that Britain had open borders and was a soft touch for asylum seekers. Such beliefs were fantasies, but dominant political classes accepted them as gospel and used such dishonesty to encourage punitive attitudes and policies. Regarding the Home Office decisions to arrest and even deport citizens whom they had dubbed illegals, Malik concluded: 'The cavalier detachment with which these big decisions are made cannot be isolated from the general corporate cheapening of human life that has set in over the past decade.'[24]

In anticipation of the routine controls from which a newborn would need to be protected, Northern Irish poet Louis MacNeice appears to have anticipated Weber's and Kafka's warnings, Havel's analysis and British migrants' fears. At the height of the Second World War, in the seventh verse of his poem *Prayer Before Birth*, MacNeice wrote,

> I am not yet born; O fill me
> with strength against those who would freeze my
> humanity, would dragoon me into a lethal automaton,
> would make me a cog in a machine, a thing with
> one face, a thing, and against all those
> who would dissipate my entirety, would
> blow me like thistle down hither and
> hither or hither and thither
> like water held in the
> hands would spill me.[25]

Routine, unreflective and consequently potentially cruel attitudes in bureaucracies also appear to contribute to the worldwide imprisonment of children. A Human Rights Watch 2016 report shows that around the world children languish behind bars, sometimes for protracted periods, and in many cases face brutal conditions.[26] UNICEF estimates that one million children are held behind bars for acts that should not be crimes: skipping school, running away from home, having consensual sex, throwing stones at military vehicles, having or seeking an abortion. Even if a juvenile court system exists, the practice of treating juveniles as though they were adults can drag on undisturbed until a sensation occurs which attracts media attention.

It is not just developing countries which lock up children and throw away the key. The Human Rights Watch report of 2016 records the US as leading the industrialized world in the number and percentage of children it locks up in juvenile facilities. The US government also sends an extraordinary number of children to adult jails and prisons, more than 95,000 in 2011.

From April to June 2018, over 2,000 children were separated from their parents at the Mexican border and then placed inside an old warehouse in southern Texas where they waited in cages made of metal fencing. An automatic policy of referring all cases of alleged illegal entry for criminal prosecution was called 'zero tolerance'. America's former first lady Laura Bush compared the scenes of immigrant children locked in cages away from their parents to the internment of Japanese Americans during the Second World War. The cries of caged children were jokingly described by an immigration official as 'an orchestra'.[27]

The Human Rights Watch report of 2016, on incarceration in response to crime, concluded, 'Girls face specific restrictions on their freedom of movement, enforced by criminal law. In Saudi Arabia, girls as well as adult women may be jailed and flogged for ill-defined offences of "seclusion" and "mingling", which one official described to Human Rights Watch as a girl or woman "being in an apartment by herself, or with a group of others, or sitting in a place where it is not natural for her to be".'[28]

The ill treatment of children includes sentences of death. Although international law flatly prohibits sentences of death for crime committed under the age of 18, since 2016, juvenile offenders have been sentenced to death in Egypt, Iran, the Maldives, Pakistan, Saudi Arabia, Sri Lanka, Sudan and Yemen.

The Israeli military's imprisonment of Palestinian children could be regarded as an unusual example of sadism but it has been continuing for so long that it appears routine. Each year Israel arrests, detains and prosecutes 500–700 Palestinian children suspected of criminal offences in the West Bank. This is the only country that automatically prosecutes children in military courts. Human Rights Watch reports that Israeli security forces 'have choked, beaten, threatened and interrogated children in custody without parents or lawyers present'.

A deeply embedded political–militaristic culture encourages Israeli citizens and their supporters overseas to perceive such cruelty as necessary, even normal. Normality for Palestinians includes 'the usual intolerable litany of daily frustrations, military checkpoints and the familiar sight of burgeoning Israeli settlements surrounding and choking Palestinian towns'.[29]

Israel justifies what it does to children in a series of Military Proclamations, 'in the interests of security and public order'. Thousands of such orders provide a 'legal' basis for arresting and charging Palestinian children.

What is meant by 'legal'? Claims about legality even when breaking international law, or being above the law, lead to a Kafkaesque world in which the cruel, the bizarre and the illegal can be promoted as not unusual. In contemporary politics, at least in Western democracies, there is an obsession with interpretations of the legal. The law is constantly reworked, whether in terms of the law itself or the processes by which it is applied, to the advantage of the powerful. In commentary on governance, we have to get beyond an obsession with law. For example, in spite of a slaughter of innocents, Israel likes to claim that it has legal, self-defence justification for such killings, allegedly carried out by the most humane army in the world.

In late December 2017, following repeated invasions of her parents' home in the village of Bilim, and after her cousin had been shot in the face by a member of the Israeli military, 16-year-old Palestinian Ahed Tamimi slapped an Israeli soldier and was filmed doing so. She was arrested. A judge confirmed that she was a threat and should be imprisoned.

Conditioned to regard Palestinians as not really human, Education Minister Naftali Bennett said Tamimi should spend the rest of her life in prison. Ben Caspit, a prominent Israeli commentator, said he would like to see Ahed sent to a dungeon to be tortured in such a fashion that no one should witness it.[30]

Israeli journalist Gideon Levy observed the automaton-like behaviour of the judge who ruled that Ahed Tamimi's imprisonment should be extended. 'Even the independent hand of the judge, Major Haim Baliti, didn't shake when he determined that the "danger" posed by Tamimi, an unarmed girl of 16, justifies her continued detention. The judge, too, is a small cog in the machine, someone who does his job, and returns to his own daughters and sons at night proud of his day's contemptible work.'[31]

The cruel treatment of powerless children, refugees and asylum seekers has been justified by claims that such policies had been approved by electorates. In an immigration repeat of Margaret Thatcher's dictum, 'The lady's not for turning', Australian governments have felt secure by repeating their policy slogans. 'No one on Manus Island or on Nauru will ever come to Australia', 'We will not restart the people smuggler trade.'

The politicians making these pronouncements dared not act in any other way. Cruelty, fuelled by a determination to avoid offending what they thought voters in key constituencies wanted, motivated those who said they would do what they had always done. Sticking to routine meant playing to electorates, to convey strength, or at least avoid appearing weak.

Regarding countries' attitudes to asylum seekers, the automatic rejectionist responses have been evident in a range of policies concerned with mandatory detention, the secret turning back of asylum-seeker boats and the provision of temporary visas. Such documents have offered no hope of citizenship or permanent resettlement. Even the Australian High Court caught the automatic justification mood, as in decisions that it was lawful to detain asylum-seeker children and lawful to detain someone indefinitely, if they could not be deported.[32]

When journalists reported that members of an Australian government department, Immigration and Border Control, had refused an asylum seeker's access to medical help on the mainland, the staff don't appear to have considered saying 'we do not agree', or, 'there must be humanitarian policies better than this'. Public servants who found the government's policies distasteful had probably been moved from the department or had left of their own accord. Those who remained faced the challenge to disobey or conform.

The American poet Theodore Roethke (1908–63) pictured the greyness of work in bureaucracies where automaton-like behaviour made it almost inevitable that the cruel outcomes of policies would not be considered. The poem was written before the arrival of computers. He called his composition *Dolor*, meaning suffering or anguish. He pictures office routines characterized by the paraphernalia of communication, 'the sadness of pencils', 'the misery of manila folders', 'the endless duplication of lives and objects'. As in current cases of refugees who have no idea which other humans sit at distant desks poring over applications for temporary visas, the insightful poet captures a sense of desolation, loneliness and 'unalterable pathos' in workplace cultures which may contribute to an end to others' freedom, even to their lives. He describes an office atmosphere 'more dangerous than silica', the grey, standard staff having something in common with 'Silt, almost invisible, through long afternoons of tedium'.[33]

Australia is not yet a police state but the May 2015 Border Force Act enabled prosecution and possible imprisonment of any offshore detention staff member who spoke about conditions in the detention centres on Manus and Nauru. In *The Drum*, Greg Barns and George Newhouse argued that the Department of Immigration had been turned into a secret security organization with police powers. Section 24 of the Act required that any departmental workers or contractors to the Department of Immigration and Border Protection should subscribe to an oath not to reveal operations. Staff could not fulfil ethical and professional obligations. Individuals such as doctors and social workers would be deterred from collecting information about detention centre conditions.[34]

Two years later, following public protest and politicians' acknowledgement that the system did not work, sections of the Act, such as those concerning the definition of protected information, were repealed. Personal information could be disclosed.

In a police state, dissent can be stifled, automatic suppression is an essential mechanism of control. In total institutions, such as prisons, psychiatric hospitals, detention centres, boarding schools, monasteries and even on merchant ships, sociologist Erving Goffman stressed that control was a permanent feature of daily life and easily exercised.[35]

Policies of dehumanization can be easier to implement if a substantial proportion of a population remain ignorant of such practices or have been schooled into becoming supporters. Such practices are even more likely to be accepted if the spirit of democracy is not honoured, or if democracy has been ridiculed and systematically destroyed, as in Cambodia in November 2017.

On 17 November 2017, the Cambodian Supreme Court dissolved the main opposition party and imposed bans of five years on 118 of that party's members. Radio stations had their licences revoked, the influential English-language newspaper *Cambodia Daily* had been forced to close after 24 years, the US National Democratic Institute was expelled and the opposition leader Kem Sokha was arrested and charged with treason.

To bolster his one-man, one-state rule, and in imitation of the violent stances and policies of the President of the Philippines, Rodrigo Duterte, Cambodian Prime Minister Hun Sen said to his opponents, 'To ensure the lives of millions of people, we are willing to eliminate 100 or 200 people.'[36]

Identifying sadism

A third and overlapping explanation concerns sadism, a pleasure in exerting control by hurting a person or an animal. Identity forged from satisfaction in exerting harmful control over others appears to have sadomasochistic features, both parties experience cruelty and it is possible both consider such actions rewarding. That claim borders on psychologism, but it is more illuminating to consider the convergence of cultural background and social context which gives men that sense of identity which makes sadism towards others look like a mission.

Individuals who have suffered torture and lived to express their understanding of the torturers' behaviour make observations about individual psychological traits, but they also emphasize the contexts which gave individuals a licence to be cruel, issued with an assurance there will be no accountability for cruel actions. In an incisive analysis of his years of being chained to radiators by fundamentalist Shi'ite militiamen during the Lebanese civil war, the former Irish school teacher Brian Keenan refers to his captors being as captured as he was. They were imprisoned by their religious beliefs. Their insistence on the absolute correctness of their own systems and way of life made compromise and acceptance of other people's traditions impossible.

Keenan says that cruelty and fear are man made, that the men who imprisoned and beat him were ruled by fear. On his release after four years of captivity, he wrote, 'Such men are only half-made things. They live out their unresolved lives by attempting to destroy anything that challenges the void in themselves.'[37] He concluded that the absolute judgements of his captors were without logic, reason, understanding or humanity, and that they had devalued him beyond comprehension.

In similar reflections about brutality by men, Gary Younge has emphasized the destructive capacity of masculinity. He observed issues of misogyny and inadequacy driving male violence. Political cultures influenced by a dominating patriarchy coupled to religious and tribal traditions provided the extra elements that guaranteed systematic violence, as seen in America with the rise of the political hard right. Younge argued that potentially violent and cruel men 'have a role model in the White House in a president who was accused of rape by his first wife, boasts of grabbing women by the genitals and openly disparages their looks and intellect'.[38]

Regarding an apparent taken-for-granted sadism in the acts of individuals carrying out the orders of specific states, I can only surmise that the Iranian hangman, the Saudi flogger, the Israeli jailers of children and the US police who shoot to kill have not found their tasks distasteful. In the case of the Iranians and Saudis, citizens of those countries, albeit critics, have explained that the cruelty would have been justified as expressing honour for God, even as a gift for that imaginary being. In obedience to an imagined divine authority, the individuals concerned could return home to maintain the pretence of a normal world, their beliefs maintained, their thirst for cruelty satisfied, at least temporarily.

Previous listing of mass murders included reference to the Iranian Supreme Leader Ayatollah Khomeini's orders for the elimination of as many as 5,000 prisoners. Sadism could cleanse the new Islamic Republic and create fear in the minds of any citizen who might think of opposing the regime.[39]

A cursory look at sadism enjoyed by rulers, their henchmen and rebel opponents in African countries would have to include reference to atrocities in apartheid-era South Africa, in the wars in the Democratic Republic of the Congo, in the civil war in Sierra Leone, the 14 years of civil war in Liberia which killed a quarter of a million people, the mass murder by Janjaweed militia of half a million civilians in the Darfur region of western Sudan, the bombings, kidnappings and assassinations by the Boko Haram terrorist group in Nigeria plus the deadly attacks by the al-Shabaab Islamist group in Somalia.

In the civil wars in South Sudan, from 2013, estimates from the UN and from aid workers are that up to 300,000 have been killed. The manner of their deaths is horrific: 'shot, speared, burned, castrated, hung, drowned, run over, suffocated, starved, and blown up, their corpses abandoned where they fell, bulldozed into mass graves'.[40] Large numbers of South Sudanese eventually found refuge in Kakuma refugee camp located in rocky, scorching hot desert country in northern Kenya. Built for 60,000 people it now is home to 180,000, only 5% of whom can ever expect to leave.[41]

The influence and consequences of state-organized violence have been expressed with characteristic courage and frankness by a former leading opponent of President Mugabe's regime in Zimbabwe. In 1999, Sekai Holland was arrested and tortured, her arm and leg broken, her ribs smashed and parts of her body so lacerated as to need skin grafts. Yet in my conversations and correspondence with her, she has avoided demonizing the individual who wielded an iron bar and the policewoman who stomped on her. Instead, she warned about the culture nurtured by state violence. 'It was my personal, gruesome experience, always denied by state-sponsored violence, which successive governments worked continuously to make more efficient, to dish it out more painfully on carefully selected victims.' The gutsy Sekai also speaks of prospects for a future of non-violence and of her hopes that human rights will be respected. 'My worry is how to balance my horrid experience with my knowledge of the resistance and generosity of Zimbabweans and their courage living with such a terrible reality. That reality includes the deeply ingrained culture of fear as a result of state-sponsored violence.'

Given the December 2017 replacement of President Mugabe by his former Deputy, Emmerson Mnangagwa, it is timely to consider the state-organized violence to which Sekai refers, which began Mugabe's governance of Zimbabwe. Massacres in Matabeleland, in western Zimbabwe from January 1983, show a fertile ground for sadism, for conditions for torture subsequently experienced by Sekai Holland and thousands of others.

Within the first five years of Zimbabwe's independence, a government force, trained in North Korea and known as the Fifth Brigade, received orders from Mugabe and his Security Minister Mnangagwa to remove all political opposition. This meant massacring Ndebele people who supported Zapu, an opposition party led by Joshua Nkomo. In the Shona language, the massacre was called Gukurahundi, 'the rain that washes away the chaff before the spring rains'.[42]

An estimated 20,000 people were killed by an elite Zimbabwean army unit which had much in common with Chilean dictator Pinochet's 'Caravan of Death'. The word 'killed' disguises the nature of the Fifth Brigade's brutalities, such as burying children alive, bayoneting pregnant girls to death, herding entire families into grass-roofed huts then setting them alight.[43]

No one has been held accountable for the massacres. Impressive evidence indicates that the British and US governments knew of the massacres but calculated that it was best to turn a blind eye. Following his inauguration in December 2017, President Mnangagwa said, 'let bygones be bygones'.

Powerful nations' collusion with South American and African dictators has contributed to torture, slaughter and to other human rights abuses, never more so than in Chad under President Hissène Habré from 1982 to 1990. Retrospective diagnosis shows Habré's brutality being fed by his warlord narcissism, by specific ethnic groups being stigmatized, by the willing compliance of state bureaucracies which ran police and armed forces, by supply of arms from France and the US and by the non-interventionist attitudes of those powers.

Habre seized power in 1982 and received support from France and the US because the French and American foreign policy architects considered Chad a bulwark against the military ambitions of the dictator of Libya, Colonel Gaddafi. Dressed in Cuban cap, Ray-Ban sunglasses, tightly fitting uniform and with a Colt revolver at his side, Habré pretended to be a Che Guevara, posed as a modern-day all-conquering macho Rambo but was subsequently dubbed 'Africa's Pinochet'. He is reported to have become obsessed with internal enemies, in particular the Zaghawa ethnic group, whose leader Idriss Deby had been Habré's deputy and had led a rebellion against him. The dictator's aptly named Directorate of Documentation and Security (the DDS) aided him with torture as the means of governance. During his eight-year rule, an estimated 40,000 were killed and another 200,000 tortured.[44]

On 30 May 2016, in Dacca, Senegal, a three-judge panel of the Special African Tribunal sentenced Habré to life imprisonment for crimes against humanity, war crimes, torture and rape. The case had been brought by 4,000 victims of the oppression. From the DDS bureaucracy, prosecutors obtained secret police archives that recorded the names of 12,321 prisoners, interrogation reports and information about the deaths in detention of more than 1,200 people.

A former prisoner, Clement Abaifonta, said that he could not forget the horrors he had seen in jail. He had worked in a prison kitchen and laundry before he was ordered to take on a new role as a gravedigger.

'What broke my life is the fact that I buried about 1,000 people. With all that Habre did, we could cut him into pieces and it wouldn't satisfy everyone.' A former DDS agent, Bandjim Bandjoum gave evidence at Habré's trial: 'When we arrested people we took them directly, we had to interrogate them. The interrogations were violent and the people cried … the sessions were unbearable … inhumane indeed.'[45]

Such cruelty is only partly explained by targeting groups as a threat to powerful rulers and to their usually male collaborators, those mostly uniformed characters who know about the top-down use of power. Before the targeting of specific groups as enemies, these targets for cruelty had been depicted as detestable, not worthy of life, a process which led to an apparent justification of and pleasure in sadism. Such punishments are not confined to the African continent.

Reference has already been made to the traditions of lying and fabrication conducted by Count Potemkin in the Russian court of Catherine the Great and to the Katyn practice of concealing massive atrocities and simultaneously blaming someone else. A culture of deceit, brutality and non-accountability continues in the Russia of Vladimir Putin, where sadism is practised by individuals who torture and kill, and by compliant behaviour in bureaucracies.

In his novel *Gulag Archipelago*, Alexander Solzhenitsyn said of the prison guards that they carried out their orders exactly and that they were impervious to suffering, 'that is what they do and who they are'.

Since the era of the Gulag, apparently little has changed. Putin's alleged jargonistic remark about inmates, 'We'll waste them in the outhouse', confirms Solzhenitsyn's observations. In numerous Russian prisons in faraway places, there's widespread evidence of everyday violence. Physical force against a prisoner makes him or her obedient and dependent on prison administration. Journalist Anastasiya Zotova says, 'Just about anyone who lives in provincial Russia will tell you that prisoners are beaten up, and that this is normal. Ex-prisoners report experiences of torture through violent sexual abuse, mass beatings and punishment by forcing heads into toilets. Russian prison staff, while seeing themselves as crime fighters, become criminals and instil in their charges the idea that no one respects the law, not even those who enforce it.'[46]

A culture of indifference to human rights and non-accountability would encourage lawlessness by lawmakers. Dissent can't be tolerated. Oppressive practices and laws by Putin and his security forces have included jailing prominent figures, persecuting artists whose work reflects poorly on Putin, restricting the advocacy of non-government organizations, expanding the definition of treason to turn virtually any government critic into a 'traitor'. This Putin-fed culture criminalizes the actions of the LGBTI community and intimidates human rights defenders.[47]

Putin's techniques for suppressing dissent have ranged from imprisonment to murder. In August 2012, members of the punk rock band Pussy Riot were arrested following their filmed performance in the Moscow cathedral, Christ the Saviour. Clad in colourful clothes and wearing balaclavas the three young women sang 'Mother Mary, please drive Putin away'. Their action was said to go against tradition and was a great insult to the church and the people. Charged with hooliganism for singing this song critical of Putin, they were sentenced to two years in prison, though on appeal one of the performers was freed on probation.

In Putin's Russia, journalists and opposition politicians risk their lives. Since 2006, the Russian Committee to Protect Journalists, and the US-funded organization Freedom House, recorded the killing of 20 journalists and 63 violent attacks on reporters.

In September 2001, the crusading journalist Anna Politkovskaya wrote *Disappearing People*, in which she blamed Russian policemen for the murder of peaceful residents in Chechnya. In a subsequent book, *Putin's Russia*, she accused the President of turning his country into a police state. On 7 October 2006, someone ordered the murder of Politkovskaya. She was shot dead in the stairwell of her Moscow apartment. The Chechnyan leader Ramzan Kadyrov, a close ally of Putin's, was suspected of sending the gunman to kill the journalist.[48]

Natalia Estemirova, a journalist who sometimes worked with Politkovskaya, had specialized in uncovering human rights abuses carried out by the Russian state in Chechnya. In July 2009, Ms Estemirova was kidnapped outside her home before being shot in the head and dumped in nearby woodland. Her friends say this was a vile, cowardly, state-sponsored execution.[49]

In 2003, a Russian politician, Sergei Yushenkov, was shot dead as he tried to gather evidence proving that President Putin was behind the bombing of a residential apartment block. Yushenkov was killed just hours after his organization, Liberal Russia, had been recognized by the Justice Ministry as a political party.

A vocal critic of President Putin, Alexander Litvinenko, had also accused him of blowing up that apartment block and of ordering the murder of Politkovskaya. On 1 November 2006, in London's Millennium Hotel, he drank cold green tea left behind by his Russian visitors. The teapot had been poisoned with polonium 210, a rare radioactive isotope. Investigative reporter Luke Harding wrote,

'Seventeen days later, Litvinenko was lying in hospital, mortally ill.' He died on 23 November.[50]

On 27 February 2015, two days before he was to lead a protest against the war in Ukraine, the Russian opposition leader Boris Nemtsov was gunned down outside the walls of the Kremlin. Although five men were convicted of the murder, Mr Nemtsov's family and his lawyer were certain that neither those who ordered or arranged the murder had been found.[51]

A 37-year-old lawyer, Sergei Magnitsky, worked for Bill Browder, creator of the Hermitage company, the largest private equity firm investing in Russia. Magnitsky was arrested in 2008 after uncovering evidence that Russian Interior Ministry officials had repeatedly authorized millions of dollars in fraudulent tax refunds to themselves and their relatives. Placed in pre-trial detention, Magnitsky was held for 11 months, tortured, beaten up by police, denied medical help and died in custody in November 2009.[52]

Responses to the brutality meted out to the brave and principled Sergei Magnitsky are significant for several reasons. Bill Browder was deported from Russia for revealing massive corruption at the highest levels in the Russian state. Embarking on a human rights campaign on behalf of his murdered colleague, Browder took the case to Washington and negotiated with US Senators and members of Congress to pass the 2012 Magnitsky Act, which punished Russian officials responsible for Magnitsky's death. The legislation also allowed the US government to sanction foreign officials implicated in human rights abuses anywhere in the world.

Events which followed Magnitsky's murder provide evidence that Russian state-ordered cruelty is coupled to stage-managed denials and a determination to pin blame on someone else. The Katyn Forest murders provided the precedent. In the Magnitsky case, Russian deception reached a new level when prosecutors convicted Bill Browder in absentia of fraud and claimed that Magnitsky was actually murdered by Mr Browder.[53]

In subsequent elaboration of ways in which successful politics depends on cruelty, there's convincing evidence that the practice is unashamed, deliberate and known, even if denied. Such deliberate acts can be nourished in cultures which are corrupt, fascinated with violence and secrecy. In his detailed human rights investigation, Bill Browder explains that judgement.[54]

Suppression by fear and cruelty in Putin's Russia looks like a revival of the taken-for-granted authoritarianism in the republics of the former Soviet Union, where people feared secret police and few dared to challenge official rules. Kazakhstan has been ruled by the same leader since 1991, while Tajikistan and Turkmenistan are reported to have grown more repressive. Uzbekistan still has chilling ways of punishing citizens who believe in freedom of speech. Since 2017, a freelance Uzbek journalist, Bobomurod Abdullaev, has been held in detention following charges of 'conspiracy to overthrow the constitutional regime'. His lawyer reported that Abdullaev 'was beaten repeatedly, and then kept naked for six days in a freezing cell without sleep. He said he was given food only on the fifth day of his detention, and even then, only after he had collapsed. Officials warned him that unless he confessed, his wife and daughter would be raped.'[55]

The latest Human Rights Watch Uzbekistan Report says that under a new leader, President Shavkat Mirziyoyev, a loosening of authoritarianism is occurring and widespread human rights abuses might cease. These abuses had included the compulsory dispatch of doctors, nurses, teachers, students and children to work as slave labour during the cotton harvest.[56]

Curbing the sadism inherent in decades of brutal repression depends on powerful officials ceasing their top-down use of power and on citizens overcoming the fears and suspicions which have dominated their lives. When considering humanitarian alternatives to cruelty in Chapter 5, those issues of power, fear and suspicion will be addressed. Even in countries where icy years of repression are beginning to thaw, education about human rights and about the benefits of non-violence has a long way to go, not least in a country where collective punishment of opponents is still treated as normal.

Sadism can presuppose an individual acting alone, but if the ideology of an institution and of a nation-state promotes cruelty, regimes act with impunity, an international community behaves as though it is neutral but numerous innocent people are punished. Collective punishment, such as house demolitions, is a serious violation of international law. Once thought to be an Orwellian fantasy, in Israel it has become routine.

In January 2017, a Palestinian, Fadi Qunbar, crashed a truck into Israeli soldiers and four were killed. Israeli officials then sealed the Qunbars' home with cement. The family became homeless. As preparation for expulsion, 12 relatives were stripped of their residency papers. Journalist Jonathan Cook commented, 'None of those people had done anything wrong. Their crime is simply to be related to someone whom Israel defines as a terrorist.'[57]

The Israeli human rights organization B'Tselem reported that officialdom acted with impunity, never to be held accountable.

Palestinians' homes could be destroyed and owners charged for the costs of the clear-up. Massive financial compensation was demanded from someone who might have been defined as a terrorist. Homes were stolen under the eyes of Israeli police. Ethics were buried, laws redefined, inhuman acts legitimized and promoted.[58] The argument that Israelis were the real victims facilitated sadism. Victims did not have to justify their actions.

The misery of people made homeless is matched by sadists' satisfaction. The settlers who celebrated that prisoners' hunger strike with a barbecue displayed the same sort of cruelty as those who, through the ages, have enjoyed punishing those they considered unworthy, people whom the Nazis called 'untermensch', or sub-human. Israeli journalist Gideon Levy argues that if one group of citizens consider themselves human and other citizens non-human, the former can mourn their dead and simultaneously rejoice in the killing of those they despise.[59]

Indifference to people suffering life-threatening illnesses illustrates another sadistic act. In an echo of the pain of Howayda, whose story of her dying days began this book, the *Middle-East Monitor* of 28 September 2017 reported that 'five female cancer patients in the Gaza Strip died in August after Israeli forces refused access to treatment outside the Strip'. According to the World Health Organization, the five women who died were aged between 26 and 53. Two suffered from colon cancer, one from ovarian cancer, one from breast cancer and one from a rare cancer known as a primitive neuroectodermal tumour. The chief executive officer of Medical Aid for Palestinians said, 'Denying access to potentially life-saving treatment is indefensible.'[60]

High-ranking individuals may have made these decisions to deny treatment but transferring responsibility from an individual to a nation-state is not the end of the story. The sadism does not stop there. Israel's collective punishment has been aided by consistent US support and by other Western countries turning a blind eye. Israel's entitlement to play the victim and thereby justify its cruelty has been indulged by the West.

Sadism involves huge financial investments in being cruel. In his comprehensive study, *American Torture*, Michael Otterman showed that sadistic practices had been used by American administrations for decades, 'From the Cold War to Abu Ghraib and beyond'.[61] After the Second World War, Americans began their official interest in extreme methods to obtain information by funding medical studies which built on Soviet and Chinese torture techniques.

Torture at Guantanamo Bay included the forcing of prisoners into stress positions, exposing them to harsh lights, extreme hot and cold temperatures, sexual humiliation, nudity and water-boarding that inflicted partial suffocation. President George W. Bush is alleged to have said that such torture represented only 'an alternative set of procedures' and that unjustified interrogation techniques were the action of a few bad apples.

In his analysis, *Official American Sadism*, Anthony Lewis documented details of the torture of a 17-year-old Afghan, Mohammed Jawad, even though prison officials knew that this young man had no valuable information to give. Lewis says that Jawad was tortured 'for sport, to teach him a lesson, perhaps to make an example of him to others'.[62]

Meanness in domestic policies can display sadism as much as in foreign affairs. A free market ideology has promoted a view of life as a competition in which only the strong, the rich and the efficient deserve to succeed. Applied to the management of societies, free market economics has provided numerous opportunities to bully and to penalize the weak.

In 2014, in an influential essay, 'The United States of Cruelty', Charles Pierce argued, 'There is a new kind of systematic cruelty in our daily lives, in how we relate to each other and in how we treat our fellow citizens, and, therefore, there is a new kind of systematic cruelty in our politics as well ... We practice fiscal cruelty and call it an economy ... We make war based on lies and deceit because cruelty is seen to be enough, seen to be the immutable law of the modern world.'[63]

New York Times columnist and Nobel Prize recipient Paul Krugman echoed Pierce's conclusions. He showed that the American Republican Party had maintained its tough, nationalist identity by wanting to appear strong in relation to citizens with limited resources. Krugman concluded that the Republicans were hostile towards anything that protected families against catastrophe.[64]

In 2017, in an effort to comprehend Republican cruelty, Krugman analysed the Republican Party's several months of trying to replace Obamacare with 'Trumpcare'. This, he said, 'required taking health insurance away from tens of millions, making it much worse and far more expensive for millions more and then using the money saved to cut taxes on the wealthy'. Krugman added that more than 40% of the Senate's proposed 2017 tax cuts would go to people with annual incomes over $1 million. Warren Buffet denounced this Senate bill as the 'Relief for the Rich Act'.[65] In these actions, the US Republicans have been consistent. The poor and the working-class have been punished, the already-rich rewarded.

In his mid-July 2018 analysis, 'The G.O.P.'s war on the poor', Krugman is explicit about the cruelty inherent in policies consistent with neoliberal ideologies. He shows that although blue-collar white Americans think that the poor are lazy and prefer to live off welfare, the hostility towards poor people is driven mainly by political elites, such as representatives of the US Republican Party. Krugman concluded that the identity and the careers of these politicians 'was wrapped up in the notion that more government is always bad. So they oppose programmes that help the poor partly out of a general hostility toward "takers" but also because they hate the idea of government helping anyone.'[66]

A comprehensive documenting of cruelties fostered by neoliberal social and economic policies has also been crafted by Nobel laureate economist Joseph Stiglitz. He identified a US political system which gave inordinate power to the top 1%, who used that power to limit redistribution, to shape the rules of the game in their favour and thereby advance inequality. He has shown the success of corporations, in particular in the finance sector, in targeting the weak, the poorly educated and the poor. Moral scruples, he says, have been set aside in a grand quest to move money from the bottom to the top. 'Justice for all has been replaced by justice for those who can afford it.'[67]

Stiglitz' research showed that a large proportion of Americans could barely meet the necessities of life. Concealed by this statement was a potentially lifelong powerlessness suffered by vulnerable children. The 2011 US Census reported almost a quarter of American children, but nearly 40% of Afro-American children, living in poverty.

In this overview, there glowers a relationship between selfishness and cruelty. Stiglitz argues that if the top percentage of individuals and corporations have too much power, they will always succeed in obtaining policies that benefit themselves, not policies that might benefit society as a whole. Tax cuts for large corporations, for example, divert much-needed revenues into the pockets of a few instead of society at large.

In terms of future policy deliberations which could limit the cruelties associated with large inequalities, two concepts are crucial. Deregulation has given a free hand to the wealthy to do what they like in their interest. Decommodification should encourage politicians, and the economists who advise them, to cease seeing every individual and every aspect of the environment as an item to be traded in a financial marketplace.

Stiglitz joined with fellow economist Krugman in arguing that laissez-faire economic policies had produced disempowerment, disillusionment and, in terms of low turn-out in US elections, disenfranchisement. Krugman warned that extreme concentrations of income were incompatible with the healthy operation of democracies.[68] A few years later, in her work *Democracy in Chains* (discussed in Chapter 5), Nancy MacLean echoed the warnings of Stiglitz and Krugman. She concluded not only that the powers exercised by a few had eroded democracy but that economic freedom and political liberty were incompatible.

Abusive power

In this range of explanations there is a common denominator: an abusive exercise of power over the vulnerable which derives from the selfish motives of politically and financially powerful organizations and the individuals who represent them. Philosophers, political scientists, sociologists and psychoanalysts have long predicted such behaviour.

In 1513, Machiavelli forecast the importance of generating fear of punishment in order to keep people docile and obedient. 'So long as he keeps his subjects united and loyal, a prince ought not to mind gaining the reputation for cruelty.'[69]

In 1651, in his dystopian view of the world, following 30 years of widespread European conflicts, Thomas Hobbes assumed that only in death would mankind cease a 'restless desire for power'.[70]

In 1984, sociologist and psychoanalyst Erich Fromm insisted, 'There is no greater power over another person, than that of inflicting pain on him, to force him to undergo suffering, without his being able to defend himself.' In his argument that pleasure in the complete domination over another person was the very essence of the sadistic drive, Fromm referred to the Marquis de Sade.[71]

Chilean poet and Nobel Prize recipient Pablo Neruda (1904–73) scorned bullies and the countries which encouraged them. In lines from *The Dictators*, he warned,

> *Between the coconut palms the graves are full*
> *of ruined bones, of speechless death-rattles.*
> *The delicate dictator is talking*
> *with top hats, gold braid, and collars.*
> *The tiny palace gleams like a watch*
> *and the rapid laughs with gloves on*
> *cross the corridors at times*
> *and join the dead voices*
> *and the blue mouths freshly buried.*
> *...*
> *Hatred has grown scale on scale,*
> *blow on blow, in the ghastly water of the swamp,*
> *with a snout full of ooze and silence.*[72]

History is peppered with accounts of cruel and dominating power exercised in dictatorships and democracies. From the time of the Russian Czar Ivan the Terrible to the operations of Stalin's secret police and the KGB to the Chinese communists' delight in public humiliation, cruelty has been a key means of control. In Iraq's Abu Ghraib prison, Saddam Hussein built torture chambers, rooms with gallows complete with hidden trapdoors. The American CIA refurbished that prison and developed their Debility, Dependency and Dread techniques plus the presence of dogs to obtain confessions from prisoners.

Punishment of prisoners by individual torturers had been preceded by oppression and subjugation of large populations. Almost every Kurd in northern Iraq could trace a family history stained by treachery and dispossession, a story of murder and banishment. Human Rights Watch records that between 1977 and 1987 more than 4,500 Kurdish villages had been razed, thousands of dissidents removed to detention camps. In the same period, Human Rights Watch claims that Saddam had executed 100,000 Kurds. In 1988 in Halabja in northern Iraq, Saddam Hussein's chemical attack on that Kurdish town killed at least 5,000 people.[73]

As a 19-year-old Israeli soldier, Ruchama Marton participated in the 1956 Israeli invasion of the Sinai Peninsula. Sufficiently courageous to blow the whistle on powerful interests, she would have been one of the first Breaking The Silence soldiers. She reported,

> The Egyptian soldiers would come out of the sand dunes, sometimes barefoot, black from the desert sun, dirt and sweat with their hands up. Our soldiers shot them. Dozens of them, maybe more. That's just what I saw. They would come down from the dunes and the soldiers lifted their guns and killed them.
>
> I wanted to tell about what happened. I wanted to publish it, but nobody agreed. They (the military authorities) told me to leave it alone.[74]

The notorious 1968 My Lai massacre by US soldiers in Vietnam illustrates the adrenalin rush that accompanies an exercise of power over defenceless people. US Army Captain Ernest Medina allegedly said of people in the Vietnamese hamlets, 'They're all Vietcong, now go out and get them.'

Anti-war activist and poet Denise Levertov observed the consequences of war in Vietnam. Her poetry suggests that she anticipated the My Lai massacre. In the first two verses of *In Thai Binh (Peace) Province*, she wrote,

I've used up all my film on bombed hospitals,
bombed village schools, the scattered
lemon-yellow cocoons at the bombed silk factory,

and for the moment all my tears too
are used up, having seen today
yet another child with its feet blown off,
a girl, this one, eleven years old,
patient and bewildered in her home, a fragile
small house of mud bricks among rice fields.[75]

In the My Lai operation under the command of Second Lieutenant William Calley, between 350 and 500 unarmed citizens were murdered. Investigative journalist Seymour Hersh reported that the victims included men, women, children and infants. Some of the women were gang raped and their bodies mutilated.[76]

It is tempting to believe that such orgies of violence occur only in wars. The convenient and lame excuse, 'It's war, anything can happen' prompted Denise Levertov to identify consequences for the warmongers, not just for the victims. In *Weeping Woman*, she imagined a warning from a woman whose arm had been blown off.

In the wide skies over the Delta,
her right arm that is not there writes indelibly,
                    'Cruel America,
when you mutilate our land and bodies,
it is your own soul you destroy,
not ours'.[77]

In Afghanistan, the terrorist organizations ISIS and the Taliban murder and maim. In early 2018, in a series of attacks aimed at undermining confidence in Afghans' Western-backed government, hundreds were killed and many more wounded. On 5 January 2018, a suicide bomber blew himself up near a crowd of police and protesters in Kabul. Eleven were killed and 25 wounded. On 20 January, gunmen attacked Kabul's Intercontinental Hotel, killing 20, injuring 25. On 24 January in Jalalabad, staff members of the charity Save the Children were killed. On 27 January, by placing a bomb in an ambulance, the Taliban killed over 100 people and injured 158.[78]

Such massacres are reported to be carried out by attackers or suicide bombers, also described as militants, extremists, terrorists or fanatics. The language is easily adopted. The content of attackers' minds remains to be unravelled.

A fascination with violence displays difficulties in shifting to an interest in non-violence. Entertaining ideas about a common humanity will require an unmasking of motives to be cruel. Sadism, the pleasure in hurting someone, is evident in the view that the ends justify the means. This gets close to explaining many atrocities. What to do about such actions is for politicians, policy makers, media personnel and NGO leaders to consider.

Efficiency and civil war in Colombia

So far this analysis has not aimed to produce an exhaustive record of cruelties but it would be remiss to ignore almost 60 years of fighting, from 1960 to 2017, between Colombian government forces and the Marxist Fuerzas Armadas Revolucionarias de Columbia, the FARC rebels.

In a letter written reputedly by Che Guevara to his mother, dated 6 July 1952, he described his experiences of life in Colombia: 'There is more repression of individual freedom here than in any country we've been to.' Guevara's observation raises questions about cruelty which go beyond the banality of evil, automaton behaviour in democracies and pleasure from sadism.

Atrocities in Colombia included the killings of an estimated quarter of a million people (including at least 45,000 children), and the displacement of six million.[79] Private militias engaged in slaughter. FARC rebels tortured and killed their kidnapped hostages. Drug cartels practised their own extortion and violence. Paramilitary supporters of Colombian government forces murdered peasant leaders who had returned to stolen lands. Evil was banal. Among government and rebel forces, sadism was widespread, but I want to explore another explanation for the Colombian government – FARC cruelties.

A culture of violence had been nurtured by centuries of dramatic inequalities, by militaristic assumptions that governance could operate only through top-down, one-dimensional power, and by a need for outside interference. That interference came from multinational companies interested in the drug trade, and in particular from US administrations which believed that any home-grown initiative that could be termed even slightly socialistic should be suppressed.

Colombian leaders' and influential outsiders' assumptions about efficient ways to run an economy and to maintain orderly government also give insight into forces which sustained the vicious, decades-long civil war. Efficiency can sound like an incontestable term. Inefficiency is easily derided. Cruelty persists in the middle of an efficiency/inefficiency tug of war, a claim which I'll apply in a brief appraisal of *La Violencia* in Colombia.

At the beginning of the civil war, an oligarchy representing establishment interest ruled the lives of peasants and wage earners living in rural areas. At stake were the rewards of governance by conservative, church and business leaders who maintained their influence in defiance of any idea of democracy, let alone equality. To achieve those latter goals would have required consultation with and representation of landless, poor and powerless people. Instead, maintenance of the oligarchy by force of arms could be deemed efficient. Any move towards genuine democracy was time consuming, required a different set of values and could be considered inefficient. The late Colombian political scientist Ana Maria Bejarano lamented that even while Colombians held free and fair elections whose outcomes were usually respected, its politicians, journalists, civil rights activists and union leaders were still regularly assassinated.[80] A form of efficiency ruled.

In the 1960s, the US intervened to squash anything that looked like democracy, let alone socialism. Supported by American business and political interests, a US Special Survey Team encouraged the creation and deployment of a paramilitary force to commit sabotage and terrorist acts against alleged communists. The FARC rebels became more efficient by increasing their weapons training, their skills in making landmines and in surprise attacks on Colombian military bases. They improved techniques of imprisonment, such as chaining hostages by the neck to a tree, in some cases for years.

To implement the ideology of efficiency, state military and non-state paramilitary had to be strengthened.

Injustices associated with massive social and economic inequalities motivated FARC leaders and followers. Efficiency needed violence. To reframe the problems of alleged inefficient people, such as campesinos, rural labourers and chronically poor Indigenous people, required steps towards a recovery of humanity, including respect for human rights. Taking those steps required a different way of thinking and acting. In a comment about the wretchedness and inefficiency of poverty, Alex, aged 25, explained that at age 15 he ran away to join the FARC, 'No money, no work, no chance to study, my family so poor.'[81] When a peace process made progress in 2017, a leader of a rebel group repeated the blindingly obvious: 'If they want to stop the guerrilla, they need to take away the arguments for our existence.'[82] Until a peace agreement was reached in 2017, removing arguments for the existence of rebel groups had been a step too far.

The efficiency–inefficiency conundrum also appeared in controversy over landownership. Small-scale farms producing for local consumption gave identity and livelihood to peasants and to other small landowners. In conventional economic policy terms, such ways of working and living could be perceived as inefficient. As a consequence of such judgements, peasants were pushed off their land, forced to migrate to cities and to work for low wages. Under the guise of efficiency, small farms were replaced by large-scale industrial farms which could produce for export.

In explanations about inhumanities in the Colombian civil war, there's no explicit reference to efficiency or inefficiency, yet steps to achieve a peace deal had to address issues which had sustained the conflict. Peace through respect for a common humanity required challenges to allegedly efficient but cruel practices. Proposals for a Colombian peace, which materialized in 2017, assessed the brutal forms of efficiency which had kept the civil war going and foreshadowed ways to encourage a de-escalation of violent values, policies and practices. The eventual peace agreements included land reform through redistribution to benefit the poor, political representation for FARC, a commitment to non-violence through the demilitarization of FARC and proposals for reparation to victims of violence.[83]

Policy pointers

A wide but random choice of examples reveals common themes. Sadism has included Mugabe's brutality in Zimbabwe, Russia's brutal penal system and elimination of critics, Israel's collective punishment of Palestinians, American governments' social policies which punish the poor and reward the rich, and the ISIS and Taliban atrocities in Iraq and Afghanistan.

From the banality of politicians pretending that they champion human rights, yet abuse them, to the commitment of atrocities by dictators such as Saddam Hussein, Bashar Al-Assad and the leaders of former Soviet republics, maintaining an apparatus to maintain abuses of power is a common theme. The fears and cruelties experienced by the people of Colombia during 60 years of civil war expose concerns with efficiency as another priority. In that country and elsewhere, maintenance of social and economic inequalities has been treated by powerful elites as inevitable. Criticism of efficiency may seem absurd, but in the conduct of bureaucracies and in the deliberations of governments the notion is used uncritically and can be addictive.

Cruelties have crossed countries and cultures, democracies and dictatorships. No moral assessment exercise should ever say that one abuse is so awful that it justifies forgiving or forgetting allegedly lesser crimes. That statement carries an important policy implication, a repeat of the thin-end-of-the-wedge argument: if an example of cruelty is labelled minor and therefore not worth considering, such a blasé attitude will encourage dangerous and destructive practices. Once a germ enters the policy bloodstream, it will foster disease which could be difficult to control, let alone eradicate.

Cruelties take place under diverse state responsibilities: governments, politicians and representatives of state agencies from defence to social security, from penal and religious affairs to immigration and border control. State institutions include surrogate organizations such as well-resourced political, religious and cultural groups.

Ethics, rules of international law, let alone any concern with a common humanity have been discarded. Such principles and rules appear to be acknowledged only when the mainstream media does its job, and when representatives of powerful institutions are so exposed that they need to save face. These points will be evident in the following chapter's illustration as to how cruelty becomes policy.

4

Cruelty as policy

What passing-bells for those who die as cattle?
Only the monstrous anger of the guns.
. . .
What candles may be held to speed them all?
Not in the hands of boys, but in their eyes
Shall shine the holy glimmers of good-byes.
The pallor of girls' brows shall be their pall;
Their flowers the tenderness of patient minds,
And each slow dusk a drawing down of blinds.
(Wilfred Owen)[1]

Wars don't decide who's right. They only decide who's left. (Bertrand Russell)[2]

Today we know more than ever that without respect for the rights of the individual, no nation, no community, no society can be truly free. (Kofi Annan)[3]

Policy can refer to a plan to achieve a particular objective. This simple statement suggests that policy goals would not be cluttered by considerations other than to achieve a specific task.

Beyond a policy statement, if it is ever explicit, implementation occurs that is often messy at best and sinister at worst. Into the mix of messiness comes a politics of contest and ambition, of denial and hubris, of shortage of resources and reinterpretation of goals. The number of policy players could increase astronomically, from politicians and bureaucrats to military and non-military operatives, from the intended beneficiaries of policies to the losers and victims, from state publicity machines to the partisan attitudes of diverse branches of media.

Even without the complex numbers of policy players, even if state representatives claim to have good intentions, their different objectives can lead to confusion and conflict. For example, the erosion of civil liberties has become a consequence of policies allegedly intended to achieve greater security for citizens. Efforts to deter criminality by increasing prison sentences have hindered policies to encourage the rehabilitation of prisoners. Under the influence of free market economic policies, the promotion of private business interests has eroded the resources of public institutions. In times of war and peace, countries' foreign policies have been ambiguous, as in statements by an Australian Foreign Minister about her country wanting to shape an external environment and increase influence in a region, whatever that was supposed to mean.

Those examples suggest a process of cracks and ambiguities. Official goals can be deflected, reinterpreted or ignored. In the ambiguities and through the cracks, cruelties emerge and may persist without ever being acknowledged. Even when acknowledged, they can be shrugged off as collateral but necessary.

Previous accounts of cruelty have included non-state actors. The following analysis confronts policies made largely by states and their representatives in state institutions. In those policies, cruelties have been formed and fomented in four ways.

(a) They may be direct and *deliberate.*
(b) They may *enable* cruelty to occur, albeit without being seen to openly promote cruel practices.
(c) They rely on *deception*, as in insistence that all is well even as cruelty occurs.
(d) They involve *collusion* between countries and with officials whose cruelty is deliberate.

All four processes display inhumanities which destroy lives and have other destructive human costs.

Deliberate

In *Violence*, German poet, playwright Bertolt Brecht (1898–1956), described factors which contribute to violence but which may not be immediately obvious.

> *The headlong stream is termed violent*
> *But the river bed hemming it in is*
> *Termed violent by no one.*
>
> *The storm that bends the birch trees*
> *Is held to be violent*
> *But how about the storm*
> *That bends the backs of the roadworkers?*[4]

From Kenya to Mexico, from Thailand to El Salvador, Mongolia to Guatemala, street children are the object of policies whose architects have been unapologetic and unashamed about their determination to remove the offending sight of such children by whatever means. Amnesty International has reported that millions of children live in fear, many of whom are beaten, disappear, are sexually exploited, detained or are killed by agents of the state. Compared to a country's interest in trade, or to the need, via diplomats, to present and maintain images of respectability, vulnerable children are of no consequence. They can be discarded and forgotten.

Examples of the deliberateness of such policies have been documented regarding the treatment of street children in Guatemala. Kate Millett has repeated accounts of Guatemalan 'police policy of unrelenting brutality toward homeless and addicted children'. Anything could be done to the children. Ears were cut off, eyes gouged out or burned and 'as if in admonition, tongues were cut out as well'.[5]

Perhaps the most deliberate of cruel policies concerns the ultimate punishment, state execution. China, Iran, Iraq, Saudi Arabia and Pakistan lead the world with the US not far behind. North Korea also favours capital punishment but publishes no records. Noting that in 2016 China executed more than all the other countries in the world put together, Amnesty International argued that China should come clean about its grotesque levels of capital punishment.

Such punishment derides human rights standards, undermines the value of human life and, under international law, is illegal. The International Covenant on Civil and Political Rights, resolved at the UN in 1966, coming into force in 1976, rules that capital punishment can be imposed for only the most serious crimes, which would exclude the drug-related offences for which Indonesia, Saudi Arabia, and until recently Iran, impose death sentences. A report by the human rights organization Reprieve found that 41% of those executed in Saudi Arabia in 2017 were killed for non-violent acts such as attending political protests.[6]

The question needs to be asked, what is the point of international law if it has severe limitations, is an inadequate protector of rights and does not appear to hinder cruelty? Nation-states continue to assert strength, and laws can be so easily ignored.

In January 2015, Indonesia shot six people for drug-related crimes and four months later eight more. The latter included the convicted Australian drug traffickers Andrew Chan and Myuran Sukumaran, even though they had proved to be model prisoners, had made amends and asked for mercy.[7]

The cruelty of the death penalty includes not just botched executions, as in an agonizing death by lethal injection in US prisons, but also the long wait for execution, which one commentator has named 'death before dying'.[8] In the US, since 1984, the time between an individual's sentencing and their execution has almost tripled from 6 to 15 years. Numerous courts, including the Supreme Court of California and the Inter-American Court of Human Rights, have found that the wait for execution 'terrorizes' prisoners and thus constitutes cruel, inhuman and degrading treatment,[9] which breaches the 1985 Convention Against Torture, to which the US is a signatory.

Many of the prisoners awaiting execution in Indonesian jails have been there for over 10 years. The uncertainty of a date of execution is compounded by prisoners being teased, 'may be this week', 'imminent', 'will not be delayed'.[10]

The Islamic Republic of Iran has allowed little delay between a sentence of death and an execution, a speed which appears to be associated with a lack of any fair judicial trial preceding a sentence. Prisoners in Iranian jails have told Human Rights Watch that authorities routinely blindfold and beat prisoners and force then to sign confessions which could be used as justification for a death sentence. In 2016, Iran executed at least 10 Sunni prisoners who had been sentenced to death based on confessions extracted under torture. Those executions included Shahram Ahmadi, a Kurdish prisoner convicted for 'enmity against God'. His trial lasted only a few minutes.[11]

Officially sanctioned state executions may be complemented by killings ordered or facilitated by a state in revenge against those who challenged their authority. Murders of Russian journalists and opposition politicians, documented in the last chapter, are examples of deliberate cruelty in policies to suppress dissent.

Policy advisers and teachers, politicians and public servants need to comprehend not just a catalogue of cruelties but also the culture and context which enables such practices to continue.

Bill Browder's investigation of the murder in Russia of Sergei Magnitsky, and in a subsequent staged trial, his – Browder's – conviction in absentia for fraud, shows how legal fabrication and indifference to ethics are catalysts for cruelty. Of Russia today, Browder concludes, it is

> A place where lies reign supreme. A place where two and two is still five, white is still black, and up is still down. A place where convictions are certain and guilt a given. Where a foreigner can be convicted in absentia of crimes he did not commit.

A place where an innocent man, Sergei Magnitsky, who was murdered by the state, a man whose only crime was loving his country too much, can be made to suffer from beyond the grave.[12]

Cruelty through deprivation of life does not have to include a specific murder or death penalty. An Australian government policy to remove Aboriginal children from their families was direct. A government's acknowledgement of such cruelty came in Prime Minister Rudd's apology when he referred to a policy which inflicted profound grief, suffering and loss on families.

In Australia's case, a different form of cruelty continued in the treatment of asylum seekers and refugees. Preoccupied with appearing strong, wanting to protect national sovereignty and to send a clear message to people smugglers, an Australian government spent up to $5 billion over four years, from 2012 to 2016, in order to contain 1,500 asylum seekers on Nauru and on Papua New Guinea's Manus Island.

In October 2017, when the detainees protested the closing of the Manus detention centre and their removal to a new but unfinished centre which made them vulnerable to attacks by local people, the government ordered their removal. The men had survived for three weeks without sufficient food, clean water, power or medical care. In response, members of the Australian Medical Association (AMA) voted unanimously to call on the Federal Government to grant access to the centre so doctors could assess the men's health, well-being and living conditions.

The detainees' health was threatened. Nevertheless, in keeping faith with their slogan, 'None of these people will ever be allowed to come to Australia', the government made two significant policy refusals. They turned down an offer from the New Zealand Prime Minister to take 150 of the detainees. They refused the AMA's request to send doctors to Manus to assess the detainees' mental and physical health.

An Iranian asylum seeker, Behrouz Boochani, kept a diary on the countdown to the closure of the Manus centre. His comments convey the policy consequences for the detainees. On Saturday, 28 October 2017, he wrote, 'The situation in the toilets has become a disaster. The prison is full of rubbish and filth. The people who are contracted to clean this place have discontinued their services and there is no trace of any cleaning products.' Later the same day he wrote, 'No one can sleep until really late due to fear. Hundreds of people gather in the prison yard to talk. The prison has submerged into a state of terror, the atmosphere is full of fear and anxiety.'[13]

At issue is the way cruelty is disguised by false claims about asylum seekers' freedom to choose. The detainees on Manus were given a choice to move to another detention centre on Nauru, move into the Manus community and be at risk of attack by local residents, or return to persecution in the country they came from.

It is not only Australia that displays cruelty towards refugees and asylum seekers. In September 2016, the Hungarian Prime Minister said that asylum seekers across Europe should be deported to camps outside the EU, patrolled by armed security, perhaps to an island somewhere in North Africa.[14]

By February 2017, Poland, the Czech Republic, Hungary and Slovakia had refused to accept EU asylum quotas. Hungary had set up border fences with Serbia and would employ 6,000–8,000 border guards to apprehend those coming through the fence.[15]

In lock step with Hungary's policy, Poland and the Czech Republic also refused to take in asylum seekers. The Czech government had admitted 12, but subsequently decided to detain refugees for at least six weeks, relieve them of their belongings and charge them for their detention. A poll by Focus found that 94% of Czechs demanded that all refugees should be deported and the border sealed.

Such cruelties contradicted refugees' rights to enter the territory of other countries even without passports. Years of neoliberal economics and anti-communist right-wing regimes had eroded the value of empathy and undermined respect for international law.[16]

Focus on Hungary's Orban and the states which have imitated his anti-immigrant policies overlooks the ways in which so-called respectable mainstream democracies have promoted fear of the other. Western European governments such as Britain and France have also legitimized hostility to immigration. In Britain, Theresa May as Home Secretary had called for a hostile environment for migrants. In France, President Macron toughened immigration and asylum laws, as in his doubling to 90 days the time in which undocumented migrants could be detained.

In the islands Italian Lampedusa and Greek Lesbos, which have catered for large numbers of new arrivals, the understanding of what could be called fair has been shaped by the policies of major institutions. The Mayor of Lesbos said that initially new arrivals were treated generously by his people but when Western democracies toughened their immigration policies, the beleaguered hosts on such islands were left to cope alone. The Lesbos mayor concluded, 'Kindness turned to anger ... and where there is anger there is room for all sorts of extremism.'

Immigration politics contain huge contradictions. On the one hand, politicians consider immigration to be necessary; on the other, they have to frame it as a problem, as in seeing asylum seekers and refugees not as living, breathing human beings but as so much undesirable flotsam and jetsam. The cruel objectives in labelling migration as a problem can be seen in criminalizing migrants, in militarizing border controls and in externalizing controls by making punishment-oriented arrangements with other countries. In addition to Australia's deal with the authoritarian dictatorship in Cambodia, the European Commission signed migration deals with Niger, Mali, Nigeria, Senegal and Ethiopia so that prospective migrants could be apprehended and locked up before they reached Mediterranean shores. In an analysis for the *Observer*, Kenan Malik reports that as of June 2018, in Libya alone there were at least 20,000 migrants held in detention by the General Directorate for Combatting Illegal Immigration and thousands more were held captive by militias and criminal gangs. Malik wrote, 'Amnesty International has detailed how all are held in the most degrading conditions and many are subject to torture, sexual abuse and extortion.'[17]

The Trump Presidency's support for Immigration and Customs Enforcement Officers (ICE), their detention of migrants and the prosecution of homeless people, shows US versions of the cruelties which Australia and member states in the EU use to promote their own border protection policies. In America the zero tolerance policies to punish migrants and to create fear to deter others is nothing new. The Trump Presidency continues a long history of racism. Policies to create fear of the other, and to bash foreigners, have a sinister history. Hadley Freeman reports that the US Emergency Immigration Act of 1921 was written to prevent the country being polluted by 'abnormally twisted Jews' who were deemed 'filthy, un-American and dangerous in their habits'. As if the 1921 Bill was insufficient, in 1924 the Johnson-Reed Act passed the US House and Senate. It banned all Asians from entering the country and was intended to 'keep American stock up to the highest standard, that is the people who were born here'. In documenting this history, Freeman refers to the events from April to June 2018 as exposing 'the bottomless cruelty of the right', as when children were separated from their parents at the Mexican border, lone toddlers, knee high to immigration officials, were removed from their parents. Freeman said that the Trump administration had so successfully denounced non-white immigrants that they were not seen as families but as animals who came, in Trump's words, from 'shithole countries'.[18]

In the cruelty stakes, the US cooperates closely with Saudi Arabia. The US/Saudi alliance in the Yemen war appeared to treat the resulting Yemeni famine as of little consequence. Children would die but weapons should be sold. Destruction of people and property should continue to show violence as the best means of foreign policy.

America's alliance with Israel is even closer than its partnership with Saudi Arabia, so much so that it's sensible to ask whether Tel Aviv or Washington determines US foreign policy. As part of the US/Israel alliance, the siege of Gaza is maintained into its 14th year, settlement building continues on Palestinian lands and the imprisonment of millions of Palestinians in refugee camps shows no sign of ending. In late 2017, President Trump demonstrated his bias by announcing the removal of the US Embassy from Tel Aviv to Jerusalem, in the face of widespread international condemnation.

In 2016, consistent with a policy of collective punishment, a record number of Palestinian homes were destroyed by Israel. In that year, the Israeli human rights group B'Tselem reported that Israel demolished 274 homes in the West Bank, and in consequence 1,134 individuals became homeless. In East Jerusalem Israeli authorities demolished 73 homes.

B'Tselem reports on a policy of ethnic cleansing: 'Despite the differences between Area C and East Jerusalem, the policy is designed to minimize the number of Palestinians in as much land as possible.' This principled human rights organization contends that the policy of house demolitions 'offers decisive evidence that Israel has long term plans to continue controlling the area, while oppressing and dispossessing its residents'.[19]

Bedouin people have also been the victims of a policy of lands being seized for future Jewish settlements. In a pre-dawn raid on 27 July 2010, Israeli forces destroyed all 45 homes, animal pens and other structures in the village of al-Araqib. Bulldozers also destroyed carob and olive trees and chicken coops.[20]

In September 2015, a camp adjacent to the Jahalin Bedouin community was also destroyed. 'The forced removal took place in 42 degrees Celsius heat. One hundred and twenty-seven men, women and children became homeless.' Israeli journalists who observed the destruction said it amounted to 'armed robbery' and showed 'an appetite for destruction'. 'Nothing was left, no tent, no roofing material, not even a water container.'[21]

Governments which sanction torture have made cruelty an inherent part of policy. I am not arguing that there is a moral equivalence in atrocities. But this coupling of cruelty in policy has flourished, from

Saddam Hussein's torture chambers to the US adoption of Abu Ghraib for their own brutal purposes, from a Syrian president's torture and execution of thousands to an Iranian government's fascination with imprisonment, torture and executions.

The UN Committee Against Torture documents the sadism in Saudi Arabia's efforts to stifle critics and to promote their inflexible versions of morality. In international comparisons of cruelty, perhaps ISIS, the Taliban and Saudi Arabia would rank as the worst of the worst. The sentence on free speech blogger Raif Badawi is one of a series of brutalities. In 2016 a Saudi man was sentenced to 2,000 lashes, 10 years in prison and a fine of US$5,300 for making tweets critical of Islam and for denying the existence of God.[22]

Torture in North Korea includes starvation, forced abortions and ordering prisoners to dig their own graves. In Justice Michael Kirby's UN report, first-hand testimonials from former guards and prisoners gave details of starvation, rape, mutilation and arbitrary detention. One former guard told the inquiry, 'When you get to this prison you are not human, you are just like animals, and as soon as you get to the prison, you have to crawl, just like animals.'[23]

In an important caveat to the usual blanket condemnation of the Pyongyang regime, Michael Pembroke, in *Korea, Where the American Century Began*, stresses that if contemporary cruelties are to be understood, but not excused, history should never be forgotten. He writes that the Korean war resulted in the 'incomparable devastation (of North Korea) and civilian tragedy north of the thirty eighth parallel. Most of North Korea was levelled, systematically bombed town by town. In the rebuilt streets of Pyonyang, the legacy is bitterness ... The country lives with a constant fear of invasion, subjugation and occupation.'[24]

A further challenge, amounting to a disproving of assumptions that cruelty as policy was and is confined to practices of the one-party regime in North Korea, comes from Pembroke's salutary reminders about the treatment, during the Korean war, of Chinese and North Korean prisoners. He refers to a UN Command camp established in 1951 on the island of Koje-do where more than 150,000 prisoners were kept in four vast, wired enclosures. The guards, 'admittedly the least impressive manpower in the US and (South) Korean armies ... treated the prisoners like animals, with casual brutality and with hostility and contempt ... It was a damning historical precedent for bad behaviour 50 years later by another generation of the US Army at Abu Ghraib, Bagram and Guantanamo Bay ... And when the American authorities began a concerted program of exploiting prisoners for psychological warfare purposes to influence opinion and encourage defections, the volatility and violence in the compounds rose to new levels.'[25]

Enabling

The Australian Aboriginal poet Kath Walker, also known as Oodgeroo Nunucaal, wrote in 1970 about officials who, under the guise of being called '*The Protectors*', enabled cruelty to occur.

> *While many despise and would exploit us*
> *There are good white men will help us.*
> *But not the appointed paid officials.*
> *Not the feudal police Protectors,*
> *The protectors who do not protect.*
>
> *The police of the little far inland towns,*
> *The Protectors of Aborigines*
> *Who move us about at will like cattle*
> *At the request of graziers and their wives:*
> *We feel like owned animals of the Sergeant,*
> *The protector who does not protect.*[26]

Policies which enable cruelty often involve acts of omission rather than commission. The enabling can be seen when governments and their representatives facilitate yet deny abuses. Usually government leaders share the attitudes and values of the abusers, and parody the three wise monkeys, neither seeing, hearing nor speaking evil.

In Ireland during most of the 20th century, for a young unmarried woman to get pregnant was the worst thing on earth. The girls were banished, their children regarded as illegitimate and placed for adoption, often to wealthy couples from America. Unmarried mothers lived in homes as a punishment and the lives of their infant children could not be guaranteed. Catherine Corless, a local historian, revealed that between 1925 and the 1960s, as many as 800 infants were buried beneath the former Bon Secours Mother and Baby Home in Tuam, County Galway. The children had died in the convent-run home and were buried without markers in mass graves.[27]

A persistent cruelty occurred in the enslavement of thousands of women in the notorious Magdalene Laundry system which existed from the 18th century until the late 1990s. Between the 1920s and 1990s, as many as 10,000 women, labelled 'Maggies', were stripped of their names and dumped in the Irish Catholic Church-run laundry, 'where nuns treated them as slaves, simply because they were unmarried mothers, orphans or regarded as somehow morally wayward'.[28]

It's debatable whether, in the treatment of unmarried mothers, the practice of the Irish government and the Catholic Church were one and the same. Even if they were administratively separate, the government enabled the cruelty to thousands of young women and their children. Mothers were placed in institutions as a form of social welfare outsourcing, accompanied by payments to the homes, albeit small ones.[29] Religious judgements and corporate interest permeated politics. Police had a free hand to round up the fallen young women. Institutions received lucrative laundry contracts to wash linen and clothes for hotel chains and for the Irish armed forces.

Similar policy enabling occurred when Australian governments failed to intervene to protect British children sent to live in Australian institutions after the Second World War. To say they 'enabled' cruelty lets them off lightly. Federal and state governments contributed to the running costs of organizations which housed and abused the children.

In 2013, the British and Australian governments apologized for the removal, decades earlier, of children from unmarried mothers. The apologies acknowledged that such cruelties had been allowed because officialdom influenced and complied with the morality of the times. Mothers and children's voices were not heard. Influenced by church and government, an arrogant society decided it knew what was best.

In previous chapters, accounts of cruelty to animals and within the Indian caste system have been referred to only briefly. In Western democracies such as the US, the UK and Australia, cruelty to animals has been tolerated until media outcry brings at least a temporary halt. In experiences of cruelty, is there any difference between cutting off electricity to citizens of Gaza and abandoning pets, between denying financial help for food and accommodation for refugees in Australia and in US cities and starving animals to death? Is there a difference between ISIS beheading men in front of their families, the targeted murders of journalists in Russia and condemning thousands of sheep to death by suffocation in the oven-like air on live-trade transport ships?

In *Animal Liberation*, philosopher Peter Singer has answered those questions by indicating that justification for cruelty to human beings has been matched in attitudes which lead to the subjugation and abuse of animals.[30] Once an animal can be judged inferior, stigmatized as an unworthy object, cruelty could be inevitable, even taken for granted. Singer links the overcoming of prejudices against black people, women and gays to the task of improving the interests of non-human animals by striving to overcome prejudices against them.[31] His is the utilitarian argument that the welfare of animals should be considered because of their ability to experience suffering. He argues that giving less consideration to beings based on their species should be no more justified than discrimination based on skin colour.

Animal protection societies in the US, Britain and Australia define a neglected animal as one not provided with proper food, water, veterinary care, shelter and socialization. Obvious deliberate cruelty has included beatings, shootings and even setting animals on fire.

The US Humane Society has published well-documented links between individuals convicted of cruelty to other human beings in terms of beating, bullying, starving and similar behaviour to animals. In many cases of cruelty, the victims are allegedly cherished pets. In an account titled 'The animal cruelty syndrome', Charles Siebert sees signs of animal abuse in the US as a possible indicator of other abusive behaviours: illegal firearms possession, drug trafficking, spousal and child abuse, rape and homicide.[32]

The British Royal Society for the Prevention of Cruelty to Animals, the RSPCA, was founded in a London coffee shop in 1824 and gained royal patronage in 1837. In the 19th century, bear baiting and cock fighting were outlawed and protection was gradually extended from cattle to dogs and other domestic animals. The end of the 20th century saw laws to protect laboratory animals, to improve conditions in slaughter houses and to forbid fox hunting with dogs.

A history of the RSPCA suggests that initial action to protect animals came from concern about efficiency in the workplace and in the military. The health of pit ponies and of millions of horses serving with British and Commonwealth forces in two world wars was crucial, if economies were to be productive and armies successful.

In Britain in the 21st century, despite laws and public concern, the RSPCA reports cruelty to animals as a national shame. Approximately 150,000 complaints of cruelty and neglect are handled each year. Most of the suffering is experienced by 'man's best friend, a dog'.[33] In Australia, animals raised for food have been excluded from laws that protect cats and dogs, but 500 million animals are raised every year in factory farms.

Public awareness of the cruelties inherent in the live animal export trade occurs when extremes of cruelty are publicized. Pictures of cattle bludgeoned to death with sledgehammers in a Vietnamese abattoir are described by a television newsreader as 'something which viewers might find distressing'. A similar warning is broadcast when cattle with their legs tied are shown having their throats cut in an Indonesian abattoir.

Charges of cruelty to animals have been deflected with the argument that animals are less than human, another example to bolster Jensen's thesis about the myth of human supremacy.[34] Policies which turn a blind eye to cruel practices enable powerful people and institutions to behave as they choose and make it unlikely that they'd ever be held responsible for acts of cruelty. Peter Singer has argued that people should feel as responsible for the things they don't do as for the things they bring about. If such arguments go unheeded, prejudices persist, cruelty flourishes. If individual human beings or animals can be labelled inferior, perceived as less than human, then pleasure, profit and other self-interests take over and ethical considerations are not raised.

Perceiving other people as less than human also characterizes the feudal and deeply entrenched Indian caste system. There's no official government policy which says 'Let's promote such means of punishment and exclusion', but a conniving, blind-eye approach to the consequences of old customs indicates cruelty inherent in the reverence for control, order and compliance. Such reverence facilitates opposition to efforts to achieve justice for the vulnerable and powerless.[35]

In an untouchable family's story of the making of modern India, Sujatha Gidla pictures life in villages where everyone has a role and a place to live, but untouchables, whose special role – whose hereditary duty – is to labour in the fields of others, or to do other work that Hindu society considers filthy, are not allowed to live in the village at all. They must live outside the boundaries of the village proper. They are not allowed to enter temples. Not allowed to come near sources of drinking water used by other castes. Not allowed to eat sitting next to a caste Hindu or to use the same utensils. There are thousands of other such restrictions and indignities that vary from place to place. Every day in an Indian newspaper you can read of an untouchable beaten or killed for wearing sandals, for riding a bicycle.[36]

Indian governments don't deny the caste system but resist any attempt by foreigners to embarrass the country over such cruelty. The system affects 165 million Dalits, who are made to feel small. Every day they are degraded by being forced to do filthy work, or by social exclusion.

In 2009, when the UN Human Rights Council declared that discrimination based on caste was a 'human rights abuse', India fought to stop the resolution. Upper-caste Hindus live in denial and have never apologized.

Indian governments have claimed they do not agree with the caste system. Laws and policies have been adopted which provide means of protection for Dalits, but there's a huge difference between the crafting of a policy and its implementation. For example, when Dalit student Rohith Vemula at Hyderabad University protested about discrimination on the campus, a cabinet minister in the Federal Government wrote to the university's vice chancellor to request that the Dalit student's activities should cease and his stipend be cancelled. In his writings about the contemptuous treatment of Dalits, Vemula had asked for 'a nice rope' to be put in the rooms of all Dalit students. He added, 'Please give us poison at the time of admission, instead of humiliating us like this.'

Vemula committed suicide. In his suicide note he wrote, 'My birth is a fatal accident.'[37]

Deception

In a characteristically humorous but revealing poem, *Statement from the Secretary of Defense*, Clive James reveals a tradition of governments' secrecy and deception.

> *This one we didn't know we didn't know:*
> *At least I didn't. You, you might have known*
> *You didn't know. Let's say that might be so.*
> *You knew, with wisdom granted you alone ...*
>
> *So leave no room for doubt: now that we know*
> *We might have known we didn't know, let's keep*
> *Our heads. Give history time, and time will show*
> *How flags wash clean, and eagles cease to weep.*[38]

Policy making via deception occurs when governments claim that all is well, that no one could doubt a country's high standards of civility and respect for human rights, a narrative vigorously reinforced by compliant and conservative media. A cloak of denial and deception is used to obscure cruelties and simultaneously facilitate them. A government-sanctioned distortion of events which heralded significant changes in the course of history came in Britain on 2 November 1917 when Foreign Secretary Arthur Balfour issued his Balfour Declaration.

On that November day, the British Foreign Secretary wrote to Lord Rothschild, a leader of the British Jewish community, 'His Majesty's Government views with favour the establishment of a national home for the Jewish people, and will use their best endeavours to facilitate the achievement of this object, it being clearly understood that nothing shall be done which may prejudice the civil and religious rights of existing non-Jewish communities in Palestine, or the rights enjoyed by Jews in any other country.'[39]

In his meticulous analysis of the background to British colonial policy in Palestine and its current effects on the Palestinian people, Bernard Regan concludes, 'The wording of the Balfour Declaration was deliberately ambiguous to obscure its true intent or mislead those on whose lands the homeland was to be established, but it also revealed that the protagonists themselves were uncertain about how it might be achieved and what it might mean.'[40]

Britain never kept its promises. 'Clearly understood' suggests that the British would insist on equal treatment for Indigenous Palestinians and the minority Jewish population. A year later, in an openly racist letter, Balfour wrote to his successor, Lord Curzon, 'Zionism is of profounder import than the desires and prejudices of 700,000 Arabs who now inhabit this ancient land.' In a letter of October 1915, the UK had already promised the creation of an Arab state, including Palestine, in return for support (which was given) against the Ottoman Turks.

In the case of the Balfour Declaration, British capacity for deception has stretched over 100 years. In 2015, the Mayor of London, Boris Johnson, wrote that the Balfour Declaration was 'bizarre', 'a tragically incoherent document', 'an exquisite piece of Foreign Office fudgerama'. In 2017, on becoming Foreign Secretary in Prime Minister Theresa May's government, Johnson declared that Balfour's letter reflected 'a great tide of history'.[41]

Deception to aid the powerful over the powerless continued. In August of 2017, during an alleged 'family holiday', British International Development Secretary Priti Patel held unauthorized, secret meetings with the Israeli Prime Minister, with the Director General of Israel's Foreign Ministry and with Gilad Erdan, the Israeli minister in charge of public security, strategic affairs and information. As a government minister, Patel had already cut aid to humanitarian projects in Gaza, including emergency aid for sewerage and electricity. She is said to have made these cuts in response to pressure from pro-Israeli groups.[42]

Evidence suggests that Patel's first meetings would have considered further cutting of British aid to the Palestinians and to the significant Israeli human rights group, Breaking The Silence. Patel's meeting with Gilad Erdan could hardly have ignored that minister's aims to use the Israeli foreign intelligence agency Mossad and the domestic intelligence agency Shin Bet to target individuals and organizations who unduly criticized Israeli policies and who supported the international Boycott, Divestment and Sanctions (BDS) movement.[43]

Two significant dates, 1788 and 1948, foreshadow the Patel meetings. Each year marked an unashamed commitment to policy by deception. Each marked the perception by invading forces that Indigenous peoples did not exist, or should be regarded as of no consequence, even if their presence was obvious.

By 1788, Australia had been inhabited for tens of thousands of years but was 'discovered' as an empty land, 'terra nullius', to be acquired for the British monarchy. That terra nullius doctrine was reversed only in 1992 when the Australian High Court recognized the existence of Indigenous inhabitants in 1788 and in consequence, through the Mabo decision, identified native title to land.

The year 1948 tells a similar story. Similar because the leaders of Zionist forces claimed that Palestine was a land without a people for a people without a land. This perception provided the moral rationale for expelling over 700,000 Palestinian landowners and erasing 500 small towns and villages.

The year 1948 differs from 1788 in that no Israeli High Court ruling has nullified the pretence that the catastrophe for the Palestinian people, the Naqba, did not happen. No Israeli Prime Minister has ever apologized for the wrongs done to the Indigenous people who were driven from their lands in 1948. The cunning business of writing and rewriting history facilitates policy by deception. Cruelty is not admitted. Huge resources are invested in promoting an image of a country's civility and normality. The promotion of one narrative and stifling of another allows cruelty to continue.

Saudi Arabia bombs Yemeni civilians but gets elected to the UN's Human Rights Council. The UN Commission on the Status of Women is dedicated 'to the promotion of gender equality and the empowerment of women', but in April 2017, Saudi Arabia was elected to serve on that Commission. The Saudi male guardianship system forbids women from obtaining a passport, marrying or travelling abroad without the approval of a male guardian – their husband, father, brother or son.

To avoid annoying this major oil-exporting country, the UN Commission overlooked hypocrisy, refused to disturb a status quo and allowed cruelty to women to continue. Such cruelty had been fostered by male-dominated tribal and religious traditions and by the preceding 30 years of reverence for neoliberal economics, promoted in particular by the US.

The following observations about social and economic policies show that cruelty as policy is not limited to a country's foreign affairs. At the entrance to New York harbour, the Statue of Liberty, dedicated in 1886, bears the inscription, 'Give me your tired, your poor, your huddled masses, yearning to breathe free, the wretched refuse of your teeming shore. Send these, the homeless, tempest tossed to me.' Every morning in American schools, students pledge allegiance to the flag of the US and 'to the Republic for which it stands, one nation under God, with liberty and justice for all'.

There's a mismatch between those aspirations and a government's free-market ideology which claims that all citizens would benefit if everyone acted selfishly. That ideology indicates that an answer to all problems is economic growth nurtured via tax incentives for large corporations whose sole objective is to maximise profit. This policy has so glorified selfishness that the crowd at a 2016 US Presidential debate cheered the idea of letting someone without health insurance die on the street.[44]

Somehow fooling themselves with their version of freedom, representatives of the Trump Presidency have attempted to abolish Obamacare and so deny health insurance to millions. They have supported the rounding-up of migrants and the prosecution of homeless people. In that respect the Trump administration has much in common with Theresa May's UK Conservative government. Growing numbers of homeless people in England and Wales have been fined and given criminal convictions and even imprisoned for begging and for sleeping rough. They have been banned from town centres, routinely fined hundreds of pounds and sent to prison if caught repeatedly asking for money. In one case a judge admitted, 'I will be sending a man to prison for asking for food when he was hungry.'[45]

In December 2017, Republicans in the US Congress passed a Bill to make a huge tax giveaway to wealthy individuals and large corporations. Democrat Senator Bernie Sanders predicted that the Republicans would subsequently return to the Congress and say, 'Oh my goodness, the deficit is too high. We have got to cut social security, Medicare, Medicaid, education and nutritional programmes.'[46]

To give tax cuts to billionaires and to large, profitable corporations it was obvious that programmes for the elderly, for children, for working families and for the poor would have to be cut. In this respect the Republican leaders were 'blunt about their motivation: to deliver on their promises to wealthy donors ... and to ... use the leverage of huge deficits to cut and privatize Medicare and Social Security'.[47]

British governments have also crafted policies which contribute to inequality and poverty. The administrative purpose of the Conservative government's Universal Credit system, rolled out initially between 2015 and 2017, was to merge six benefits – such as a Job Seeker's

Allowance, Child Tax Credit and Housing Benefit, into one. As part of an efficiency drive, payments were made in arrears, so that even parents without money to feed their family were turned away, 'leaving children to suffer in hunger for weeks'.[48]

A political purpose of the chaotic Universal Credit system was to use instant impoverishment to force people into work or into cheaper housing. Such a policy continued even if there was neither available work nor alternative accommodation. The British NGO Shelter reported that the only practical options for poor families were debt or starvation.[49]

The inhuman features of these practices were influenced not only by free market ideology but also by the adoption of a brave new world digital system of communication. Social work online had replaced face-to-face encounters. Of people whom he knew were suffering 'poverty, hunger and suicidal despair', one caseworker reported, 'We sit behind a computer screen, we have never met them.'[50]

The catastrophic fire on 14 June 2017, in London's high-rise Grenfell Tower in affluent North Kensington, displays the consequences of policies which allow poverty and inequality to grow. Seventy-two people lost their lives and 70 were injured. Under the enforcement of austerity as an ideology, local authority councils had felt obliged to spend as little as possible. In a refurbishment of Grenfell Tower, £300,000 had been saved by removing the fire-prevention sprinkler system.

In August 2017, the British government admitted that the Grenfell Tower disaster was no once-in-a-life-time event. One hundred and eighty-one other high-rise buildings had also failed fire safety tests.[51]

In an economic free market's property-owning democracy, social housing and tenants were problematic; the buildings they lived in an eyesore which hindered private development. Poor people could be vilified and condemned to second-class status. By contrast, privileged citizens were said to be able 'to buy their safety, their security, their legal representation and can kid themselves that they're clever and know the answers'.[52]

By stigmatizing citizens of North African origin, the economic and social policies of successive French governments have also ensured families' sense of isolation and their experience of the consequences of huge inequalities. After the Second World War and after the Algerian War of Independence, hundreds of thousands of Algerians were imported to help rebuild France. The new arrivals existed on low wages. Nabila Ramdani reports, 'Most were stuck in run-down, out-of-town housing estates where today, their children and grandchildren continue to face anti-Muslim discrimination on the margins of the Republic.'[53]

The Australian self-image of fair go, mateship and respect for human rights corresponds to the inscription on America's Statue of Liberty. Yet for the first decades of the new century, Australian governments' indifference to the plight of asylum seekers peppered newspaper headlines. In October 2001, 353 asylum seekers drowned following the sinking of a crowded asylum-seeker boat, *SIEV X*, somewhere between Indonesia and Australia. The Australian government's subsequent withholding and misrepresenting of vital evidence compounded the tragedy of lives lost.[54]

For as long as possible several government agencies worked to conceal evidence that the boat sank in international waters, denied that Australian Federal police and navy were involved, and that Australia had any duty of care. To conceal the truth, deception and denial continued to the point where the government wanted to wear people down so that they would give up and move on.[55]

Secrecy and deception also characterize an Australian government's aims to become a commercially successful exporter of arms. The government approved four military exports to Saudi Arabia in 2015, with five more permits in 2017, but refused to disclose the details. The Defence Minister used the predictable excuse that national security would be affected by the ability to 'effectively regulate the export of military goods and technology'.[56]

This export of arms coincided with chaos in Yemen. On 8 November 2017, a UN official warned that if the siege of Yemen was not lifted, it would result in 'the largest famine the world has seen for decades with millions of victims'. In November 2017, a UNICEF official said, 'Yemen is one of the worst places on earth to be a child. More than eleven million Yemeni children are today in acute need of humanitarian assistance.'

The sale of arms is accompanied by refusals to say it is happening. The sale of arms is coupled to boasting about modest humanitarian assistance to a people who are starving because of a blockade from which countries such as Australia, Britain and the US profited. Cruelty by deception flourished. An Australian government denied. The opposition stayed silent. A sanctimonious stance was maintained by giving a pittance in humanitarian aid.[57]

Collusion

The poem *Tell Me the Truth About War* depicts the false claims of leaders who colluded in the 2003 invasion of Iraq.

A coalition of the willing declared war
but did not explain why,
or the reasons they gave
were not the real reasons
and something called a dodgy dossier
became as smelly as the exam papers
of a schoolboy who cheated.

One leader is an evangelist,
another a true believer,
each hooked on the catechisms of their convictions
and would be lost without reference to their Gods
though non-believers
have questioned the sacred texts
and have asked for evidence.[58]

States may maintain that they do not openly promote cruelty, yet they support and cooperate with countries which do. Such cooperation has been displayed by indifference to the human rights of leftist opponents of military regimes, to the rights of refugees, by participation in the international arms trade and by close cooperation between countries which torture and practise rendition of alleged terrorists.

Brazilian military governments from 1964 to 1985 sanctioned the elimination of opponents by torture and execution.[59] Dilma Rousseff, a subsequent President of Brazil, had been imprisoned for three years, beaten and tortured with electric shocks. In 2014, she wept as she unveiled a Truth Commission Report on the military dictatorships' abuses. The Report concluded that a share of the blame went to the UK and the US, who were found to have trained Brazilian interrogators in torture techniques. A witness before the Commission confirmed the collusion. A Brazilian officer who had been a torturer explained, 'psychological torture was best, and England was the best place to learn it'.[60]

From the 1960s to the early 1990s, an alliance among authoritarian regimes in South American countries (Uruguay, Paraguay, Argentina, Brazil and Chile) facilitated the oppression and elimination of those they labelled leftists. Dictators demanded conformity. Policy making by collusion was open and acknowledged. Under Chile's 1974 Operation Condor, the secret police, DINA, were able to pursue opponents into exile in neighbouring countries.[61]

On the African continent, where commercial gain and the lives of white inhabitants have been at risk, governments have regarded human rights as of secondary importance or have ignored such principles. New documents reveal US and UK collusion in the 1983 massacres in Matabeleland, western Zimbabwe. These documents contain evidence that the British diplomatic and military teams in Zimbabwe during the Gukurahundi massacres ignored the victims of gross abuses. The documents included minutes of meetings and other relevant communications between the British High Commission in Harare, Prime Minister Thatcher's office, the British Foreign and Commonwealth Office, the Cabinet Office, the Ministry of Defence in London, plus the US Department of State and the US Embassy in Harare.[62]

The British knew that elimination of Ndebele people was official Zimbabwean policy. In receipt of solid intelligence, the UK government's approach was nevertheless said to be influenced 'solely by consideration for the white people who were in the affected regions but were not affected by the violence'. One cable to the British Foreign Office in London said that events in Zimbabwe were important on account of British and Western economic and strategic interests in southern Africa. The Gukurahundi massacres were referred to as 'occasional Zimbabwean perversity'.[63]

Between 1982 and 1990, Hissène Habré, the dictator of Chad, used imprisonment, torture and murder – of at least 40,000 Chadian citizens – as his means of government, but to become an effective torturer and killer, he needed a supply of arms and blind-eye attitudes from major powers France and the US. Roland Dumas, the French Minister of Foreign Affairs during Habré's rule, explained, 'From the moment that Hissène Habré became a strategic leader in a strategic country, we had a tendency to take a laissez faire attitude: "We simply ask for you to keep your country going, do what you want".'[64] An evaluation of US policy concluded, 'The Americans didn't have an interest in Chad per se, but they had very strong feelings about reining in the ambitions of Colonel Gaddafi in Libya, so the US government armed Habré's regime.' The head of a commission into crimes committed by Habré made the judgement, 'Whether it's France or the US, they gave Habré the means to rule and it's their responsibility.'[65]

Cruelty by collusion is practised by many countries and comes in several colours. In the case which follows, governments in Thailand, Britain, the US and Libya cooperated. Operatives from Britain's MI6, America's CIA and Libyan leader Gaddafi's police and prison staff interpreted and carried out orders. In Thailand in 2004, following information from Britain's MI6, members of the CIA seized a Libyan couple, Abdel Hakim Belhaj and his pregnant wife, Fatima Boudchar.

In a textbook rendition process, the couple were hooded, shackled and flown to prison in Libya. Belhaj and Boudchar, in addition to be known opponents of the Libyan dictator Muammar Gaddafi, were suspected of having links to al-Qaida. On the basis of that suspicion, Belhaj was tortured and imprisoned for six years. Initially imprisoned in a cell where she could hear her husband being tortured, Boudchar was released to give birth to her son.[66]

In May 2018, via a speech from her Attorney General in the British House of Commons, Prime Minister Theresa May issued an abject apology for the cruelty and collusion of the British state and its representatives. She acknowledged that Britain, through the government of Tony Blair and Foreign Secretary Jack Straw, had colluded in torture. 'We should have understood much sooner the unacceptable practices of some of our international partners ... We shared information about you ... We should have done more to reduce the risk that you would be mistreated. We accept this was a failure on our part.'[67]

In June 2018, the UK Parliament's Intelligence and Security Committee (ISC) concluded that the country's intelligence agencies were complicit in hundreds of incidents of torture and rendition, mainly in partnership with the US in Iraq, Afghanistan and Guantanamo. The report found 13 incidents where intelligence officers witnessed first-hand a detainee being mistreated by others, 25 where UK personnel were told by detainees how they had been abused and 128 where torture was reported by foreign intelligence officers. Leading investigative reporter for the *Guardian*, Ian Cobain, writes that in the years after 9/11, British intelligence agencies were involved in 598 cases in which prisoners were being tortured or placed at risk of mistreatment. He explains the nature of collusion with US authorities. 'Intelligence officers were giving consent or watching the torture or supplying questions and receiving answers. And this does not include the 2–3000 interrogations they conducted at Guantanamo.'[68]

The UK's ISC report concluded that it was difficult to believe that those at the top of office, the leaders of intelligence agencies, including the Foreign Secretary of the time, did not recognize the pattern of mistreatment by the US. They say, 'the evidence clearly suggests that the UK saw itself as the poor relation to the US and was distinctly uncomfortable at the prospect of complaining to its host'. The refusal of governments to reveal cruelties continued. Dominic Grieve, a Conservative MP and Chair of the ISC, and former Attorney General, maintained that Prime Minister Theresa May had denied the ISC access to evidence from four intelligence officers who were central to the events involving collusion with US interests. Britain's leading human rights groups, including Amnesty International, Reprieve and Liberty, have argued that the findings of the ISC report were just the tip of an iceberg.[69]

In early 2016, in the interest of discarding refugees from the offshore detention centre on Nauru, Australia colluded with one of the world's poorest countries ruled by one of the most authoritarian regimes. Australia paid Cambodia $55 million to settle three refugees, even though Cambodia acknowledged there were no social programmes to support them. The refugees left in Phnom Penh said they felt abandoned, wanted to quit the country but could only return to the countries from which they had fled in the first place.[70]

On 6 December 2017, despite evidence of the Cambodian government's authoritarian anti-democratic policies, Australia's Department of Foreign Affairs and Trade said, 'settlement in Cambodia remains an option for Nauru-determined refugees'. Australia insisted that Cambodia was a safe place for refugees to resettle, despite the Cambodian government's crackdown on basic rights and freedoms. Prime Minister Hun Sen had already imprisoned the opposition, shut down newspapers and said that to stay in power he'd be prepared to sacrifice 200 lives. His military chief vowed to 'smash the teeth of anyone who does not support the Prime Minister'.[71]

Human rights are easily set aside not only through indifference to refugees, but also in the interest of selling arms. If commercial gain is possible, British governments seldom hesitate to collude with countries whose human rights record they usually oppose. Values can be ditched, or sold to the highest bidder. Where corporatism enters politics, cruelty grows.

In 2015, the UK government made a list of repressive regimes, then invited them to a Defence and Security Equipment International Exhibition in London. That list included Colombia, Iraq, Pakistan, Saudi Arabia, each invited to go shopping in London for weapons.[72]

Following the UK general election of 2016, British manufacturers exported almost US$5 billion worth of weapons to countries judged to have repressive regimes and controversial human rights records: Saudi Arabia, Azerbaijan, Kazakhstan, Venezuela and China. Critics of such arms sales also accused the government of making deals with the United Arab Emirates to sell cyber surveillance technology which that government would use to spy on its citizens and use 'to commit war crimes in Yemen'.[73]

In early 2017, thousands were being killed in Yemen and millions subjected to famine and disease. Arms-manufacturing countries perceived such a disaster as a commercial opportunity. In May 2017, as the US/Saudi alliance prosecuted the Yemen war, President Trump visited Saudi Arabia and announced the sale of $7 billion of precision-guided munitions from US defence contractors. This was part of a $110 billion weapons sales agreement which also coincided with Trump's visit.[74]

Saudi Arabia, the US, Britain, Israel, Russia, Syria and Turkey are committed to sustaining violent militaristic policies for their own political advantage. In alliance with the Syrian President, Russian arms dealers have also seen wonderful commercial opportunities. By early 2016, the Kremlin admitted to spending almost US$500 million in testing weapons in the Syrian civil war. Such testing was regarded as a colossal means of advertising which would result in new purchases. Kremlin insiders said that the marketing effect of the Syrian conflict would boost Russian arms sales by up to $7 billion.[75]

Policy by collusion is aided by deception. The Siamese-twin relationship between Israel and the US is sustained by double standards and double speak. In September 2016, Israel and the US signed a defence agreement worth $38 billion over 10 years, the largest pledge in US history. Such massive arms sales were said to contribute to the foreign policy and national security of the US by helping to improve the security of a strategic regional partner.[76]

The subjugation of Palestinians in the West Bank, in Gaza, let alone in the myriad refugee camps is not considered. Neither is the sale of every kind of weapon and surveillance equipment to numerous oppressive regimes. Sale of arms is crucial to powerful countries' continued ability to dominate others. In his comprehensive *War Against the People*, Jeff Halper argues that Israel lives and has always lived in a state of deep cultural militarism where reality is shaped always by the use of force.[77]

Israel is not only concerned with manufacturing weapons of suppression and surveillance to defend itself but has become an ally and arms supplier to the most contemptible and hated regimes in the world.[78] This sale of arms remains Israel's most successful foreign policy instrument. Halper argues that the Uzi machine gun, the Galil assault rifle and smiling Israeli officers can be seen in numerous repressive regimes. The policy collusion is evident in familiar claims that even arming dictatorial regimes is a means of confronting terrorism and defending the West.

Cruelty has been facilitated by the collusion which Israel has enjoyed with the US, the EU and even the UN. Despite its crucial role in setting human rights standards, the UN has been silent over the destruction of Bedouin homes by Israeli forces. In 2015, after my visit to the Jahalin Bedouin community, whose school has since been bulldozed for land on which to build another Israeli settlement, the following judgement appeared in *New Matilda*: 'Cruelty as policy persists because the so-called international community has chosen never to hold Israel accountable, always to turn a blind eye to enable successive Israeli governments to behave as though they are above the law.'[79]

US collusion is so open that some American leaders appear to see Israel as a US state. In December 2017, in violation of UN Security Council resolutions, in disregard of international law and in total indifference to any notion of justice, President Trump recognized Jerusalem as Israel's capital. The illegal became legal.[80] Since the 1970s, the US had vetoed Security Council resolutions critical of Israel 43 times, more times than all other countries have used their veto on all other issues combined. Almost half of American military assistance each year goes to Israel.[81]

The EU has also continued to fund major Israeli weapons projects. NATO has judged Israel as a major non-NATO ally. Israel is accepted into the Organisation for Economic Co-operation and Development, the exclusive club of advanced economies, despite a human rights record that should have excluded it. Halper shows that virtually all the agreements and protocols Israel has signed with the 157 counties with whom it has diplomatic relations contain military and security components.[82]

For many countries, peaceful coexistence with Israel depends on a trade in arms which overlooks cruelty to Palestinians. Trade trumps human rights. The politics of security through weapons sales stifle even whispers about justice. In his study of countries to whom Israel sells weapons and why, Benjamin Beit-Hallahmi concluded,

> What Israel has been exporting to the Third World, is not just the technology of domination but a world view that undergirds that technology. In every situation of oppression and domination, the logic of the oppressed is pitted against the logic of the oppressor. What Israel has been exporting is the logic of the oppressor ... Israel advisors have much to offer in the technology of death and oppression and that is why they are in such demand.[83]

The mainstream media establishment have also been massive policy colluders. They could raise public awareness of the cruelties inherent in policies facilitated by collusion but have seldom done so. In their infatuation with the war against terror and the need for Western countries to participate in regime change in the Middle East, the media in many countries have ignored their responsibilities. Instead of making siren calls for justice, they have become the mouthpiece of governments. Jeffrey Sachs argues that the mainstream media in the US have been no match for what he calls 'the American Security State'. The mainstream US media, he says, have not even tried to play their professional roles. '*The New York Times* and *The Washington Post* have utterly failed to track, investigate and report on covert American operations in the Middle East.'[84]

Policy pointers

Over many years, cruelty as policy has been accepted in diverse countries. Examples from Britain, Russia, China, Israel, the United States, Chile, the Philippines, Syria, Saudi Arabia, Australia, Indonesia, Zimbabwe, India and Ireland show a global spread. Professor Jeffrey Sachs' 2018 essay 'Killer Politicians' confirms this conclusion and recalls the main findings of Pitirim Sorokin and Walter Lunden's *Power and Morality: Who Shall Guard the Guardians?*, 'The behaviour of ruling groups tends to be more criminal than that of the people over whom they rule.'[85]

Evidence that the business of doing harm to others is a consideration in domestic and foreign policies comes, paradoxically, from efforts to deny this is happening. Apart from cases where cruelty is deliberate, visible and direct, efforts to conceal or disguise oppressive practices take as much time and energy as would the implementation of socially just and humanitarian goals.

By ignoring policies, by their advocacy of stereotypes about friends and enemies and even by their collusion with policy makers, the media can play a significant role. Damning conclusions from American journalist Seymour Hersh show the sinister consequences when media personnel fear to fulfil their responsibilities. In his memoirs, Hersh writes that his years of observation revealed three crystal-clear phenomena.

(i) The powerful prey mercilessly on the powerless up to and including mass murder.

(ii) The powerful lie constantly about their predations.

(iii) The natural instinct of the media is to let the powerful get away with it.[86]

Denial and concealment is apparent when governments enable cruelty by finding it convenient to ignore or to be indifferent to harmful practices. Deception, as in claims about freedom to be enjoyed from privatizing public assets, runs parallel to policies of collusion where, for example, commercial gain is considered desirable by arms trading with countries whose human rights abuses can't be denied.

Before answering questions about humanitarian alternatives, it's time to review the composition of the cultural seedbeds from which cruelty grows. For example, although individual prison guards, civil servants, soldiers, security personnel, members of terrorist groups, powerful men in and out of uniform can be perceived as perpetrators of cruelty, the culture which gives them ideas, weapons, legitimacy and protection from accountability exists within hierarchies of policy making, order giving and control. Cruelty agendas appear to be spawned by men who are arrogant, racist and self-important, who are convinced of their correctness and are unwilling to revise their views, let alone say sorry. To a questioning public, these men are invisible. It is not always known which cities they work in, what offices they occupy, the sort of ideological and theoretical baggage they carry in their heads or what their qualifications are for making decisions about powerless people. Such a culture builds without question in state bureaucracies, within the top echelons of private corporations and drug cartels, in military and scientific establishments, within the cabinets of democratic and authoritarian governments. These claims could refer to deliberations about the use of biological, chemical or nuclear weapons by American, Japanese, Syrian, Korean or Russian governments. They could refer to decisions about capital punishment in Saudi Arabia, the US, Egypt, Indonesia or by ISIS and Taliban operatives in Iraq, Syria and Afghanistan, or to the disproportionate use of firepower by several states and terrorist groups intent on destroying countries, cultures and citizens.

Authoritarian cultures can also be identified in Australian, British and US treatment of asylum seekers and in several European governments' determination to disobey the rules of international law in relation to the human rights of refugees. In Washington, London, Paris, Tel Aviv, Rome and Canberra, the promotion of policies which reward the rich and penalize the poor fosters cultures of inequality and cruelty.

It should be politically rewarding to advocate the humanitarian alternatives to cruelties which have persisted, sometimes openly, usually disguised and for so long. Such advocacy should encourage those who craft and implement policies to wake up to the place which cruelty has in the many strands of governance and in non-state organizations' reactions to the power of governments and to the influence of state institutions. In an economically and ecologically globalized world, the nation-state is increasingly dysfunctional. Assumptions about the nation-state need scrutiny plus imagination to craft diverse ways to oppose cruelties and to promote humane governance.

5

Humanitarian alternatives

> I believe in the equality of man, and I believe that
> religious duties consist in doing justice, loving mercy, and
> endeavouring to make our fellow creatures happy.
>
> All national institutions of churches, whether Jewish,
> Christian or Turkish, appear to me no other than human
> inventions set up to terrify and enslave mankind and
> monopolize power and profit. (Tom Paine)[1]

> Whereas recognition of the inherent dignity and of the equal
> and inalienable rights of all members of the human family is
> the foundation of freedom, justice and peace in the world.
> (Preamble to the Universal Declaration of Human Rights)

Utopian thinking requires creative, non-harmful conduct in individual
relationships. It imagines socially just practice in institutions and in
the manner in which policies are crafted and implemented. These
challenges also confront those who derive pleasure by promoting fear,
discrimination and brutality. The persistence of cruelty worldwide
makes it urgent to respond with humanitarian alternatives. Overcoming
the fatalism that nothing can be done is a first task.

Oscar Wilde insisted that a map of the world that did not include
utopia was not worth even glancing at, so he challenged his public to
consider the ideals of a common humanity. Gary Younge's response
to the Oscar Wilde challenge is a vision of a community without
border guards, barbed wire, passport control, walls, fences or barriers.
But Younge commented, 'Sadly desperate people are turned away at
borders all the time. Others are incarcerated for having the audacity
to cross borders we have created, to escape wars we have started,
environmental chaos we have contributed to or poverty we have
helped create. Others die trying.'[2]

In deliberations about policies towards asylum seekers and refugees,
constant reverence for borders becomes an obstacle to conceiving the
importance of sanctuary and asking why the powerlessness of millions
persists. Fixed borders are an idea of modernity and the nation-state.
An humanitarian agenda needs to look beyond the binary of the
border and the nation-state.

A common humanity refers to a quality of living, as in the enjoyment of political and economic rights, and to a set of values, as in the acknowledgement of responsibility to care for others. Commitment to 'humanity' includes a moral imperative to respect such rights and to live by such values and begins by assessing the ways in which power is exercised.

Envisioning the interdependence of people in pursuit of justice introduces another way to change consciousness and to influence conversations. Imagination also needs to be freed from the shackles of thinking that life's purpose is economic and that superior force is the way to achieve security. The philosophy, language and practice of non-violence offers the fulfilling alternative to a global fascination with punishment and other forms of violence.

Creative, non-destructive power

The English romantic poet William Wordsworth observed the benefits of a natural environment and, in contrast, the oppressive reality of lives dominated by the drudgery of work in factories. He forecast the evils of an economic system in which concern with profits ruled out thinking about the rights of people. In *Humanity*, written in 1829, he questioned why, in commercial enterprise to achieve financial wealth, putting time aside to think was a least-valued use of power:

> *What a fair world were ours for verse to paint*
> *If Power could live at ease with self-restraint*
> ...
> *For the poor Many, measured out by rules*
> *Fetched with cupidity from heartless schools,*
> *That to an Idol, falsely called 'the Wealth*
> *Of Nations', sacrifice a People's health,*
> *Body and mind and soul; a thirst so keen*
> *Is ever urging on the vast machine*
> *Of sleepless Labour, 'mid whose dizzy wheels*
> *The Power least prized is that which thinks and feels.*[3]

Wordsworth's observations, made as the Industrial Revolution gained pace, highlight a need to think differently about ways to live, beginning with an exercise of power which is creative, fulfilling and harms no one. Consideration of that goal follows a pendulum-like movement from one-dimensional to multi-dimensional uses of power.

Examples of cruelty have been characterized by a one-dimensional, top-down assertiveness. The man who is violent at home, the flogger in a Riyadh square, the invisible Immigration bureaucrat who delays decisions and plays with refugees' lives, the politicians and military personnel who love bombs and bombing, all appear to think that force by them and compliance by others is the only option. The pendulum of their thinking is stuck in a one-dimensional, destructive position.[4]

Abusive power is shown by those who need to be in charge and in control, who want to appear masculine, who would consider empathy a sign of weakness. Rebecca Solnit argues that underlying the warped US idea of the alleged freedom involved in owning guns, mass shootings in that country mark a lack of empathy, a will to dominate and an entitlement to control, to harm and even take the lives of others. Such killers are prisoners of their selfishness before they are punishers of others.[5]

In *Poetry* (1996), the pacifist American poet William Stafford has shown why he rejected the top-down, rule-based way of thinking.

> *Sometimes commanders take us over, and they*
> *try to impose their whole universe,*
> *how to succeed by daily calculation:*
> *I can't eat that bread.*[6]

In *The Bread of the People*, Bertolt Brecht, another highly significant commentator on ideals for humanity, wrote,

> *Justice is the bread of the people.*
> *...*
> *As daily bread is necessary, so is daily justice.*
> *It is even necessary several times a day.*[7]

The 'bread' which Stafford and Brecht found palatable was the multi-dimensional perspective which lauded equality, human rights and deep respect for nature. I'll elaborate that perspective after the pendulum has swung away from commanders' top-down views.

To move from that destructive, one-dimensional attitude requires consideration of the points of view of women as well as men, children not just adults, Indigenous peoples as well as mainstream rulers, people with disabilities as well as the 'able bodied', non-English speakers as well as the Anglosphere, civilian organizations as well as military and corporate interests. A prescription for a more open and vigorous democracy recommends that the seldom-consulted be heard and heeded.

Even that movement of the pendulum from one-dimensional to two-dimensional ways of thinking may flatter to deceive. It represents the arrival of greater solidarity with the other, but is still caught within the confines of an officialdom committed to bolstering borders, respecting age-old hierarchies, needing to keep secret unsavoury practices and fearful of rejecting military solutions for complex conflicts.

Freeing imagination in order to move to multi-dimensional ways of thinking represents a liberation for people and their ideas. They will experience diverse ways to express identity: activities which are creative and fulfilling, from pop and classical music to dance, from poetry to fashion, pottery to sculpture, let alone by deploying all the ingredients of hospitality.

The alternative 'bread' referred to by William Stafford and Bertolt Brecht requires that multi-dimensionality which I have described as an invitation to promiscuity: not just crossing cultural and discipline boundaries but questioning their validity, an exercise to combine arts with science, poetry and philosophy with politics, to search and find any sources of inspiration.[8]

Such a stretching of imagination has been described by the philosopher/international lawyer Professor Richard Falk in his vision of a just peace for Palestinians and Israelis. 'In effect, we need to free the political and moral imagination from the dead-end characteristics of feasibility, acknowledge the necessities of a just peace with dignity, and by so doing set our sights high above the horizons of desire.'[9]

Interdependence and belonging

The emergence of pandemics which cross national boundaries, the threat of global warming from which no country may escape, are reminders of an interdependence across the globe. This interdependence needs a language to promote horizons which stretch beyond a protective nationalism. In that respect, and in the interests of a common humanity, the ideals of solidarity and interdependence promise so much.

In his memorable (1624) *No Man Is an Island*, 17th-century poet John Donne expressed this interdependence.

> *No man is an island entire of itself; every man*
> *is a piece of the continent, a part of the main;*
> ...

> *any man's death diminishes me,*
> *because I am involved in Mankinde;*
> *And therefore never send to know for whom*
> *the bell tolls; it tolls for thee.*[10]

Similar sentiments were expressed by Australia's Indigenous peoples at the Garma Festival in Arnhemland in 2017. In their recommendations to the Federal government for policies of greater inclusiveness for Aborigines, they referred to a common good, as illustrated by the notion 'Makarrata', a coming together, a making of peace. Over the centuries, poets have also expressed Makarrata-like visions of interdependence and belonging. In *All One Race* the Indigenous poet Oodgeroo Nunucaal wrote,

> *I'm for human kind not colour gibes;*
> *I'm international, and never mind tribes ...*
>
> *I'm international, never mind place;*
> *I'm for humanity, all one race.*[11]

In *Human Family*, written in the 1990s, Afro-American poet and civil rights activist Maya Angelou explained,

> *We love and lose in China,*
> *we weep on England's moors,*
> *and laugh and moan in Guinea*
> *and thrive on Spanish shores.*
>
> *We seek success in Finland,*
> *are born and die in Maine,*
> *in minor ways we differ,*
> *in major we're the same*
>
> *I note the obvious differences*
> *between each sort and type*
> *but we are more alike, my friends*
> *than we are unalike.*[12]

The thesis about an interdependence between the world's peoples presupposes common attributes in being human. In Archbishop Desmond Tutu's words, this is best expressed by the African word 'ubuntu' which conveys respect for the indivisibility of people and for the qualities of a common humanity. Tutu explained that if someone has ubuntu, it means they are human because they belong. 'A person with *ubuntu* is open and available to others, affirming of others ... has a self-assurance that comes from knowing that he or she belongs in a greater whole and is diminished when others are humiliated or diminished, when others are tortured or oppressed, or treated as if they were less than who they are.'[13]

Associated with perspectives about the interdependence of all people and all living things is a concern to end the destructiveness to people and planet, a goal for which Naomi Klein is a highly influential advocate. The task, she says, is 'to articulate not just an alternative set of policy proposals but an alternative worldview to rival the one at the heart of the ecological crisis – embedded in interdependence rather than hyper-individualism, reciprocity rather than dominance, and cooperation rather than hierarchy'. This objective means, 'an unshakeable belief in the equal rights of all people and a capacity for deep compassion will be the only things standing between civilization and barbarism'.[14]

This vision also demands that humanitarian perspectives should not remain anthropocentric, people centred. Comprehensive accounts of cruelty must include the maltreatment of animals. Consideration of compassion as a policy objective would emphasize a human rights issue never to be overlooked: the responsibility to afford protection and dignity to animals. The fascination with violence shown by governments and armies, by corporate and religious organizations, by political and religious extremists requires a universal antidote. That prescription exists in the philosophy, language and practice of non-violence. In the spirit of Pachamama, the goddess revered by the Indigenous people of the Andes, non-violence is also practised towards the non-human world, to trees, rivers, earth, mountains, rocks, a reverence for all living things which sustains life on earth.

Non-violence

The 19th-century English poet Shelley protested any form of authoritarianism, whether in the guise of military or political institutions, through religious intolerance or in the tyranny of poverty and ignorance. His lauding of a common humanity showed that if citizens came together in non-violent protest, they would experience solidarity and even undermine the force of armies.

In *The Mask of Anarchy*, he wrote on behalf of those who had been killed, in Manchester in August 1819, while participating in a rally in support of parliamentary reform. Here are three verses.

Rise like Lions after slumber
In unvanquishable number
Shake your chains to Earth like dew
Which in sleep had fallen on you —
Ye are many — they are few ...

Stand ye calm and resolute,
Like a forest close and mute.
With folded arms and looks which are
Weapons of unvanquished war, ...

And these words shall then become
Like oppression's thundered doom
Rising through each heart and brain,
Heard again — again — again —.[15]

Influential activists have espoused non-violence. Mahatma Gandhi argued that non-violent practice was not only a way of living but a law for life. Martin Luther King maintained that for practical as well as for moral reasons, non-violence offered the only road to freedom for his people.

Expressions of non-violence contribute to a quality of living which I have called peace with justice, a process and outcome which can be experienced in personal relationships, in dialogue across cultures and in international relations. Such a philosophy and language are always interesting and usually rewarding because such qualities enhance others' sense of opportunity, security and fulfilment.[16] That contention can be explored regarding non-violent opposition to the worst threat of global violence, from the use of nuclear weapons.

Japanese survivors of the atomic bombing of Hiroshima and Nagasaki are known as the Hibakusha. For as long as they are physically able, they intend to campaign against nuclear weapons. One survivor, Sunao Tsuboi says, 'On behalf of all the atomic bomb victims, I will ask the Japanese Prime Minister to do everything possible to rid the world of nuclear weapons.'[17] Tsuboi and his comrades have been encouraged by support for a treaty to abolish nuclear weapons, but are dismayed by the refusal of nuclear powers to endorse that treaty.

The Nuclear Non-Proliferation Treaty of 1970 was recognized by five nuclear-weapons states, but with no plan to abolish their nuclear arsenals. In July 2017, in the UN General Assembly, 122 nations voted in support of a Treaty on the Prohibition of Nuclear Weapons. This ban the bomb initiative was judged 'a circuit breaker in the search for a dependable, rules-based security order outside the limits of what the nuclear armed countries are prepared to accept'.[18]

Despite diplomatic game playing to protect the interests of nuclear powers, by politicians who refused to recognize the Prohibition Treaty, its birth marks a significant step in the history of non-violent actions to respect a common humanity. In October 2017, the Australian-based group ICAN (International Campaign to Abolish Nuclear Weapons), which had argued the humanitarian case for abolishing nuclear weapons, was awarded the 2017 Nobel Peace Prize. In the Nobel Lecture given in Oslo on 10 December 2017, representatives of ICAN said, 'Ours is the only reality that is possible. The alternative is unthinkable ... The only rational course of action is to cease living under the conditions where our mutual destruction is only one impulsive tantrum away.'[19]

Sadists and bureaucratic automatons, banal policy makers, dictators and arms traders have mastered their familiarity with and literacy about violence. To question the consequences of such cruelties depends on confidence in showing what non-violence has achieved and the promise it holds. That record and this promise require enthusiasm and literacy.

Literacy usually refers to an ability to read, write and converse in a specific language, but does not always rely on words. Self-expression may be conveyed in dress, in hospitality through the preparation and presentation of food, and in the freedom communicated through theatre or other art forms. Understanding the powerful symbolism of dress, food and music illustrates a literacy about non-violence, a familiarity with the many ways of generating energy on behalf of others.

Musical expressions of people's non-violence have crossed countries and cultures. In my Colorado University days, a colleague from Columbia taught a course called 'the sociology of dance'. She traced a history of dance to show how people across South America had danced to experience solidarity and oppose dictatorships.

In his performances, the Pink Floyd singer-songwriter Roger Waters aimed to increase public awareness of human rights issues. From the song *Each Small Candle*, he sang,

> *Not the torturer will scare me,*
> *nor the body's final fall,*
> *nor the barrels of death's rifles,*
> *nor the shadows on the wall,*
> *not the night when to the ground the last dim star of pain,*
> *is hurled but the blind indifference of a merciless, unfeeling world.*[20a]

In anticipation of appearing at the site of the wall on the US/Mexican border, Waters said, 'There will first need to be an awakening against these far-right policies. The sewers are engorged by greedy and powerful men.'[20b]

In not dissimilar vein, composers of symphonies have known how to use their genius to dramatize the plight of the vulnerable and to challenge oppressive regimes. In his Fifth Symphony (1937) and with poetic subtlety, Dmitri Shostakovich challenged the oppression of the Stalin regime. His listeners got the message.

In 2015, through his foundation Pianos for Peace and in his composition *Syrian Symphony*, the Syrian concert pianist Malek Jandali remembers his country's half a million civil war dead, including 55,000 children. His empathic works show how music remembers the slaughtered and surviving refugees. His language also speaks opposition to the Syrian dictator Bashar al-Assad and to those who carry out his orders. 'Nothing else seems to work,' says Malek.[21]

Beethoven wanted his final symphony, the Ninth (1824), usually referred to as the peace symphony, to be a victory for humanity, inside and outside the concert hall. This work is. The words in the last movement, sung by the chorus and by soloists, came from the German poet Friedrich Schiller's work, *Ode to Joy*, written in 1785 and revised in 1803 during the Napoleonic Wars. To express peace through an interdependence of peoples, Schiller wrote that he wanted his words to be a kiss for the whole earth.

In terms of the EU's insistence on being generous to refugees, it is worth remembering that the final movement of Beethoven's Ninth Symphony is the EU's national anthem, and that the goal of achieving peace through inclusiveness was a key motive in the creation of the EU. The British people who voted for Brexit could take notice, so too the East European governments, Poland, Hungary, Slovakia and the Czech Republic, which refuse to admit asylum seekers. So too the indifferent, money-rich but values-poor dictatorships of Middle East Arab states.

Pete Seeger's 1961 song *If I Had a Hammer* conveys aspirations for peace with justice, the exact opposite of divisive nationalism. Seeger began, 'If I had a hammer, I'd hammer in the morning, I'd hammer in the evening, all over this land.' He ended,

> *Well I've got a hammer*
> *And I've got a bell*
> *And I've got a song to sing*
> *All over this land*

It's the hammer of justice
It's the bell of freedom
It's the song about love between my brothers and my sisters
All over this land.[22]

Technology: help or hindrance?

Being inspired by music, poetry, dance, numerous other art forms and by generous hospitality could make humanitarian alternatives to cruelty seem easy to attain. But in contexts in which violence is a dominant language, and where generations have been constrained by that way of thinking, it could be difficult for perspectives to change.

Reliance on top-down ways of exercising power and seduction through the false claims made by free market economists will not go away. In addition, it may be assumed that values don't need to change because future benefits for humanity will depend on mastering technology. Assumptions that technology will produce more efficient and even socially just lifestyles may hinder any capacity for reflection, let alone finding time to ponder the conditions which facilitate cruelties.

In her appraisal of the creation of the Soviet gulags, Kate Millett warned that the application of technology could be seductive because it suggested to states' operatives an easy and almost limitless form of surveillance and control. Millett wrote: 'Technology completes, even perfects the powers assumed by government, brings them toward an omnipotence previously imagined only in connection with the deity. The state now aspires to the condition of divine power, as its citizens, every day more subject, are inspired to fear and accept it with the unquestioning awe they once felt for God.'[23] But Shoshana Zuboff warns that in the West, the state is being effectively contracted out to corporate giants, Google and Facebook, so it is not just the state which 'aspires to the condition of divine power'. Zuboff shows that in terms of individuals' freedoms, the influence of these corporate giants through their surveillance capitalism is seductive, largely invisible and therefore more dangerous and pernicious.[24]

Technology which is used to observe citizens' movements, to control and repress their behaviour may be most evident in openly authoritarian regimes. The coronation of Xi Jinping as President for life promises to entrench China's high-tech authoritarianism.[25]

Chinese scholar David Brophy has observed China's north-west region of Xinjiang, 'where a panoply of checkpoints, digital monitoring and political education camps keep the local ethnic group, the Uyghurs, in line'. He has observed police stations at every major intersection, elderly men and women trudging through the streets on anti-terror drills, television and radio broadcasts haranguing Uighurs to love the party and blame themselves for their second-class status.[26]

The UN estimates that up to one million Uighurs may be held involuntarily in extra-legal detention in camps in Xinjiang. The Chinese government says the camps are vocational training centres which provide language teaching and re-education of extremists, yet Michelle Bachelet, the UN High Commissioner for Human Rights, has been refused permission to travel to the region to assess these claims.

Modern means of communication – smartphone technology – may appear to be less intrusive on freedoms than hidden cameras on street corners, yet even major promoters are warning of the dangers of dependence on a potentially addictive appliance. Children and adults who can't put their smartphones down are replacing conversation with a need to check the gadget hundreds of times per day. Smartphone use is said to take the same cognitive toll as losing a full night's sleep.[27]

If relationships are routed through smartphones, daily lives are distorted, users' behaviour is constrained to react to cues and to keep that process going. Instead of technology liberating people to become socially aware and to think differently about governance, their behaviour is constrained. They are confronted with a mess of alerts, likes, messages, retweets and internet use so pathologically frantic that it inevitably makes far too many people vulnerable to pernicious nonsense and real dangers.[28]

A former Facebook executive has warned, 'The short term, dopamine-driven feedback loops that we have created are destroying how society works ... No civil discourse, no cooperation, misinformation, mistruth ... So we are in a really bad state of affairs ...'.[29]

When asked about the prospect of global self-destruction through the use of nuclear weapons, novelist and human rights advocate Arundhati Roy referred to her 'paranoia' about the technology of artificial intelligence (AI).

> Perhaps AI can do better surgery than surgeons, write better poetry than poets and better novels than novelists. But what it does is make the human population almost surplus ... when human beings become surplus, that's where these smart nukes and chemical and biological warfare – these things that are genocidal – begin to really

worry me. Because I do see a time when the masters of the universe will decide that the universe is a better place without most of the population. Artificial intelligence is a way of becoming the perfect human being, which fascists have always thought about: the supreme human being. If you can think of that, if that is your goal, then certainly you can't think of the other. I worry about it.[30]

In addition to worrying about a dependence on a technology that reduces humanity and appears to give little time for contemplation, let alone for equanimity, observations from a couple of poets highlight the value of being sufficiently still to ponder life's purpose. Australian poet Les Murray wrote about *Equanimity*. He argued that the experience of equanimity gave 'lifelong plenishment'.

> *Whatever its variants of meat-cuisine, worship, divorce,*
> *human order has at heart*
> *an equanimity. Quite different from inertia, it's a place*
> *where the churchman's not defensive, the indignant aren't on the*
> *qui vive,*
> *the loser has lost interest, the accountant is truant to remorse,*
> *where the farmer has done enough struggling-to-survive*
> *for one day, and the artist rests from theory —*
> *where all are, in short, off the high comparative horse*
> *of their identity.*[31]

William Stafford's *You Reading This Stop* provides another reminder of the value, not of reliance on technology but of contemplation in quiet places.

> *Don't just stay tangled up in your life.*
> *Out there in some river or cave where you*
> *could have been, some absolute, lonely*
> *dawn may arrive and begin the story*
> *that means what everything is about.*
> *So don't just look, either: Let your whole self drift like a breath*
> *and learn*
> *Its way down through the trees. Let that fine*
> *waterfall-smoke filter its gone, magnified presence*
> *all through the forest. Stand here till all that*
> *you were can wander away and come back slowly*
> *carrying a strange new flavour into your life.*

Feel it? That's what we mean. So don't just
read this — rub your thought over it.

Now you can go on.[32]

A different economy

There's no chronological order to the tasks of crafting humanitarian alternatives to cruelty, but it's time to consider proposals for societies freed from thinking that life's major purpose is economic. A rethink about social purposes and social values requires a reversal of the market-oriented convention that economic management must precede efforts to build a just society: economy first, society later.

In *Democracy in Chains* (2017), Nancy MacLean shows how manipulation of economic interests was secret and alien to democratic ideals of openness, trust and sharing. She documents relentless American right-wing initiatives to promote selfishness by eliminating unions, suppressing voting and privatizing education. She shows how citizens' freedom depends on struggles between the free marketeers who argue that no one should be taxed against their will and those who insist that democracy demands intervention to achieve equity. MacLean concludes that a society's choice is between unfettered capitalism and democracy, that we cannot have both.[33]

Almost a decade earlier, Tony Judt warned of the dangers of the narrow economic terms which determined policies and constrained conversations. He wrote of the difficulties of even imagining a society different from the one characterized by inequalities and injustices. He showed that in countries influenced by free market ideologies, by trickle-down economics, key policy questions had been — is the policy efficient, is it productive, will it contribute to growth? Instead, he argued, promotion of a common good would require asking whether policies were fair or unfair, good or bad, contributing to justice or to injustice.[34]

Concern to craft societies not preoccupied with financial gain has a long history. In the 18th century, Adam Smith was arguing not for untrammelled wealth but that moral sentiments should be uppermost in conversations. In 1930, during the Great Depression, the philosopher-economist John Maynard Keynes wrote that for the first time since creation, 'Man will be faced with his real, his permanent problem — how to use his freedom from pressing economic cares ... to live wisely, and agreeably and well.'[35]

In the US in 2017, Rabbi Michael Lerner advocated a national security strategy, a global Marshall Plan that would dedicate 1–2% of

US gross domestic product for the next 20 years to eliminate domestic and global poverty, inadequate education and inadequate healthcare and repair damage to the environment by 150 years of ecologically irresponsible forms of industrialization and 'modernization'.

He argued the need to overcome a global system of selfishness and materialism, of respect for militarism and for economic growth whatever the human costs. Such humanitarian-oriented policies depend on a new bottom line, a perspective 'that judges every sector, system and institution ... by the extent to which they maximize love and caring, kindness and generosity, empathy and compassion. This new bottom line would prioritize the well-being of the planet and all its inhabitants.'[36]

In a visionary analysis of what he calls a 'large scale post capitalist project', Paul Mason speaks of an interdependence of social and economic policies to remove uneven power relationships. This would require networks of like-minded people, consumers, lovers and communicators, working to sustain the environment, to maximize the power of information to address poverty and disease. Such problems would be attacked from all angles, not just in states, corporations and political parties. Mason concludes: 'There's one change which anybody in charge of a state could implement immediately and for free: switch off the neo-liberal privatization machine.'[37]

Cruelties derived from free market policies are evident in the consequences of inequalities, as in the negative effects of poverty on early child development, and in the realization, the fewer the years of education, the higher the risks of early death. In his deliberations about combatting the consequences of inequalities, Professor of Epidemiology and Public Health at University College, London, Sir Michael Marmot, stressed two policy priorities: the need to promote equal educational opportunities and a need to defend and extend universal healthcare, not least by paying attention to mental health and dental services.[38]

A historical view of societies which have reduced inequalities shows progressive income taxation as a positive phenomenon, as in Nordic countries whose commitment to strong economic growth included investment in people, by regulating working conditions and by providing substantial welfare services. These achievements display ways to build a rights-with-responsibilities obligation of citizenship as a means of confronting inequalities and as a crucial building block of civil societies.[39]

The French economist Thomas Piketty has shown the destructive consequences of immense inequalities of wealth. He advocates a reinvigorated democracy as the way to influence alternative forms of governance and thereby promote social and economic justice. This philosophical and political narrative requires the resuscitation of old ideals. In common with Marmot, Piketty advocates the promotion of collective interests over private ones. He repeats Nancy MacLean's warnings about the cunning efforts by powerful lobbies to promote their privileged version of freedom; and she was repeating Kenneth Galbraith's famous identification of the dangers of private affluence and public squalor.[40] Galbraith was bringing up to date the phrase first used by R.H. Tawney in 1911: private affluence and public squalor.[41]

Consistent with an understanding of interdependence and belonging, any reinvigorated democracy would also need to emphasize the importance of being an international citizen, committed to supporting universal human rights in foreign and domestic policies. Such a commitment would mean substantial increases in wealthy countries' contributions to overseas aid, a socially just and non-violent policy initiative, evidence of compassion, altruism and kindness. Those attributes should become the bottom-line criteria which human beings have always valued, but which have never been quantified by economists.

Belief in justice through the attainment of universal human rights will also depend on courage to stand up to the bullies of international politics. Advocacy of the human rights of oppressed peoples such as Tibetans, West Papuans, Palestinians and the people of Western Sahara would have little financial costs but considerable social justice and political benefits.

Courage is crucial

Considerable courage is needed to challenge the cruelties which flourish unhindered around the globe. To participate in non-violent protest, to emphasize the imperatives of interdependence, to seek alternatives to neoliberal economics and to face up to violent repression, takes mental and physical courage.

Courage is not just an account of individuals' characteristics but appears linked to a culture of curiosity and creativity in which virtues such as friendship, loyalty, courage and humour are linked. Alasdair MacIntyre has described Greek, Medieval and Renaissance cultures in which a chief means of moral education lay in telling stories which showed courage and friendship as qualities necessary to sustain a household and a community. Courage also had meaning as a feature of citizenship in the city-state. He concluded that there should be no separation between the promotion of a common good and the behaviour of the virtuous person.[42]

Reserves of mental and physical courage see well-known and less well-known humanitarians on public platforms when it would have been easier to have retreated, to mull over ideals but only as private citizens. The need for courage confronts anyone who struggles for peace with justice but who may be tempted to think they should protest only occasionally, who may think that passivity is the best form of protection.

A poem which depicts the stands taken by the late Muhammad Ali shows courage in the boxer's non-compliant response to the heavy-weight demands of establishment authority. In *True to Himself* the American poet and nuclear disarmament campaigner David Krieger reflects:

> *Muhammad Ali was graceful and strong*
> *and he had no quarrel with the Vietcong*
> ...
> *That he had courage there was no doubt,*
> *facing giants in the ring and taking them out.*
>
> *When called upon to fight in the Army's ranks,*
> *he said in so many words, 'no thanks.'*
> ...
> *They took away his well-earned crown,*
> *threatened him with jail and called him a clown.*
>
> *Through it all, he stayed true to himself,*
> *not allowing his deepest beliefs to be put on a shelf.*
>
> *Finally, the man who I call a hero*
> *won at the Supreme Court eight to zero.*
>
> *Muhammad Ali was graceful and strong*
> *and he had no quarrel with the Vietcong.*[43]

No one should be seduced by the idea that only the famous struggle for human rights. Even Nobel Prize recipients have been relatively unknown before their recognition by the Nobel committee. These recipients have included the gutsy Indigenous leader (1992) who insisted that her people should participate in building democracy in a country such as Guatemala,[44] campaigners (1997) for an international treaty to abolish land mines,[45] and the individuals (2012) who created safe havens for children who were victims of war.[46]

Conquering fear is as much a feature of the activities of unheralded and unknown humanitarians as it is of someone as internationally well known as Muhammad Ali. A common denominator in those activities is a philosophy of small victories in which relatively unknown people made a difference, in the home and the schoolroom, in the office and on building sites, in sporting events, in the performance of music and song and in political campaigning. Even inspiring leaders such as Nelson Mandela and Martin Luther King achieved outcomes for justice because they were supported by people who did little things to contribute to leaders' success.

Reference to small victories needs a caveat. Protesters for human rights take much greater risks in police states, under military or religious dictatorships, than they do in democracies. Without some consideration of the bravery of protesters who risk their lives in making even the slightest challenge to rulers, the ideals of humanitarianism will seem hopelessly unrealistic.

In Indonesia during President Suharto's repressive New Order government from 1967 to 1998, the national poet Rendra had been imprisoned several times for having the courage to express dissent. He is remembered as a daring humanitarian and his poetry as the voice of political conscience, an integral part of the opposition to the regime in Suharto's Indonesia.[47] Rendra's poetry readings were mass events. For example, in April 1978 at the Jakarta Arts Centre, he spoke in opposition to military power and against the suppression of free speech. He read *I Write This Pamphlet*.

> *I write this pamphlet*
> *because the institutions of public opinion*
> *are covered in cobwebs.*
> *People talk in whispers*
> *and self-expression is suppressed,*
> *ending up as mere acquiescence.*
> ...
> *I see no reason*
> *why we should sit here in enforced stupor.*
> *I would like us to engage in a fair exchange of views.*
> *Sit and debate honestly when we agree and when we don't.*[48]

Such poetry reading was a significant feature of Indonesian public culture. Performances by Rendra encouraged opposition and contributed to a sense of solidarity among young people trying to confront an unchecked exercise of power.[49]

Another poet in another country was also a leader for opposition to an uncompromising authoritarianism. The 2010 Nobel Peace Prize was awarded to the very brave and principled Chinese literary critic, poet and human rights campaigner Liu Xiaobo. An 11-year prison sentence for demanding an end to one-party rule meant that Liu could not travel to Oslo to receive his award. An empty chair symbolized his presence at the ceremony. The specific 'crime' that led to his spending his final years behind bars was *Charter 08*, a 2008 declaration inspired by *Charter 77*, a manifesto published by Czechoslovakian dissidents in 1977. Liu dedicated his Nobel Prize to the lost souls of 4 June, a reference to victims of the Tiananmen Square massacre.[50]

On receiving notice of the Nobel award, the Chinese government placed Liu's wife, the poet and artist Liu Xia, under house arrest, since which time she has been living under surveillance and in almost total isolation. Suffering in prison from liver cancer, Liu Xiaobo was not permitted to seek medical treatment abroad. He died in prison in July 2017. The last verse of *The Empty Chair* recognizes the significance of Liu Xiaobo.

> *This poetic protester*
> *has cultivated freedom's blooms*
> *but languishes distant*
> *in a prison cell and cannot hear*
> *the applause for the vacant seat*
> *from an audience grateful*
> *for the courage of the prisoner*
> *who should be sitting in that winner's chair.*[51]

The bravery shown by Liu Xiaobo has been repeated by unknown protesters in other countries where the exercise of freedoms is stifled and punished. Late December 2017 and early January 2018 saw country-wide protest in Iran against economic hardship, corruption and the oppressive rule by mullahs, by the Grand Leader Ayatollah Khamenei, by the Revolutionary Guards and the Basij Militia. Protesters were suppressed with water cannon, tear gas, rubber bullets and live fire. Thousands were arrested and 22 killed.[52]

The Centre for Human Rights in Iran reported that some detainees faced charges which carried the death penalty, and that relatives of detainees were threatened with arrest for staging peaceful sit-ins outside the Evin prison. Relatives said that armed forces 'told us we should leave, or we will all be arrested. We said we are ready to join our kids inside the prison. We will not go anywhere until we get some news about our kids. All we know is that they are on hunger strike.'[53]

Under Chinese rule in Tibet, protesters display amazing courage. They seek freedom without the potential oversight and protection from foreign news media and human rights organizations, both banned by the Chinese governments. In September and October 2013, Tibetans who protested against being forced to fly Chinese flags on their houses were shot by security forces while seeking the release of arrested villagers. Singers had been jailed for singing songs of freedom. Others were jailed just for having those songs or the Tibetan flag on their phones.[54]

On 12 October 2019, Hevrin Xelef, the 34-year-old Kurdish leader of the Future Syria Party, was murdered by Turkish-backed Ahrar al-Sharqiya militants. Hevrin was remembered by her people as 'a symbol of courage, security and peace'. Her grieving friends said that their brave leader 'gave her life for the brotherhood of nations'.[55]

The courage of such activists for justice is pitted against powerful individuals and governments, against extremist groups such as ISIS and the Taliban in Afghanistan, who establish identity by committing atrocities, almost always against civilians. Such individuals and organizations continue to be fascinated with violence, greed, corruption, deceit and cruelty. In dialogue about the humanitarian alternatives, they can be offered agendas which would not be destructive but would be far more life enhancing, health promoting and interesting.

Poetic epilogue

Judith Wright, the Australian poet, championed Indigenous people and the environment. In *The Flame Tree*, she suggested the infinite benefits of a non-violent way to live.

> *How to live, I said, as the flame tree lives?*
> *— to know what the flame tree knows; to be*
> *prodigal of my life as that wild tree*
> *and wear my passion so.*[56]

At the end of the 20th century, the Nobel Prize-winning Polish poet Czeslaw Milosz looked back on a time of inhumanities. In *This World*, he imagined that brutalities never took place and that humanity could be recovered in spite of the past.

It appears that it was all a misunderstanding.
What was only a trial run was taken seriously.
The rivers will return to their beginnings.
The wind will cease in its turning about.
Trees instead of budding will tend to their roots.
Old men will chase a ball, a glance in the mirror –
They are children again.
The dead will wake up, not comprehending.
Till everything that happened has unhappened.
What a relief! Breathe freely, you who have suffered so much.[57]

6

Cruel or compassionate world?

To be hopeful in bad times is not just foolishly romantic.
It is based on the fact that human history is a history not
only of cruelty, but also of compassion, sacrifice, courage
and kindness. (Howard Zinn)[1]

I am convinced that for practical as well as moral reasons,
non-violence offers the only road to freedom for my people.
(Martin Luther King Jr)[2]

Wise owls dream of peace. Wise people make it happen.
(Stella Cornelius)[3]

On 26 February 2018, the UN demanded a resolution for a 30-day
ceasefire across Syria and the allowance of humanitarian convoys
for the 400,000 people besieged in the Damascus suburb of Eastern
Ghouta. The following day Iran said it did not care about UN
resolutions. Turkey declared that its operations in northern Syria
would not be affected. Russia said a ceasefire could last for five hours
not 30 days. UN Secretary General Antonio Guterres pleaded for an
end to wartime activities. The Syrian government and their Russian
allies continued the slaughter. Humanitarian law and UN resolutions
were of no consequence.

The Syrian civil war bred cruelties. The siege of Ghouta had
been under way since 2013. Hundreds of thousands of people lived
underground, beneath bombs, under gunfire, with little food or water
and no medical supplies. The Syrian Observatory for Human Rights
reported that by mid-March 2018, 1,000 people had been killed
in pulverized buildings, described by UN spokespersons as a 'hell
on earth'.

Disbelief about Syria raises questions whether a worldwide
malignancy of cruelties will end. If the leaders of states, if powerful
people in institutions, if key members of extremist groups think that
their actions should be influenced only by what they can get away
with, the idea of policies governed by ethics and laws looks absurd.

Slaughter in Ghouta highlights conditions which have nurtured
cruelties: indifference to human rights and non-violence, plus derision

about humanitarian law and other ethical considerations. In reaction to threats of terrorism, and as the product of an economics-based encouragement of selfishness and inequality, cruelties seem bound to increase. If so, do those who influence public opinion allow the trend to continue, or would they support a counter humanitarianism?

The question, are some cruelties worse than others, takes us nowhere. But reminders should be made of the atrocities of ISIS, the Taliban and other extremist groups, of executions without trial in Iran, of President Duterte's arbitrary killings across the Philippines, Indonesian abuses in West Papua, the Myanmar military's expulsion of the Rohingya people, Israel's decades-long occupation of Palestinian lands and their inhumanity in the siege of Gaza, let alone the US and Saudi decimation of Yemen, or China and Russia's continued suppression of dissent. The economic policies of the US, the UK and other European governments which ensure that poverty persists should be included in that list, so too the states which cast aside the rules of the 1951 Refugee Convention and close their doors to refugees.

To confront such a catalogue, an education for humanity would identify principles which seem lost but must be recovered. Those who craft policies could support areas of public life which either have not appeared on their radar or have not been perceived as having anything to do with cruelty. To that end, priority tasks in education concern issues which I have previously omitted, or which have been given insufficient emphasis:

(i) the erosion of human rights principles;
(ii) reminders about the ways in which free market economic policies enable corporations to contribute to poverty and to cruelty to children;
(iii) evidence of the increase in cruelty to animals;
(iv) the cruelties associated with the possession and threatened use of nuclear weapons.

Stories derived from poetry, such as Brecht's 'Justice is the bread of the people', or Oodgeroo Nunucaal's 'I'm for humanity all one race', can find a place in citizens' values and in leaders' minds. That contention underlines the responsibilities of teachers, in schools, in colleges and universities, plus journalists of every description, to educate about rebuilding civil societies through advocacy of human rights, including protection of a precious planet, and by supporting public institutions and services.

Erosion of human rights

In response to the slaughter of 60 million people in the Second World War, an edifice of human rights principles was built to ensure no repeat of the years of violent disregard for a common humanity. Embodied in the UN Charter, the Universal Declaration of Human Rights and the Geneva Convention, those principles expressed a respect for universal values, as opposed to the notion that nation-states would always be entitled to act alone.

In the first decades of the 21st century, states' acknowledgement of universal principles has been replaced by a post-modern notion of a freedom to act according to the dictates of pragmatism and self-interest. When states, institutions, organized groups or individuals ignore human rights principles, they do so because the risk of being found out may be the only restriction on their so-called freedom.

Such freedom has produced legislation to suppress dissent and even to legitimize torture, provided it is carried out in secret. In different countries, repressive legislation appears under various names: special powers acts, suspension of constitutional rights, emergency provisions, martial law and extraordinary detention statutes. In Northern Ireland during the 1970s Britain passed a Special Powers Act 1971, an Emergency Provisions Act 1973, a Prevention of Terrorism Act 1975, and in 1978 another Emergency Provisions Act.

In 2016 in the UK, the Investigative Powers Act introduced a mass surveillance system, permitting the interception, access, retention and hacking of communications without even a requirement of reasonable suspicion. In his commentary on that legislation, the UN High Commissioner for Human Rights said that nation-states that had previously respected human rights could become indistinguishable from the terrorists they were fighting. 'Our world is dangerously close to unmooring itself from a sense of compassion, slowly becoming not only a post truth but also a post empathic world.'[4]

In an echo of the Commissioner's warning, Professor Kevin Clements has advocated 'a politics of compassion in a world of ruthless power'. This politics, he says, would place the welfare of the community first and the state second, would aim at solving problems non-violently, collaboratively, empathically and altruistically. To achieve that goal, it would be imperative to replace political pathologies such as domination, fear, inequality, poverty and war.[5]

Nevertheless, states continue to use the language of morality to defend immoral practices, to pursue national priorities in violent ways: killing citizens in Syria to maintain the sovereignty of a state, imprisoning asylum seekers on offshore islands as a way of protecting refugees in other parts of the world, collectively punishing Palestinians to show respect for a biblical inheritance given by God, abolishing any semblance of democracy in Cambodia, stifling dissent in Turkey to show that government must be uncompromisingly authoritarian. Oppression is fomented by fear, fabrication and a paranoia which is publicized as strength.

Rewriting rules to suit the convenience of states disguises cruelty and the horrors of state violence. In the campaigns against the Taliban in Afghanistan, President Obama wanted to minimize the evidence about the number of civilian casualties killed by drones. Early in 2012, he decreed that all males killed in a drone-strike zone should be counted as enemy combatants, unless there was evidence proving them as innocents. A flimsy argument maintained that if Afghanis were sighted in a particular area, they must be up to no good. A US officer observed that counting casualties required deception, that corpses could be counted but no one could be sure who they were.[6]

Nikki Haley, the 2017–18 US Ambassador to the United Nations claimed that other countries violated international agreements, yet the US showed contempt for UN resolutions and for the UN Charter. The US has never signed the Convention on the Law of the Sea, nor the Rome Statute of the International Criminal Court, has withdrawn from the Paris agreement to combat climate change, and in order to prevent Israeli governments from being held accountable for their treatment of Palestinians, had in May 2018 withdrawn from the UN Human Rights Council. By promoting the transfer of the Israeli capital from Tel Aviv to Jerusalem, President Trump thumbed his nose at the international community and at humanitarian law.

When Israel enacts legislation to justify the military occupation of Palestinian lands, the US defies international law by always siding with Israel. Yet the Fourth Geneva Convention says, 'Individual or mass forcible transfers as well as deportations of protected persons from occupied territory to the territory of the Occupying Power, or to that of another country, occupied or not, are prohibited regardless of their motives.' Nevertheless, a 2018 Israeli Ministerial Committee for Legislation has presented a Bill to amend entry to Israel by a Law which allows the Interior Ministry to revoke the residency status of Palestinian Jerusalemites for 'breach of loyalty; or for committing a criminal act'.

The Palestinian educator and human rights campaigner Dr Hanan Ashrawi shows that Palestinian Jerusalemites are the Indigenous peoples of the land and have lived in the city for centuries. Their lives should not be dependent on the whims of Israeli policies of occupation and apartheid, and Israel should not be given licence to enhance its illegal and extremist settler population.[7]

Appeals to nationalism, to a need for countries' security in a fight against terrorism, are used to justify the protection of borders and to foster indifference to human rights. References to nationalism, security and terrorism have become the prescription for do-what-you-like policies. Ethics have been drowned, imagination stifled, fences and walls erected.

Before the January 2019 controversy in the US over President Trump demanding billions of dollars to build a wall on the Mexican border, the Chinese artist Ai Weiwei reflected on the use of walls to punish powerless people. Such actions, he said, were an injustice which reflected the consequences of social and economic inequalities. Ai Weiwei wrote,

> If we map the 70 plus border walls and fences built between nations in the past three decades, we can see the extent of global economic and political disparities. The people most negatively affected by these walls are the poorest and most desperate of society. ... How do we think the poor, displaced or occupied can exist when their societies are destroyed? ... There are many borders to dismantle, but the most important are the ones within our own hearts and minds ... These are the borders that are dividing humanity from itself.[8]

Respect for the idea of an interdependence of peoples has been replaced by support for destructive nationalism. Britain voted for Brexit irrespective of the idea for European union, that it should be a bulwark for peace. Slogans about regaining independence and becoming great again give a green light to authoritarianism. As a boastful public spectacle, an American President has flaunted his wealth, and in the name of citizens' alleged security, supports the murderous violence facilitated by a National Rifle Association. This might-is-right claim is based on a version of freedom which says that nothing should hinder my choice of how I wish to maintain power. Such a disdain for the values of a civil society is also expressed by Tayyip Erdoğan in Turkey, Viktor Orbán in Hungary, Vladimir Putin in Russia and the leader of the Law and Justice Party, Jarosław Kaczyński, in Poland.

The go-it-alone, forget-about-ethics, do-what-you-like policies are also evident in South East Asia. Respect for human rights and for the precepts of democracy has been buried beneath authoritarian rule in Cambodia, in the Philippines, by the generals in Thailand and by Buddhist-led brutalities in Myanmar. In the latter country, in spite of evidence that starvation is used to drive remaining Rohingya from their country, and that military bases have been built to conceal the destruction of Rohingya villages, the Myanmar representatives at the UN have claimed that nothing unusual had happened.

Politics post the Geneva Conventions is used to manipulate others in the quest for power. The practitioners with the most power can rewrite history, or ignore it, can formulate laws and make new policy regulations for their own purposes. In anticipation of this discarding of human rights principles, the philosopher Alasdair MacIntyre forecast that the modern state would behave 'towards those subject to it as if it were no more than a giant monopolistic utility company and part of the time as if it were the guardian of all that is most valued. In one capacity it requires us to fill in appropriate forms in triplicate. In the other, it periodically demands that we die for it.'[9]

Corporate contributions

Previous discussion of ways to build a democracy freed from the influence of neoliberal economics contained no explicit reference to the cruelty sustained by the policies of corporations. Yet corporations have been compliant in policies which have punished the vulnerable, the unemployed or the underemployed, those who allegedly are not contributing to economic growth, including migrants who are rounded up and the homeless who are prosecuted.

In *Profits of Doom*, a damning record of how corporations are becoming more powerful than the state, Antony Loewenstein shows the links between multinationals and states and the consequent lack of accountability that arises from those links.[10] He shows how business is conducted on the backs of others' misery, by cashing in on emergency relief, from contracts to incarcerate the vulnerable and from the processing of asylum seekers.

In *Disaster Capitalism*, Loewenstein continues his research into systems which make vulnerable people among the world's most valuable commodities.[11] Via carefully concealed contracts, companies such as G4S, Serco and Haliburton obtain massive profits from running privatized prisons and detention centres and from militarized private security, by siphoning profits from overseas aid budgets and from destructive mining. His analyses are a fitting overture for an appraisal of corporate responsibility for privatization and poverty.

In 2017 in the United States, and without any opposition from major businesses, the Congress attempted to deny health insurance to millions. In December 2017, the US Congress passed a Bill to give huge tax rewards to wealthy individuals and corporations, the politicians and their business allies somehow indifferent, or denying the reality, that financial wealth to the top percentile would require cuts to essential services.

Companies' contributions to poverty and poor living conditions, by paying low wages, has been concealed by a public sector's willingness to top up low pay. In an analysis of the high public cost of low wages in America, the Labor Centre at the University of California Berkeley reported that when jobs don't pay enough, workers turn to public assistance in order to meet basic needs. Public programmes were subsidizing employers. At state and federal levels, more than half the total spending on programmes such as Medicaid, the Children's Health Insurance Program, Temporary Assistance for Needy Families, Earned Income Tax Credit and food stamps went to working families.[12]

In Britain, the public sector tops up and thus conceals the poverty facilitated by companies' aims to limit costs and maximize profits. Businesses which pay poverty wages are claimed to be costing taxpayers 11 times the amount lost by benefit fraud. The UK's four large supermarkets, Tesco, Asda, Sainsbury's and Morrisons, have been costing annually just under £1 billion in tax credits and extra benefit payments.[13]

Factors contributing to poverty are concealed by the transfer of public sector resources to private interests, the rest of society virtually paying a country's large businesses. The *Guardian Sustainability Report* says that, to put the figure in perspective, the total cost of benefit fraud in 2015 was £1 billion, but corporate scrounging was 11 times that figure. Almost one quarter of British employees earn below living wages, which means they are likely to be living in or near poverty. It looks as though employers set their pay rates on the expectation that there will always be a top-up from governments.

Dependence on child labour

Corporate responsibility for cruelty is more obvious when questions are raised about child labour. The International Labour Organization (ILO) estimates that in the fashion industry 170 million employees are children. Although this practice is forbidden in most countries, it continues to be rife in some of the poorest parts of the world. The ILO estimates that at least 11% of the world's children live in situations that deprive them of their right to go to school without interference from work.[14]

Fast fashion has engendered a race to the bottom, pushing companies to find ever cheaper sources of labour. A 2017 Stop Child Labour report says that children are seen as obedient workers, easy to manage, and that countries like India and Bangladesh bring young girls into the textile industries under false promises of earning decent wages. In the textile and garment industry, Uzbekistan, Egypt, Pakistan, India, Bangladesh, Thailand and China are notorious for child labour.

In the fashion-industry supply chain, the practice of multiple outsourcing to subcontractors enables companies to claim that they don't know where their materials or their finished textiles are coming from, and whether children are employed. In the demand for cotton, child workers are valued but highly vulnerable. They are employed to transfer pollen from one plant to another, subject to long working hours, exposure to pesticides, and must harvest a delicate crop. They sow cotton in the spring, weed in the heat of long summer months and in the next step of the chain, labour in yarn and spinning mills.[15]

Ten major companies, Nestlé, H&M, Philip Morris, Walmart, Victoria's Secret, GAP, Apple, Disney, Forever 21 and Hersheys have been identified as using child labour which allows for cutting production costs and boosting profits.[16]

Walmart has been accused of employing child labourers to work up to 19 hours a day. GAP knowingly outsources production to sweatshops which employ workers as young as eight years old. Apple has factories in Thailand, Malaysia, China, Taiwan and the Philippines in which poor working conditions and worker abuse are said to have been rife. With factories in China, Bangladesh and Haiti, Disney has been paying employees as little as 33 cents an hour.[17]

Poverty cycles

An intergenerational cycle of poverty makes children from Indigenous groups and from lower castes particularly vulnerable to exploitation. If parents have no education, they end up in low-paid work, their children forced to work, so they miss out on education and end up in low-paid work as adults. Vulnerability persists, so does cruelty. A 2017 UNICEF report refers to slavery-like conditions such as forced and bonded labour, child soldiering and sexual exploitation. The latter abuse happens in homes, institutions, schools, workplaces, in travel and tourist facilities. The 2014 report *Hidden in Plain Sight* estimates that around 20 million girls under 20 have been subjected to forced sexual intercourse or other forced sexual acts at some points in their lives.[18]

Children on the move, internally displaced as a result of natural disasters, armed conflicts or as refugees, are vulnerable to different cruelties. By the end of 2015, 28 million children had been forcibly displaced by violence and conflict, of whom 17 million were internally displaced, 1 million were asylum seekers, 10 million were refugees. The European Commission's inquiry into the fight against the trafficking of human beings reports that children seeking to survive when on the move, or in related conflict situations, are often compelled to exchange sexual services, and girls are even forced to marry for food, shelter, protection or safe passage.[19]

In conflicts in Iraq and Nigeria, children forced to become combatants have been used as human bombs and human shields. In Iraq, ISIS and other extremist groups have trafficked boys and young men, including members of the Yazidi minority, into armed conflict. Using deception, death threats or the offer of money and women, ISIS attempted to radicalize their captives into committing terrorist acts. In Nigeria between 2014 and 2016, 90 children – 70 girls and 20 boys – were used by Boko Haram in 56 suicide bombings.[20]

There is a silent children crisis in Central America where, in March 2018, the UN High Commission for Refugees (UNHCR) reported that thousands of children were running for their lives. In Honduras, El Salvador and Guatemala crime syndicates known as 'maras' have recruited children as young as six years. In 'join or die' confrontations with families, ransoms or 'war taxes' are demanded and parents are pursued for payments. UNHCR reports that families are too frightened to let their children leave home, knowing they may never return. Under cover of night, families flee to southern Mexico, to a relatively impoverished state where aid organizations can provide essential but bare minimum help with food, beds, blankets and clothing plus some cash assistance and offers of counselling.

A UNHCR staff member in Mexico, Francesca Fontanini, reported in March 2018 that the violence by maras gangs had contributed to a refugee crisis in southern Mexico. Although some aid could be given to the fleeing new arrivals, 'There are many families we cannot reach. We have more and more mothers and children arriving on their own. We don't have enough space. We urgently need more shelter, more beds, more food.'[21]

Corporations and the arms trade

Destructive, death-promoting polices come from corporations which grow wealthy by feeding on the edict, 'there's no business like the arms business',[22] even if the consequences are devastating. Dangerous, lucrative deals have included US companies' sale of bombs and missiles to the Saudis in their brutal war in Yemen, and the 10-year deal to sell arms to Israel for 'self-defence', even though that means keeping Gaza as a site tailor-made for experimenting with new forms of surveillance and warfare.

Of the world's largest arms manufactures, four are American – General Dynamics, Raytheon, Boeing and Lockheed Martin – and one, BAE Systems, is British. To be successful, each needs to watch where war and instability occurs, where sales can be made, where conflict may decline and sales diminish. War is good business, while withdrawal from conflicts sees a decline in sales. Between 2011 and 2012, when the US withdrew troops from Iraq and Afghanistan, arms companies' spending fell from $159 billion to $115 billion.[23]

In order to maintain and increase profits, arms companies must court political influence, but as though their executives might feel a trifle guilty over the sources of their profits, they appear to be relatively secret about the extent, let alone the consequences of their sales. The US Pentagon's arms sales agency is known euphemistically as 'The Defence Security Cooperation Agency'. The US political system fosters contracts to companies in specific electorates, ties corporations into the crafting of foreign policies and is the key influence in facilitating sales and distributing weapons.

In July 2017, in support of a policy to increase Australian arms companies' sales around the world, an Australian Defence Industry minister said he wanted to increase his country's capacity to send a lot more weapons overseas to appropriate countries and places. He planned for Australia 'to become a major arms exporter on par with Britain, France and Germany and use exports to "cement relationships" with countries in volatile regions such as the Middle East'. Critics said that such a policy would be exporting death and profiting from bloodshed.[24]

As with other forms of cruelty, corruption plus cover-ups and denial that such practices occur is prevalent in arms company practice. Commenting on an Italian aerospace chief executive officer's fraudulent and corrupt conduct related to the sales of his companies' helicopters to the Indian government, the director of the Stockholm International Peace Research Institute programme on Military Expenditure and

Arms Production, Dr Samuel Perlo-Freeman, said that this was nothing new. 'The arms industry has always been associated with corruption both in international arms transfers and sometimes in domestic procurement.'[25]

Corporate benefits from war are associated with secrecy and corruption. David Whyte of the University of Liverpool found that neoliberal economic policies in Iraq contributed to a huge appropriation of oil revenue. The 2003 invasion of Iraq, he says, was 'one of the most audacious and spectacular crimes of theft in modern history. At least $12 billion of revenue was appropriated by the invading coalition and has not been adequately accounted for.'[26]

Animal cruelty

Notions of a common humanity could demand that policies to promote kindness, caring and generosity to animals receive as much attention as policies to eliminate cruelty to humans. Yet consideration of the lives of animals often comes as a political afterthought, when controversy can't be denied and powerful forces are shamed into acting.

The advocacy organization Animals International reports that animals in Asia are the most abused in the world. From bears captured and caged for their bile, to dogs and cats slaughtered in horrific ways for their meat, exploitation of animals in Asia is said to be common and widespread. It is estimated that in China, 10 million dogs and 4 million cats are slaughtered for their meat each year.[27]

From China and Vietnam come reports of repeated cruelties in zoos, safari parks, circuses and tourist attractions. Animals Asia claims that many wild animals, such as elephants, live their lives in chains and that in zoos and safari parks in Asia, terrified cows, donkeys, pigs and chickens are dropped into enclosures of starving lions and tigers as live prey, for the entertainment of crowds. Under-cover investigations into zoo performances have revealed gross abuse of wild animals. Satisfaction from sadism persists. Fear and punishment force animals to perform.[28]

In Britain, the Press Association reported that cruelty to pets was rising and becoming disturbingly inventive.[29] In 2017, the *Independent* reported a huge increase in animal cruelty shown on Snapchat and said that most of the abuse was committed by children.[30]

In greyhound and horse racing industries in North America, the UK and Australia, economics drives decisions as to the usefulness of animals, how to care for them and for how long. Peter Singer's significant thesis concerning suffering experienced in common by humans and non-humans is only slowly having an effect. On several continents, financial considerations transcend the suffering of animals, profit motives mean that underperforming creatures become surplus to requirements and are not worth keeping.

Animal Aid in the UK says that approximately one in every 37 horses who start a season's racing will have perished by the end of it and that as many as 10,000 horses are slaughtered each year for horse meat.[31] Prior to those 2016 estimates, an investigator for the *Guardian* wrote, 'For thousands of British thoroughbreds that are too old, too slow or not good enough jumpers, the end is brutal: a bullet through the temple or a metal bolt into the side of the brain. Then their carcasses are loaded on to freezer lorries and driven to France, where their flesh is sold as gourmet meat.' Horses which could live on average for more than 30 years are killed before their fifth birthday.[32]

In the Australian greyhound racing industry, up to 18,000 animals are killed each year because they are not considered fast enough to ever win races. Animals Australia also reports on the sadism of live baiting as a technique to motivate dogs in training. 'Terrified piglets, rabbits and native possums are victims of live baiting. Tied to lures, flung around race tracks at breakneck speeds and then mauled to death.'[33]

The Australian horse-racing industry is little different from any other animal industry. The question, 'when does use become abuse in equestrian sport?' has particular application to one of the richest races in the world, the Melbourne Cup.[34] In a 2018 report, Animals Australia concluded, 'You can count on one or two hands the Melbourne Cup winners who now graze on beautiful paddocks in their retirement. The vast majority of thoroughbred flat, jump and harness racing horses fail to run fast enough or become injured and are just discarded by the racing industry.' That report showed that failed or older racehorses were destined for slaughter or sent to knackeries to be converted to pet meat or part of the approximate 2,000 tons of horsemeat exported from Australia for consumption in Japan and Europe annually. Over 25,000 horses are killed in Australia each year.

One prominent newspaper editor argued, 'The horse racing industry is cruel, exploitative, unsafe and reliant on organized crime and rent-seeking. It should not be celebrated.'[35] A more cautious conclusion is that horses lead an unnatural and restricted life while racing, and at worst end up as 'wastage' in an industry that has no more use for them.

In the live-animal export trade, if profit motives dominate, brutal treatment of animals follows, even if a 2002 Animal Welfare Act says that a person is guilty of animal cruelty if they transport an animal 'in a way that causes or is likely to cause unnecessary harm'. Applied to accounts of 60,000 sheep transported from western Australia to the Middle East in August 2017, that legal reference to unnecessary harm reads like an understatement. Two thousand four hundred sheep died on the voyage. A whistle blower's video of transport by ship shows sheep dehydrated, distressed and dying amid decaying corpses on the boat's main deck.[36]

As a result of what is not done, acts of omission rather than commission, eyes-cast-aside-policies have enabled cruelty to animals to continue. Indifference to responsibilities for animals' welfare corresponds with authoritarianism, with disregard for international law and the consequent erosion of human rights. The persistence of cruelty to animals needs exposure, subsequent debate, proposals to outlaw barbaric practices[37] plus reminders that kindness towards animals correlates with beliefs in a common humanity; and that goal should include the Pachamama vision, referred to earlier, whose purpose is to act non-violently to all forms of life, thereby working towards a sustainable future that benefits everyone.

Nuclear cruelty

For advocates of nuclear disarmament, the revival of respect for a common humanity depends on adherence to treaties which uphold human rights and could protect the life of future generations. The Treaty on the Prohibition of Nuclear Weapons had its origins in a humanitarian initiative to promote complete nuclear disarmament by focusing attention on the catastrophic consequences of nuclear war. An unimaginable cruelty which is promised by the threat, let alone the use of nuclear weapons, merits worldwide attention. Nuclear-power states who want to keep their weapons and who refuse to sign the treaty are colluding with a cruelty which promises to be far more harmful than an aggregate of other worldwide atrocities.

ICAN received the December 2017 Nobel Peace Prize 'for its work to draw attention to the catastrophic humanitarian consequences of any use of nuclear weapons and for its ground-breaking efforts to achieve a treaty-based prohibition of such weapons'. Beatrice Finn, the first of two speakers representing ICAN at the December 2017 Oslo award ceremony, referred to continuing fear that 15,000 nuclear weapons still exist and can guarantee human destruction, a fear greater today than at the end of the Cold War. Creating fear continuously, or even occasionally, appears inherent in the policies of states which want to keep nuclear weapons and which refuse to accept the history-making Prohibition Treaty.

The second speaker at the 2017 Nobel ceremony, Setsuko Thurlow, spoke as a member of the family of Hibakusha, those who by some miraculous chance survived the bombings of Hiroshima and Nagasaki. For seven decades, she and her fellow survivors have worked for the total abolition of nuclear weapons. Setsuko described an unimaginable cruelty suffered by the victims of those bombings.

> I saw a blinding bluish white flash from the window, I remember the sensation of floating in the air.
>
> As I regained consciousness in the silence and darkness, I found myself pinned by the collapsed building. I began to hear my classmates' faint cries: 'Mother help me. God, help me.'
>
> As I crawled out, the ruins were on fire. Most of my classmates in that building were burned to death alive. I saw all around me utter, unimaginable devastation.
>
> Processions of ghostly figures shuffled by. Grotesquely wounded people, they were bleeding, burnt, blackened and swollen. Parts of their bodies were missing. Flesh and skin hung from their bones. Some with their eyeballs hanging in their hands. Some with their bellies burst open, their intestines hanging out. The foul stench of burnt human flesh filled the air.
>
> Thus, with one bomb my beloved city was obliterated. Most of its residents were civilians who were incinerated, vaporized, carbonized, among them, members of my own family and 351 of my schoolmates.

This humanitarian appeal contrasts with the attitudes of the leaders of Russia and the US, the two countries holding the majority of nuclear weapons. In a speech in the Kremlin in February 2018, President Putin boasted that Russia now possesses unstoppable nuclear weapons capable of causing widespread devastation irrespective of the destruction and cruelty to citizens who feared such sparring but felt unable to stop a potential last fight which no one might remember.[38]

President Trump had already said he wanted a tenfold increase in the US stockpile of nuclear weapons, which if implemented would give the US 'more than four times the total number of nuclear weapons currently declared worldwide by all the declared (and undeclared) nuclear powers'.[39]

In March 2018, after Putin's Kremlin speech in February, Trump joked that he wanted an army capable of fighting wars in space. He recognized that space was a war domain just like the land, air and sea. He later said he thought this was no joke because having a Space Force was really a great idea.[40]

To bolster his boasting, in April 2018, President Trump appointed John Bolton as his new national security adviser. Bolton had been a persistent critic of treaties to limit the spread of nuclear weapons, which he had described as 'unilateral disarmament'.

To the potential victims of nuclear war, the language to describe the power of the weapons and to compose treaties to limit their spread reads like macabre science fiction. These are militaristic accounts in which policies that are claimed to provide security are remote and mostly unknown to the people they are said to protect. Even the modest objectives of the New START Treaty depend on a specialist language which is confusing and threatening. Russia and the US agreed to limit the number of 'deployed strategic warheads' to 1,550 and 'fielded delivery platforms', intercontinental ballistic missiles, submarine-launched ballistic missiles and nuclear capable bombers, to 700.

Members of the Arms Control Association have said that if the treaties on Intermediate Nuclear Forces and New START (to limit the US and Russia's number of nuclear warheads and platforms to deliver them) were not renewed, this could lead to a rapid increase in nuclear arsenals. Former officials and experts from the US, Europe and Russia reported that nuclear danger loomed, that without binding limits on the world's two largest nuclear superpowers, the risk of unconstrained nuclear competition would grow.[41]

Artistic lifelines

Convention may insist that drafting and implementing policies is such a hard-nosed, rational enterprise that it's esoteric to consider how art forms could contribute to a kinder, more socially just and peace-enhancing world. But in many cultures, commentary from the world of the arts adds that indispensable non-violent dimension to life, makes it more interesting and potentially inspirational. In his 1897 work *What Is Art?*, Leo Tolstoy argued that great art 'can improve life by giving positive examples of "brotherhood and love of one's neighbour", luring men towards peace while alienating them from violence'.[42]

Tolstoy's aspirations are far removed from the tyranny used by Trump and Putin, by dictators in the Middle East, in South East Asia and in military-dominated governments such as Israel's and Turkey's. They promise continuing oppression. By contrast, poets' visions of a more compassionate, more socially just future, derive from those multi-dimensional ways of thinking which challenge authoritarianism, promote non-violence and record the beauty of all living things. Lessons can be learned from poets' pictures, the hopes they generate, even the counselling necessary to handle dark days of pessimism. W.B. Yeats' *To a Friend Whose Work Has Come to Nothing* speaks to the sentiments of people in despair in the 21st century, though he wrote at the beginning of the 20th.

> *Now all the truth is out,*
> *Be secret and take defeat*
> *From any brazen throat,*
> *For how can one compete,*
> *Being honour bred, with one*
> *Who were it proved he lies*
> *Were neither shamed in his own,*
> *Nor in his neighbours' eyes.*[43]

Yeats wrote in defence of ideals, against defeatism. His poetry describes outrage at tragic loss, surprise at institutional failure and gives pictures of betrayal and fear. His responses to cruelty have lessons for the present. A century after the violence which Yeats faced in Ireland in the early 20th century, sentiments are repeated by those who question the indifference to the human rights of the oppressed peoples of Western Sahara, West Papua, Tibet and Palestine, who denounce the genocide of Rohingya refugees from Myanmar, who oppose cruelties in the wars in Syria and Yemen. Yeats felt the despair of civil war and wrote *Meditations in Time of Civil War*. Here are the last lines from seven long stanzas.

> *I turn away and shut the door, and on the stair*
> *Wonder how many times I could have proved my worth*
> *In something that all others understand or share.*[44]

Extracts from poems have revealed aspirations for fairness and justice, or they have depicted struggles to overcome unfairness and injustice. Poems reflecting class, caste and ethnic divisions show efforts to resist the cruelty which comes from any preoccupation with militarism and violence. Yeats wrote against the English violence in Ireland. Louis MacNeice warned of the dangers of conformity in the run-up to the Second World War. Oodgeroo Nunucaal looked beyond discrimination against Australian Aboriginals. Pablo Neruda damned the brutalities which passed for governance under South American dictators. To keep hope alive, Mahmoud Darwish gave leadership and inspiration to millions of stateless Palestinians.

Poems can capture traditions of fairness which dictators, generals, terrorists, political and religious extremists have ignored. Poets' insights provide antidotes to cruelties, as in visions of policies and practices so that all citizens could live together amicably. To commemorate the 50th anniversary of the founding of the UN, Maya Angelou wrote *A Brave and Startling Truth*. She imagined how a more human world could be achieved if fingers were released 'from the fists of hostility', if 'children dress their dolls in flags of truce', and 'the aged can walk into evenings of peace'. Foreshadowing the renowned scientist Stephen Hawking's plea to reach for the stars, not look down at your feet, Angelou considered that a wonder of planet Earth was the potential of the world's people to realize the sacredness of human existence.[45]

> *We this people, on this miniscule and kithless globe*
> *Who reach daily for the bomb, the blade and dagger*
> *Yet who petition in the dark for tokens of peace …*
> *Out of our mouths come 'cankerous words',*
> *Yet out of those same mouths*
> *Come songs of such exquisite sweetness*
> *That the heart falters in its labor*
> *And the body is quieted into awe.*[46]

The Palestinian poet and playwright, Australian citizen Samah Sabawi, speaks of her besieged people in the Gaza Strip:

> *We will cultivate hope in the seeds we plant in place of uprooted trees,*
> *in the prose and the verses of our poetry,*
> *in homes we build from rubble after their demolition,*
> *in songs of love and passion,*
> *in strokes of oil on canvas and in prayers in mosques and churches …*
> *And there, within the suffocating spaces between their (Israeli) towers,*
> *walls and checkpoints, we will teach our children how to dance to the*
> *   rhythms of life.*[47]

Educational priorities

Evidence shows cruelty inherent in policies and in the motives of extremists whose violence provokes violent responses. A long overdue priority is to highlight values which would benefit refugees, oppose militarism and in economic policy terms would cast aside the wreckage of neoliberalism. Education about the human costs of abusive power can occur in family conversations, in recreational groups, in exchanges on the streets, in meetings in institutions, let alone in the usually invisible discussion between politicians and public servants who influence social and foreign policies.

Journalists can educate readers by frank appraisal of abusive individuals, governments and their policies. The cruelties promoted by an Australian Minister for Immigration have worldwide implications and were confronted in a *Saturday Paper* editorial.[48]

The editor identified the traits of a bully and the institutional arrangements by which public servants shuffled papers concerning applicants' claims to residency in Australia, but which kept tens of thousands in a state of fear and insecurity. The editorial concluded that the Minister

> is a man delusional about refugees, a man completely ill equipped for his office. ... He is so morally disfigured that his every utterance contains hypocrisy. His racism has tortured thousands of people ... [The Minister's] department continues to drag people from their homes. It continues to deport people into the hands of violence. He personally oversees the ruined lives of thousands of people, held in prisons as a warning to the rest of the world.

In *Making Peace*, Denise Levertov addressed those who seem unable to conceive non-destructive ways of exercising power. Her lines could characterize relationships between men and women, could produce awe in school classrooms and influence exchanges in boardrooms and political forums. She insists that 'a line of peace might appear' if we ceased preoccupations with profit and power, questioned needs and in this way 'restructured the sentence our lives are making'. She also warns that achieving peace would be 'an energy field more intense', and therefore more demanding, than making war.[49]

Restructuring 'the sentence our lives are making' could be enhanced by the ideal that no one should graduate from high school or university without knowing the goals of the UN Charter and the terms of all 30 clauses of the Universal Declaration of Human Rights. Such education can't be left to organizations such as Human Rights Watch, Amnesty International, Médecins Sans Frontières. The educational task addresses the lives of all citizens.

Human rights education has to cut through religious, political, tribal and economic interests and action would need to identify hypocrisy in politicians' claims about their principles. Hypocrisy was apparent in March 2018 when Australia took its seat on the UN Human Rights Council. The Australian government gave a pledge to respect all human rights findings, 'through implementation of (UN) recommendations and resolutions'. But in a reference to 1,800 asylum seekers contained on Manus Island and Nauru, the Director of the Melbourne-based Human Rights Law Centre replied, 'just saying over and over again that you respect human rights doesn't make it true. Not for the innocent human beings warehoused on Manus and Nauru for the last five years. Or the Aboriginal and Torres Strait Islander men, women and children being forced into prisons away from their families and communities at obscenely high rates. All of the people suffering injustice right now in our community need action, not just words.'[50]

Inspiration from artists, composers, musicians and poets can contribute to literacy about the philosophy and practice of non-violence. In her regret that uranium had ever been mined, that Trump, Putin and the leaders of other nuclear powers would therefore have never possessed weapons with which to swagger and threaten, Denise Levertov imagined,

> But left to lie its metaphysical weight
> might in a million years have proved
> benign, its true force being to be
> a clue to righteousness —
> showing forth
>
> the human power
> not to kill, to choose
> not to kill: to transcend
> the dull force of our weight and will;
>
> that known profound presence, untouched,
> The sign, providing witness,
> occasion,
> ritual
> for the continuing act of
> nonviolence, of passionate
> reverence, active love.[51]

A priority educational task is to oppose the political free-for-all which says that superior power is the only arbiter in human affairs. Courage to achieve that goal is evident when standing for altruism, not egoism, is apparent in support for freedom of speech by citizens in democracies and police states.

Philosopher Alasdair MacIntyre writes that any striving for a common good needs courage: 'Practitioners of a shared practice come to genuinely care about each other, and genuinely caring about others means a willingness to risk harm or danger on their behalf, and that is what courage is.'[52]

Refugees who seem completely dispossessed yet retain hope display impressive resilience. Their life-giving courage inspires others. In the Kakuma refugee camp in northern Kenya, built originally for 60,000 people, now home to 180,000, Lydia Gitau describes the character and spirit of a South Sudanese woman, Grace, 'who contracted HIV/AIDS after being raped by a soldier in South Sudan and being forced to marry him'. Grace has witnessed the slaughter of almost all her relatives and in this hot, dusty, rocky outpost she cares for 10 children. You might expect her to be depressed and suicidal, but Lydia reports, 'Amidst all she has gone through, Grace remains jovial, hopeful and good-humoured.'[53]

Courage can achieve small victories which fuel future striving against cruelties. In *Blessed Is the Man*, the eccentric, often mischievous American poet Marianne Moore wrote, 'Blessed the geniuses who know that egomania is not a duty.' She finished by encouraging the gutsy individual who had taken the risk of a decision, having asked himself or herself the question, 'Would it solve the problem? Is it right as I see it? Is it in the best interests of all?'[54]

In a philosophy of small victories, *About Political Action in Which Each Individual Acts from the Heart*, Levertov speaks of the limitless benefits from acting with and on others' behalf.

> ... *when we taste in small victories sometimes*
> *the small, ephemeral yet joyful*
> *harvest of our striving,*
> *great power flows from us,*
> *luminous, a promise. Yes! ... Then*
>
> *great energy flows from solitude,*
> *and great power from communion.*[55]

In this book's first chapter, reference was made to the silence which often greets news of atrocities. To break the silence by expressing outrage at inhumanities requires political curiosity, social awareness and literacy about the benefits of non-violence.

It is not difficult to recall denials of atrocities and of policies which have oppressive consequences. Numerous examples spring to mind: murders in the Katyn forest or at Srebrenica, the Iranian government's 1988 orgy of executions and, in December 2019, Iraqi forces killing over 1,000 people protesting against government corruption and oppression. Forty years after the end of the Vietnam war, horrendous deformities are suffered by tens of thousands of Vietnamese children as a result of their parents' exposure to the dioxin poisons from the 45 million litres of Agent Orange dropped by American forces in that war. Soil, river systems, lakes and rice paddies were also poisoned.[56]

Respect for a common humanity demands outrage so that the consequences of such atrocities are not erased from memory or from history. Nevertheless, as late as April 2018, silence or lukewarm reaction from democratic governments, the UN and the EU continued over the war-imposed famine on 20 million of the 25 million population of Yemen.

The non-reaction of a morally bankrupt West has been displayed in relation to Israel's murderous response to Gazans' protests, from March 2018 to December 2019, over their imprisonment in an almost uninhabitable strip of land. By January 2019, over 200 Gazans had been killed, some only onlookers, many shot in the back. Israel refused requests for an international inquiry. Despite self-promoting righteousness, governments said little and did nothing.

Countries' claim to be defending sovereignty is used to justify murder. In Israel's case a self-defence argument is compounded by the politically convenient, intellectually lazy, easily contrived charge of anti-Semitism against anyone who dares to criticize Israel's policies. Although anti-Semitism, in common with any other racist prejudice, should be outlawed, the almost automatic use of the anti-Semitism charge to stifle dissent must be exposed. Cowardice shown by deference to bullies amounts to collusion with cruelty. In response to the latest Gaza slaughter, one observer judged, 'In short the Palestinian people have been abandoned by a cowardly sycophantic international community.'[57]

In struggles to restore faith in a common humanity, in efforts to find the courage to recover from terrible loss and continued oppression, the fatalism that nothing can be done can be overcome by recalling those who have climbed mountains and remained hopeful. Philosopher Bertrand Russell recommended, 'Remember humanity and forget the rest.' Nelson Mandela advised, 'I learned that courage was not the absence of fear but the triumph over it.' In contemporary Russia, the lawyer-activist Alexei Navalny campaigns for some semblance of justice, even though arrested, often imprisoned and disbarred from being a candidate in Presidential elections.

Navalny follows in the footsteps of Russian poet and novelist Boris Pasternak, who found the stamina and courage to continue to write despite state controls and persecution. In 1958, when prevented from travelling to Oslo to receive the Nobel Prize in Literature, he wrote *Nobel Prize*, in which he expressed his hopes that even as he faced death, he still believed that cruelty, spite and the forces of darkness would in time 'Be crushed by the spirit of light'.[58]

7

Humanity on a bonfire

> *... We, rebellious progeny*
> *With great brainpower, little sense,*
> *Will destroy, defile*
> *Always more feverishly,*
> *Very soon we'll extend the desert*
> *Into Amazon forests,*
> *Into the living heart of our cities,*
> *Into our very hearts.*
>
> (Primo Levi)[1]

> Oppressors can justify their actions by effectively removing their victims from their understanding of 'human' and thereby avoiding the necessity of recognising their human rights. (Jim Ife)[2]

There comes a time when abhorrence over cruelty should be expressed spontaneously and passionately, separate from academic references, scholarly analytical theory, legal punctiliousness and political hypocrisy. There comes a time when an explicit verdict on the bestiality of state and non-state actors should be delivered in the court of common decency and universal human rights. That time is now.

Few states can escape the opprobrium of using cruelty as a form of governance. Motivated by religious dogma or political ideology, every non-state violent group has also dug deep into depravity. States and their opponents have fuelled one another: separate in opposition yet joined in derision of democracy and humanity, in refusing dialogue and applauding violence.

Two levels of officially sanctioned cruelty appear in states which sustain cruelty over long periods and in those whose apparent pleasure in such violence takes place in a time-limited period. In the first category, states which continue brutalities over time include Indonesia's oppression of West Papuans, Morocco's decades long containment of the people of Western Sahara, Israel's siege of Gaza, a Saudi Arabian penal system which subjugates women and promotes medieval-like punishments to anyone who challenges the state, the US fascination with weapons of all kinds, their specific states' retention of capital punishment and the inevitable botched executions, the Singhalese government of Sri Lanka's continued discrimination against Tamils, the subjugation of Tibetan people and culture by Chinese takeover, Hun Sen's authoritarianism in Cambodia and Australia's imprisonment of asylum seekers on remote islands.

The distinction between brutality which either seems endless or occurs within a time frame is blurred, though a possible time limit hints at an end to cruelties and hopes that non-violent times might materialize. Cruelty within a time frame would include military dictatorships in Brazil, Chile and Argentina, the repeated appearance of dictators in Africa – Idi Amin in Uganda, Mugabe over Zimbabwe, Habré in Chad, Sierra Leone brutalized by Charles Taylor from Liberia. Then come recent outrages, the Myanmar military government's murder, rape and expulsion of Rohingya people and Philippines dictator Duterte's summary executions of anyone suspected of being a drug addict, user or pusher.

Extremist non-state groups have the resources to operate for years and only some appear to have a short life. The 'here for ever' and the 'come and go' extremists include groups spawned from conflicts, the Christian Phalange in Lebanon, Boko Haram kidnappers in Nigeria, the ISIS murderers in Iraq and Syria, fundamentalist Islamic bombers in Indonesia, previous Hamas suicide bombers and the 'kill, steal and do what we like' Israeli settlers.

The usual victims

The victims are groups and individuals stigmatized as unworthy, as detestable, as deserving their treatment and even as not really human. A non-comprehensive list includes Palestinians in relation to Israeli government policies, Tamils persecuted by a Sri Lankan dictator, West Papuans defined as primitive, first by colonial powers, then by Indonesian forces, Coptic Christians blown up by Islamic fundamentalists in Egypt, Muslim Rohingya cleansed by a Buddhist military in Myanmar, Uighur people of Xinjiang controlled and imprisoned by the Chinese government, or Yemeni adults and children subject to Iranian interventions, then starved, bombed and destroyed by Saudi/ US forces and their allies.

There's a lesson to be learned from stigmatizing peoples as inferior. Groups experience exclusion and other forms of cruelty but such treatment motivates them to take up arms against their oppressors. The marginalization of Sunnis in post-2003 Iraq produced ISIS, the creation of a Caliphate and the malignancy of cruelties across Syria and Iraq. In policy and practice, in attitudes and relationships, beware the consequences of not being inclusive.

The victims from war-torn countries, Syria, Iraq, Afghanistan and Sudan, include refugees, their misery compounded by Arab states, by Poland, the Czech Republic, Slovakia and Hungary, which have closed their borders. Even countries which admit refugees, Australia, the UK and the US, like to demonstrate how strong they are by excluding or in other ways punishing those who arrived by the wrong form of transport – by boat to Australia – or who, in the case of Britain, could not produce the papers they were allegedly given when they arrived decades earlier. In the US, migrants accepted at one time are rounded up and threatened with deportation. Fear of the other, Islamophobia, anti-Semitism, Hindu or Buddhist racism travel hand in hand.

Where prejudice reigns, outcast peoples are demonized and punished. The vulnerable individuals include people flogged in Saudi Arabia, the gay men and young women caned in the Sharia-law province of Indonesia, gays beaten up in Chechnya and other parts of Russia, Nigerian school girls targeted by Boko Haram, journalists a focus of Taliban wrath in Afghanistan or of military-generated hate in Egypt. The demonization of Muslims in Hindu nationalist India threatens the lives of millions.

Different types of war

Cruelties practised in civil wars display a particular sadism, albeit linked to a possibility that one side might win, could display mercy and a capacity for reconciliation, or that all the parties would be so exhausted that they'd come to a bargaining table. In the Algerian independence and civil wars diverse Algerian independence groups, French forces and their settler supporters ran a revenge-without-end conflict which spawned motives to slaughter first to avoid being killed later. The Syrian civil war stages so many participants that it is difficult to establish who commits specific atrocities, let alone who commits the worst. In that war, the apparatus for lying and denying is as well organized as the purchase of bombs, missiles and poisonous gases.

Cruelty is also inevitable when one country invades another, the US in Vietnam and in Iraq, Israel in Lebanon and Gaza, Russia and its Iranian allies in Syria, Turkey in relation to the Kurds, the UK and others over Serbia and Libya. You would have to be blind not to see the cruelty and carnage in such invasions, not to anticipate the long-term destructive consequences. I would be irresponsible, naive or both not to realize how much corporations which trade in arms have been smacking their lips, rubbing their hands and counting their coffers at the mega profits to be made from other people's misery. Such warring, which looks like militaristic whoring, occurs on a precious environment subject to pollution, unexploded bombs, pulverized buildings, poisoned and disabled people, depleted and disappearing water resources. If the precious environment had a voice it would surely call out, 'life for you humans is so short and you depend on me, so please don't do this. Your lives in forests and river valleys, on the slopes of hills and mountains, in the depths of oceans and on nurturing shores are so short, so make the most of it. Listen to Noam Chomsky's advice, "If you want to end war or terrorism, stop participating in it."'

Another civil war occurs when states and their representatives decide who should benefit from social policies, which is code for saying what is normal and abnormal. These wars don't usually use military weapons, though if the populace kick up too much fuss, martial law can be declared, tanks roll in, gun-toting, baton-wielding police appear, in Ankara or Istanbul, in Moscow and Leningrad, in Beijing and Colombo, in Brixton UK, Ferguson US and in Hong Kong. Those forces arrive to restore order, to remind the protesters what is allowed, that compliance is normal and that status quo interests must be protected.

Although social and economic policy interventions are seldom so visible and are not immediately seen as unjustified, there should be no excuse for missing such wars. How mediocre have been the social scientists, the anthropologists, historians and journalists not to register these other actions as cruel, and not to be outraged by them. To breathe normality into a culture, the deviants had to be labelled, arrested, put away or even killed. Aboriginal children, orphan kids shipped from one country to another, unmarried mothers, asylum seekers, refugees, homeless people, alleged drug addicts, unregistered migrants, the unemployed, the powerless of class and caste needed to be controlled, washed into a new version of themselves or simply hidden away, so that normality could be paraded free of contamination.

That is a civil war of a different kind. An industry thrives on it. Normality is success. Abnormality is failure. State institutions, not just in one-party regimes, include police, immigration, homeland security, education, welfare, health and housing bureaucracies. They include private banks supported by public funds and the business-financed think-tanks which promote the trickle-down messages that citizens with few resources can be motivated to obtain jobs and homes even if there are none. Efficiency demands compliance. Imagination and discretion in state bureaucracies is seldom allowed. Power must be exercised in top-down fashion. Efficiency looks like violence but cloaked with claims about the best of intentions. In democracies, there's no reason to overlook the motives and outcomes of policies. If the social scientists and journalists had seen themselves as war correspondents, reporting on policy wars not the military ones, the social cruelty industry not the arms trade, there could be a comprehensive view of what is going on. It would be immoral not to recognize this but would require a different morality to do so.

Housing apparently poor, mixed-race London citizens in dangerous high-rise apartment blocks located in the midst of affluent neighbourhoods has fatal consequences, an inevitable outcome of cost-effective domestic policy. The French equivalent lies in slum-like ghettoes for largely Muslim poor, who feel of little consequence but survive not far from the cosmopolitan, tourist magnets of central Paris. American cruelty via social policy includes politicians' determination to oppose even the prospect of universal health insurance for millions of citizens. In an essay quoted earlier, Charles Pierce describes the cruelty inherent in the conduct of relationships in America, and a systematic cruelty in American politics. 'We practice cruelty and call it economy. We make war based on lies and deceit because cruelty is seen to be the immutable law of the modern world.' In India, Arundhati Roy shows how poor people have been humiliated, told the country needs atomic bombs or new dams, so the powerless lose homes, habitat and livelihood and are then encouraged to be grateful for their misfortune.

A policy language

Policies to promote domestic cruelties have been called rationalist, monetarist, neoliberal, laissez-faire and free. What's in a name? A blanket to conceal and confuse. Assumptions that any economist called rational or characterized as free must be trusted. The camouflage given by the labels is being stripped to reveal cruelty not only in foreign wars but also in the suppression and even the torture of citizens at home.

Free market economic policies have opposed public sector investment, stressed the need for everyone to become more economically efficient and have revered the magic of privatization. They have destroyed the safeguards against workplace exploitation and promoted increasing socioeconomic inequality, worldwide. Citizens are punished for their inefficiencies, for not seeing the benefits of privatizing hospitals, universities, banks, water, electricity and telecommunication companies. When the empirical evidence or inquiry report fails to support a chosen policy, it is kept secret, labelled 'commercial in confidence', or rewritten to justify the unjustifiable. By delegating policy recommendations to management consultant firms, even the policy process has been privatized, with absurd consequences. A US-based management consultant company, contracted to assess the cost-effectiveness of a large hospital, recommended that staffing in the hospital's social work department be halved because time was being wasted conversing with the families of cancer patients, even making tea for them. The initial report landed on my desk. I wrote a rejoinder for the hospital's Medical Director, mocked the management men and referred to the social workers' alleged inefficiency as an expression of humanity. The Medical Director ditched the consultants' report, at least regarding work on the oncology wards.

If cruel policies are to be presented as acceptable, camouflage and secrecy are imperative. In the US, Australia, the Middle East, the UK and other European countries, a hostile culture towards migrants thrives. Security companies are paid handsomely to capture, guard or imprison asylum seekers. In South America, the Middle East, the US and countries in South East Asia, the numbers of children in prison, who may never leave, are kept secret. State propaganda via servile media maintains images of mateship in Australia, respect for God in Iran and in the US and dramatizes Israel's humanity even as its military murders and its settlers steal. The US is still claimed to be the land of the free even as it tears up international treaties that might protect the planet and contribute to a common good. Iranian mullahs stay intent on respect for a God. One-man rule in communist China promotes a free market in which everyone is controlled, and punished for signs of disobedience.

A common denominator

Argument can be made that the cruelties documented in previous chapters are so many and so diverse that common patterns, let alone a common denominator, can't be found. A mixture of countries, contexts, contestants and commercial interests make this search too complex. Reference to complexity is usually an excuse for implying that nothing will change. I reject that view and do so by considering the details of horrendous events, which occurred mostly in the first few months of 2018: the genocide of Rohingya peoples by the Myanmar military, the slaughter of hundreds of Gazans by Israeli forces, the killing of mostly Christian worshippers by suicide bombers in Indonesia and, in the Syrian civil war, an estimated 13,000 deaths in detention, most prisoners executed in secret. At first sight it looks as though the cruelties were so different. They were not.

Like a slow drip, cruelty from social and economic policies erodes victims' lives, but cruelty from state and non-state terrorists explodes in a barbarity horrendous to watch, even from the comfort of an armchair. To escape rape, murder, throat cutting of whole families, bonfires to roast screaming children, 700,000 Rohingyas escaped to hastily erected refugee camps in Bangladesh. Films of dismembered bodies, burning villages and of Myanmar soldiers lining up victims to be shot are broadcast worldwide. Denials follow. Bare-faced lying occurs. Murders are only a counter-terrorist action. The once-worshipped Nobel Prize recipient, Myanmar leader Aung San Suu Kyi, manages blank-faced explanations. Nothing much happened. If a few atrocities were committed, it's not entirely our fault. Outside forces have a habit of undermining our image. Within Myanmar, local politicians are megaphoning, there's no such thing as the Rohingya, they don't exist.

How to manage the disappearance of conscience, incredulity at the lying and despair at the denials? At which point, collusion with the cruelty grows. China at the UN Security Council waters down a British-initiated resolution condemning the ethnic cleansing of the Rohingya.

While Rohingya people are clinging to life on muddy, treeless hillsides in Bangladesh, another barbarity is playing out on the Israel/ Gaza border. Let's not mince words. Cast aside the usual diplomatic, academic, political and journalistic care not to cause too much offence to the Israeli support lobbies. Against the rules of international law, against opposition from most UN members, the US Embassy in Israel is opened in Jerusalem. A Dallas pastor, Robert Jeffers, who once claimed that all religions other than Christianity, and presumably Judaism, lead to a separation from God, gives the opening prayer. A prominent American end-of-time preacher, John Hagel, gives the closing benediction. He had once preached that 'Hitler was sent by God to drive the Jews to their ancestral homeland'. The embassy opening is as grotesque as if Hermann Goering had been invited to open a synagogue. Israeli-American dignitaries' celebration of an illegality is accompanied by the maiming, kilometres away, of thousands of Gazans and the slaughter, confirmed in a UN March 2019 report, of 189, including 35 children, clearly identifiable paramedics, journalists and people with disabilities. Gazans killed, wounded, disabled for life, are easy, useful targets for snipers who are shown applauding their kills. By February 2020 UN estimates show as many as 250 fatalities and well over 20,000 badly injured. The Gaza border had become a fairground shooting range for sharpshooters who are said to be defending their country.

The hasbara propaganda technique to dramatize virtues went into overdrive. US Ambassador to the UN Nikki Haley said the Israelis showed admirable restraint. At the UN's one-minute silence to respect the slaughtered Gazans, Haley exited the chamber. Orwell's *Nineteen Eighty-Four* was meant to be a satire. No room for satire now. After 12 years of siege, the bloodshed of Gazans is restraint. Slaughter is self-defence. An Australian Foreign Minister appears on television to say that it's all Hamas' fault.

In several visits to the West Bank and Gaza, well-educated groups of young people have argued that the March of Return protests should be based on non-violent resistance. They have helped to organize supplies of water, tents, toilets, plus ambulances to transport casualties, even to Gazan hospitals starved of surgical and medical supplies. Of course, the government of Hamas contributed but it suits the Israeli message and the Western media's repeat of that message that all these protesters are terrorists under Hamas orders, and snipers kill only in order to defend themselves. In the months of protest, no one saw a Hamas flag. Who cares? Stereotypes must be maintained. As a triumph for all-conquering nationalism, the US President's daughter congratulates the Israeli Prime Minister for orchestrating the latest dances of death.

Simultaneous with the Gaza slaughter, in the Indonesian city of Surabaya, parents with their children have become suicide bombers. Twenty-eight people were killed and 57 injured in the bombings of Christian churches. An Islamic State group, Jamaah Ansharut Daulah, claims the achievement. How to comprehend why parents would sacrifice their children? A first temptation is to answer that only brainwashed extreme Islamists would progress from sacrificing men, then women and now children. To separate these horrendous acts from other cruelties is to pretend there's a continuum from the most grotesque to the slightly less grotesque to the least offensive acts, from the most to the least cruel, from cruelties in which state parties cooperate to abuses by individuals who appear to operate alone, their goals influenced by some religious hallucination or by a maniacal nationalism, love for country, hatred for those whose beliefs are not the same.

Before and after these specific events, the Syrian government of Bashar al-Assad had been killing on an industrial scale. Amnesty International described the Sednaya prison outside Damascus as a 'human slaughterhouse'. In late July 2018, families of the disappeared learned that their loved ones had been tortured to death or hanged without trial, but official death certificates – only 400 were issued – claimed that detainees died from heart attacks or strokes. Bodies were not being returned and grieving families were not told where they might find them.

In the search for explanations of atrocities, including the intolerance of one religion towards another, there is a connection between Gaza and Israel, Myanmar and the Rohingyas, between the Trump, Bashar al-Assad, Putin, African dictators' derision of democracies and their ridicule of human rights. From Singapore to London, from Washington to Canberra, anti-terrorist experts are wheeled out to say that 'radicalization' is the cause of the latest mayhem. They see obvious but worrying new trends in the use of children, but in trying to fathom the cruelties it's not part of their repertoire to join the dots between individual incidents and a wider political, economic and cultural backdrop. If international human rights obligations are of no consequence, if bullying has become governance anywhere, if militarism encourages assumptions that fear through superior force can be taken for granted, if dialogue is a forgotten art and if enthusiasm for violence stifles literacy about non-violence, cruelty flourishes. There's no difference between Israeli snipers, Myanmar bonfire burners, the child suicide bombers of Surabaya and executions in Syrian prisons.

Critics might say there's nothing so horrendous as the Myanmar military throwing babies and toddlers into a bonfire, a word that has referred to ancient Celts burning bones and heretics. Anyone despised, whom the powerful and orthodox wanted to eliminate, should be burned alive. As though they were desperate to follow historical precedents, and numerous analogies come to mind, the snipers on the Gaza border, the Surabaya suicide bombers, the Myanmar soldiers and Syrian torturers were all heaping humanity onto bonfires.

There could be a ritual burning of claims about some cruelties not being worth discussing and others as slightly less offensive than the next. There are common denominators. In state and non-state contexts, all leaders need to practise the language of humanity and mean 'never again'. Never cruelty as part of military and defence contract interests, cruelty never seen in foreign, social or economic policies. Humanity would benefit from admissions that cruelty is present in the motives of policy makers, in the hate-filled attitudes of religious and political extremists and in the cowardly indifference of media commentators. If cruelty is acknowledged to be significant in a range of values and policies, crucial to the operation of bureaucracies and in the conduct of international relations, there's a responsibility to ensure that such conduct is exposed, challenged and eliminated. Valuing, protecting and cherishing each other is a crucial first action which anyone can take in the development of alternatives to throwing humanity on a bonfire.

8

Language for humanity

It is early summer, 2019, a steamy evening in the public gallery of the Shoalhaven Council building in the New South Wales town of Huskisson. Elected councillors are discussing applications for commercial developments and requests for houseowners to cut down trees that hinder views. They also deliberate a motion to disqualify a community newspaper from receiving Council revenue because councillors have been offended by their critics in the newspaper.

The chair of the meeting is the town Mayor, who represents the Greens party. She conducts the meeting with dignity and professionalism but is the target of repeated abuse from half a dozen councillors, mostly male, who ridicule her rulings.

This example of democracy at work may seem only local and the implications parochial, but the chemistry of that meeting has lessons that apply internationally. Councillors' opposition to a woman and to her mostly female-elected supporters displayed intolerance, abuse, an unwillingness to listen, let alone take notice of others' views. Appearing convinced of their wisdom, the abusers drew from an apparent expectation that no one should challenge their boorish, bullying, misogynistic, self-important behaviour.

They argued that commercial developments be allowed even against the interests of local Indigenous people on whose land the new developments were to occur. They were enthusiastic about the right to remove trees and they passed the motion that, in effect, the newspaper editor should be punished for daring to allow criticism of councillors. In that debate, the councillor who moved the motion made false claims as though any concern with the truth was irrelevant.

Arrogance, bullying, a lack of commitment to democratic principles and not the slightest touch of humility captured that meeting. Even in local government in a country which is not a police state, authoritarianism flourished. The same conduct has appeared in other liberal democracies, hence a need for language which expresses liberating, non-destructive visions of the future.

A language for humanity includes questions of identity, ideals of humane governance and determination not to be cruel to future generations. The crescendo comes with a redefinition of human rights and with passion for crafting a different politics. Poets will have the last words.

Redefining humanity

If digital technology requires constant use to feel confident in a language, alternative forms of empowerment also require practice. If cruel practices are to be combatted, humanitarian perspectives merit regular rehearsal. Protecting planet Earth rests on citizens being curious, reflective, showing concern for others and being prepared for conversations about justice, which includes a conception of humanity inseparable from the health of planet Earth. In an internet age there appears to be little time for such exchanges. Instead, time is consumed with responses to likes, shares and demands, so that major issues of justice, equality and survival of the planet can be put aside.

Embracing humanity includes reaffirmation of the values of love, friendship, solidarity, trust and humour. However serious the current authoritarian trends, never underestimate the value of laughing at them. Satire about the absurdities of any form of extremism can be a cue for dialogue. Follow Australian kookaburras' early morning greetings, their apparent laughing at adversity and excitement at the prospect of the next meal. Together with their mates, these proud, defiant birds display disdain for absurdities and signal that when their and our laughter subsides, we must prepare for the next steps.

One way to redefine humanity and to show how to respond to *challenges, opportunities and responsibilities*, the subtitle of this book, is to repeat a story told by the brave and principled computer engineer turned whistle blower, Edward Snowden. Attempting to escape the attention of the world's media and arrest by US authorities, he was given refuge by four people who had nothing and were surviving in one of the poorest neighbourhoods in Hong Kong. A refugee from the Philippines and three from Sri Lanka sheltered him at considerable risk to themselves. In his gratitude to these selfless people, Snowden gives an abiding interpretation of humanity. He writes, 'These unfailingly kind and generous people came through with charitable grace. The solidarity they showed me was not political. It was human, and I will be forever in their debt. They didn't care who I was or what dangers they might face by helping me, only that there was a person in need.'[1]

Humane regard for others includes determination to avoid cruelty to future generations. That objective challenges the free market neoliberal project, requires creative stewardship of the planet, plus policies to promote equalities and to end militarism as the means of security.

Politicians have been curtailing freedoms in the interests of 'security', allegedly to make nation-states more efficient and to combat terrorist threats. These developments, coupled to a burning planet, display immediate crises. Recognizing the crises should prompt remedial action, as in the impressive October 2019, global Extinction Rebellion protests aimed at forcing governments to immediately adopt policies to curb the effects of climate change.

In *The Origins of Totalitarianism*, Hannah Arendt argued that the crises of fascism in the 20th century were predictable and, with greater public awareness of the dangers, could have been prevented.[2] Today, similar dangers affect public consciousness and political priorities. An easy-to-sloganize populist dogma is widespread, democracy and science are derided. Turkish novelist Ece Temelkuran asks her readers 'to spot the recurring patterns of populism, so that maybe they can be better prepared for it than we were in Turkey'.[3]

Warnings of dangerous threats to well-being, as in the first verse of Yeats' *The Second Coming*, may be familiar but merit repeating. In the aftermath of the First World War and at the beginning of the Irish War of Independence, he wrote.

> *Turning and turning in the widening gyre*
> *The falcon cannot hear the falconer;*
> *Things fall apart; the centre cannot hold;*
> *Mere anarchy is loosed upon the world,*
> *The blood-dimmed tide is loosed, and everywhere*
> *The ceremony of innocence is drowned;*
> *The best lack all conviction, while the worst*
> *Are full of passionate intensity.*[4]

In *Clear Bright Future*, Paul Mason warns that reacting to contemporary dangers also requires awareness of the world we live in, which, he says, 'means understanding how the elites, fascists and bureaucrats are undergoing a cumulative radicalization towards racism, xenophobia and the curtailment of democratic rights'.[5]

Shoshana Zuboff describes authoritarianism as the China syndrome, symbolizing surveillance and subjugation, characterized by intelligence services using the internet to identify, survey, monitor and track the location of all Chinese citizens.[6] Such societies are controlled by fear and the only certainty is that no one should be trusted. In an all-controlled society, debunking, satirizing, refusal and irreverence is a crime and trust an absurd notion. One million imprisoned Uighurs and brutalized minorities in Tibet know this system. Hundreds of thousands of protesting Hong Kong citizens fear that their freedoms are threatened.

In a multifaceted analysis of supposed threats to freedoms from China's military and economic expansion, Joe Camilleri has focused on the growing authoritarianism within China. He also emphasizes the peace-making responsibilities of other nations, the US, the UK, Japan, South Korea and Australia, whose policies depend on military alliances and security strategies through the deployment of tens of thousands of troops on foreign bases. Camilleri concludes, 'If we are to create a more peaceful and secure environment, we can in concert with others fashion policies for the demilitarization of our region, including reduced military budgets, zones of peace and nuclear weapons free zones and gradual removal of foreign military bases.'[7]

Questions of identity

Individuals' experience of insignificance, expendability, political isolation and loneliness contributed to 20th-century fascism. In the 21st century, violence towards the vulnerable, and demands for supposed strong men to take control, have become the conditioned responses to people's anger at not being heard, or not being taken seriously.

Frustrations and violence follow people's feelings that until their social and political identity is recognized, they will never experience justice. In Palestinians' long experience of powerlessness, acting strategically about identity requires steps towards small victories as a route to more ambitious outcomes. Income, shelter and food remain daily concerns. Longer-term planning brings questions about allegiance, to the Palestinian Authority, to Hamas, to community or family interests.

Palestinian poet Mahmoud Darwish hoped that his people could achieve an identity that did not celebrate aggression, avoided undue pride and would outlaw judgementalism.

We will become a people if we want to, when we learn that we are not angels, and that evil is not the prerogative of others.

...

We will become a people when a writer can look up at the stars without saying: 'Our country is loftier and more beautiful!'

We will become a people when the morality police protect the prostitute from being beaten up on the streets.

...

We will become a people when we respect the right, and the wrong.[8]

Palestinians' March of Return, which began in early 2018, expressed defiance against the siege of Gaza, though the fatalities and injuries to protesters were barely covered by mainstream media in the West. Such media could have been a voice for those seldom heard, a voice for communities on the West Bank, in Gaza, in refugee camps and might have reached the representatives of hostile Israeli, Egyptian or US forces.

Young Gazans appear to be following Mahmoud Darwish's hopes. They are trying to be optimistic that something is happening, stalemate has been avoided. Their ideas about transitional justice emphasize the benefits of equality for women in relation to men, Palestinians in relation to Israelis, refugees in relation to conservative, commercial interests.

Gazans have considered examples of ways to achieve justice. Oppress or resist is one story. Divide and conquer another. In thinking strategically about their futures, young Palestinians are asking, 'Do we want to imitate Nelson Mandela's vision for a unified South Africa, or the pragmatic arrangement for a partitioned India, Pakistan, Kashmir?' 'Would we support a coherent, united Europe or a go-it-alone, nationalist Brexit Britain?'

Humane governance

Avoiding cruelty to future generations could be taken for granted if humane governance prevailed and guaranteed commitments to respect human rights. Richard Falk describes the apocalyptic dimensions of nuclear weaponry and climate change as priorities for humane governance, and he castigates the inflexibility of policy priorities which ensure that private sector entrepreneurship remains central to business and finance. By contrast, humane governance would be dedicated to the security of people by improving ways to protect global and human interests.[9]

Reconsideration of what it means to live in a democracy is central to the ideals of humane governance. Rejuvenated democracy requires transparency in governance, an end to secrecy and corruption, accountability of politicians and public servants and enhanced respect for the rule of law. In foreign policy, humane governance emphasizes the benefits of multilateralism and of imaginative, respectful dialogue between nations. Faith in democracy also needs trust in alliances. If trust is absent, says Zuboff, shared values and mutual obligations slip away, 'confusion, uncertainty and distrust enable abusive power to fill the social void'.[10]

Instead of undue reverence for the integrity of nation-states, humane governance would champion the principle of the Responsibility to Protect, as endorsed by all member states of the UN at a World Summit in 2005. This refers to an obligation rooted in international law, especially regarding sovereignty, peace and security. Although treated by the UN Security Council as a measure of last resort, it challenges the assumption that outside intervention in domestic affairs is not permissible, that within their borders, nation-states can do what they like. The Responsibility to Protect values the responsibility to protect all populations from mass atrocity and human rights violations.

On questions of security, instead of a preoccupation with enemies considered terrorists, a humane interpretation of security would include fights against poverty and hunger, against environmental destruction and political oppression. These goals also reflect judgements about the destruction caused by capitalism.

Advocacy of humane governance rests on indictments of the worst effects of capitalism: worldwide inequity, the invisible powers of corporations and appropriation of resources, impoverishment, huge incidence of mental illness and vast numbers of people feeling worthless. Individual and corporate selfishness and greed influence these outcomes. Governments with business-as-usual attitudes ensure the continued use of fossil fuels, refuse to respond to the devastation caused by greenhouse gas emissions and enable a burning planet to continue to burn.

Criticism of states for fostering cruelties does not mean replacing state governance with private enterprise projects. Wise economic management should link drastic tax reform to environmental responsibility, associate international dialogue for peace with vibrant local democracies and ensure that states craft polices for a common good.

Humane governance can also be fostered by support for the UN's peace-building responsibilities. The creation of the UN included a view of sovereignty so much more cosmopolitan than noise about nationalism, so much more altruistic than the policy priorities of wealthy nation-states.

When lauding internationalization, it is not imperative to go as far back as John Donne's *No Man Is an Island*. Others have embraced the same vision. In the early 19th century, Indian philosopher and poet Rabindranath Tagore advocated 'One identity of the universe, a proud harmony of all races'.

After the 1989 Velvet Revolution in Czechoslovakia the poet, playwright, political leader Václav Havel called for the UN to become 'the platform of joint solidarity-based decision making by the whole of human kind as to how best to organize our stay on this planet'.

In 2000, political leaders at a Millennium Summit finalized their view of the role of the UN in the 21st century: 'We recognize that in addition to our separate responsibilities to our individual societies, we have a collective responsibility to uphold principles of human dignity, equality and equity at the global level.'

The glib assumption that the UN is impotent and achieves little is confounded by any appraisal of UN peace-keeping missions, staffed largely by personnel from developing countries, Ethiopia, Pakistan, India, Bangladesh and Rwanda. There have been 71 peace-keeping operations since 1948, and as of November 2019, 14 missions are spread across four continents. A helmeted blue line of UN peace keepers protects vulnerable people from others' violence. It is also important to recall that in 1988, UN peace keepers received the Nobel Peace Prize for risking their lives in working for 'the ultimate human aspiration' – peace.

In 2010, with a view to highlighting the significance of non-violence in building peace with justice, a UN task group crafted the terms of a UN Emergency Peace Service (UNEPS) with an emphasis on service, not force. UNEPS was designed to protect civilians at extreme risk and to ensure prompt starts to peace-keeping operations, as in organizing safe havens, buffer zones and humanitarian corridors.[11]

Meeting human needs and respecting human rights depends on a certain street wisdom about the context in which a member of UNEPS might be operating. Standing between Palestinian children and heavily armed, swaggering Israeli soldiers in the West Bank town of Hebron is one such context. Looking for shelter in East Timorese capital Dili following the carnage by Indonesian forces, and standing firm when threatened by Zanu PF thugs in Zimbabwean capital Harare are others. Advocacy for refugees seeking residency in Australia from a powerful but mostly invisible Department of Home Affairs is little different. The principle is the same. Human rights are identified with supporting evidence. Protection of the vulnerable is linked to visions of humane governance.

Redefining human rights

In observations about humanitarian alternatives to cruelties, faith in human rights and in international law may be assumed, as though the mere recitation of those words would stem the tide of cruelties. That faith in legalities has been unrewarding. Ethics in politics has been treated as irrelevant, requests for respect for human rights fall on deaf ears and appeals to a general public to respect human rights create false optimism.

In August 2019, the High Court of Australia endorsed the dismissal of an employee of a government department for anonymously criticizing the work of her employer, as in the staff member's critical observations about immigration policies and the detention of immigrants. The employee assumed that her anonymous criticism of government abuses would be protected by law. Brave Michaela Banerji had tweeted as Lalegale but lost her job. The High Court approved her sacking, in effect riding roughshod over her freedom of political communication. Instead of law acting like a conscientious guard dog over a chicken run, the High Court decided that the powerful should not be criticized. Better to put a fox in charge.[12]

What is legal is connected to political interest, but can be disconnected from community realities, hence an argument that the law/human rights connection is often too simple. There are socially relevant ways to explain and practise human rights. An everyday context gives meaning, connection and urgency, in the home, on the streets, in the workplace, in places of religious worship, in trade unions and NGOs, in every level of politics. Human rights can be nurtured by dignity, by empathy, kindness and reciprocity and by visions of what is socially just. Such practices don't have to be dramatic, but they could be.

In threatening times and in dangerous places, appeals to legalities would be abstract and could be pointless. In mid-1984, on a Colombo street, not long after the vicious Sri Lankan civil war had begun, angry Singhalese youths pursued a Tamil friend of mine. Instead of immediately decrying their anger and disputing their motives, I tried to communicate over issues which were not concerned with discrimination, cruelties and killing. The confrontation became a dignified exchange, expressed that we were equals, achieved a chemistry in which human rights came to be respected without any reference to legalities. The context, the respect and rapport said almost everything that needed to be said. Such a rewarding outcome does not always occur but can be tried. Paradoxically, by ignoring reference to legalities, the principles of humanitarian law could be expressed and sustained.

Redefining politics

Politics concerns power plays to influence the interests of one individual or group over another, so no one escapes political cultures, in families, workplaces or social movements. But the exercise of power by supposedly successful politicians can tell more about cowardice than courage. It can be cowardly to maintain official interests, to be secretive, ensure impunity and ignore the consequences of inequalities. Such cowardice can be coated by the veneer that says this is how democracy works.

The victimization of Julian Assange because he dared to reveal truths about murders and mayhem in US wars, illustrates a cancerous cowardice, a might-is-right doctrine peppered with lies that WikiLeaks cables put lives at risk.[13] In the controversy over US efforts to have this journalist, whistle blower, publisher extradited to face a possible 175 years in prison, US politicians demanded that Assange be taken out by a drone, shot or killed by other means. UK politicians claimed that British justice was beyond question. Australian leaders said nothing. Mainstream journalists ingratiated themselves, apparently because they thought this could curry favour with politicians and enhance their careers. As a means of hanging on to power, cowardice became infectious. Courage remains the penicillin-like quality to nourish a different politics.

Managerialism to promote alleged efficient activities irrespective of human costs also stifles a more transparent and humane politics.[14] Such practices infect relationships and policies, in private and public institutions, even in places of scholarship and scientific inquiry. Universities' one-time collegiality has been replaced by management conformities, trust replaced by suspicion, enthusiasm for education replaced by business ideology, by cost-cutting and related profit motives.

Around the world, previously elected staff and student representatives on university governing bodies have been replaced by corporate operatives who know about business and can focus on profit as the yardstick to measure performance.[15] Debunking managerialism can influence a wider politics.

To give vitality to places of learning there needs to be satire, a refusal to play hierarchical games and energy for intellectual promiscuity, as in questioning discipline boundaries and crossing them. On many campuses, 'discipline' refers to control of difficult students and disobedient staff, even though the best university traditions have no room for such discipline. Managerialism is alien to supportive workplace cultures.

Non-compliance with management absurdities may not always work but should be tried. Otherwise authoritarian leaders, their hosts on US Fox News and on other Murdoch media outlets will attempt to persuade the public that a culture of conformity depends on removing dissidents.

Machiavelli taught that tyrannical individuals could not tolerate ridicule. In *Macbeth* and *Coriolanus*, Shakespeare showed that laughing to scorn could reduce the high and mighty to a morsel of their former selves. Falstaff in *Henry IV Part I* is the great debunker of commanders who resent criticism. In response to his master Prince Hal's repetition of the belief that there is honour in fighting and dying for a country, Falstaff says that the only people who have honour are dead and it does them no good. Honour, he says, is worthless and he'll have none of it.[16]

To expose cruelty, to challenge arrogance and deception, every country needs numerous Falstaffs.

Redefining politics involves questions about the undue reverence for national sovereignty. In an economically and ecologically globalized world, the nation-state is increasingly dysfunctional and the source of so much cruelty. Discriminatory policies, solidified by walls, fences and well-policed borders, encourage a siege mentality, aggressive nationalism and associated racism. There is a need to look beyond the binary of the border and the nation-state, a need not just to cross boundaries but to question their very validity.

Epidemics such as Ebola and the coronavirus do not respect borders. Global warming threatens human existence, melts Greenland's glaciers, fuels forest fires in California, Siberia, the Amazon, across Australia and ensures the arrival of more environmental refugees, yet selfish interests dispute the value of internationalism.

At a Pacific Islands meeting in August 2019, the Australian Prime Minister appeared not to acknowledge the dangers of global warming, in particular with reference to Australia's coal industry. He was perceived as ignoring Islanders' fear of their homes being swamped by rising seas. In response, Prime Minister Enele Sopoaga of Tuvalu said, 'I'm concerned about protecting my people, … and likewise the leaders of other South Pacific small island countries, but you only want to protect your economy.'[17]

As global warming advances, so too the tidal waves of human rights abuses, somehow justified by politicians who insist they are beyond politics. Trump, Johnson, Putin, Orban, Erdogan, Netanyahu, the Saudi and other Middle East dictators, the Iranian theocrats, demagogue Bolsonaro in Brazil, far-right parties in Germany and France, in Austria and Italy behave as though there is no alternative.

Collusion with authoritarians occurs in the mainstream press and in presentations on commercial television's breakfast chat shows. Ridicule, derision, debunking of science and democracy are repeated. In Australia, Britain and the US, the Murdoch media has encouraged intolerance of others as a way of showing leaders' demonstration of their power.

A life-promoting alternative to authoritarian populism derives from language to promote a secular ideology which combines humanitarianism, non-violence and enthusiasm for meaningful human rights. Attaining these goals depends on a global conversation, an internationally shared scepticism about the nation-state plus advocacy for a more open, more trusted, more democratic politics. Citizens who may feel there is nothing they can do, could meet such challenges through a commitment to social justice and through context-based interpretations of human rights.

In personal relationships, language to describe being humane can be joyous. In policy deliberations, the language to advocate humanitarianism can be shared. Each of these objectives requires certain values and the courage to act. There needs to be a positive response to Swedish teenager Greta Thunberg's 24 September 2019 'How dare you' address to a UN forum, pleading with her audience not to continue to collude with the destruction of life on Earth.

Thunberg's challenge was echoed by UN Secretary General Antonio Guterres at the Madrid December 2019 Climate Change conference when he warned, 'If we don't change our way of life we jeopardize life itself.'

Language to envisage a different politics addresses cowardice and courage, cruelty and compassion, collegiality rather than hierarchy. Authoritarianism and sacrosanct assumptions about the nation-state can be addressed by promoting internationalization, through citizens' views, in NGO alliances, in social movements, in dialogue with supposed enemies and in governments' policies. The visionary historian Howard Zinn wondered how US foreign policies would look if national boundaries were wiped out, at least in people's minds, and if all children were considered our own. If that happened, he argued, the atomic bomb would not have been dropped on Hiroshima, no napalm would have been used over Vietnam, wars would not be waged anywhere because wars are always against children, our children.[18]

Faced with the prospect of worldwide violence, poets have warned about impending disasters and have challenged a public to wake up. It's instructive to return to them, beginning with Alfred Lichtenstein, who asked readers in *Prophecy* to think about the likely slaughter in the First World War.

> *Sometimes there comes – I have a premonition –*
> *A deathstorm out of the distant North.*
> *Everywhere the stink of corpses*
> *The great murder begins.*[19]

Prior to the outbreak of the Second World War, in his poem *September 1, 1939*, W.H. Auden warned of the choices confronting a world rushing to destruction, but he also expressed the best way to respond.

> *There is no such thing as the State*
> *And no one exists alone;*
> *Hunger allows no choice*
> *To the citizen or the police;*
> *We must love one another or die.*[20]

From a poem, *Ninety Plus Campaigner*, the last word comes from a resident of a retirement home in Gerringong, New South Wales. Ninety-two-year-old Ken O'Hara wrote letters every week to newspapers to support human rights, to question cruelty to vulnerable people and to oppose destruction of a precious environment. Here is the last-verse tribute to such a campaigner, and to millions like him.

> *He is the advocate with the deaf aid who hears,*
> *the resident with the spectacles who sees,*
> *the navigator with humanity's compass*
> *who asks other citizens*
> *to heed the noise from the unfair shore*
> *by organizing, speaking, writing*
> *about the benefits of justice,*
> *'more, more, more!'.*[21]

References

Introduction

1. Mandelshtam, Osip (1991) *Selected Poems*. London: Penguin Books.
2. Fischer, Louis (1997) *The Life of Mahatma Gandhi*. London: Harper Collins.
3. MacNeice, Louis (1988) 'Prayer Before Birth', in *Selected Poems*. London: Faber & Faber. pp 93–4.
4. Darwish, Mahmoud, 'We Travel Like Other People', in Forché, Carolyn (ed) (1993) *Against Forgetting: Twentieth Century Poetry of Witness*. New York: W.W. Norton. p 562.
5. Housman, A.E. (1979) 'The Laws of God, the Laws of Man', in *The Collected Poems of A.E. Housman*. London: Jonathan Cape. p 79.
6. Caputi, Ross, Hil, Richard and Mulhearn, Donna (2019) *The Sacking of Fallujah: A People's History*. Amherst and Boston: University of Massachusetts Press.
7. Milgram, Stanley (1974) *Obedience to Authority*. London: Tavistock.
8. Montaigne, Michel de (1910) 'On Cruelty', in *The Essays of Michel de Montaigne*. New York: Edwin C. Hill.

Chapter 1

1. Tolstoy, Leo (1951) *The Kingdom of God is Within You*. Boston: L.C. Page & Company. Book X.
2. Paz, Octavio (1988) 'Remembrance', in *Octavio Paz Collected Poems 1957–87*. Manchester: Carcanet Press. p 555.
3. Watt, Holly, Taylor, Diane and Rice-Oxley, Mark (2018) 'Drowned, restrained, shot: how these migrants died for a better life', *Guardian Case Studies*, 20 June. p 4.
4. Ondawame, Otto (2010) *One People One Soul: West Papuan Nationalism and the Organisasi Papua Merdeka*. Adelaide: Crawford House Publishing.
5. Loveday, Morris (2018) 'Turkey says it has more evidence to share in Khashoggi's killing', *Washington Post*. 6 November.
6. McKenzie-Murray, Martin (2017) 'Driven to death on Manus Island', *The Saturday Paper*. 12 August. p 3.
7. Gettleman, Jeffrey (2017) 'Rohingya Recount Atrocities: "They threw my baby into a fire"', *New York Times*. 11 October.
8. US Holocaust Museum (2018) *The Armenian Genocide (1915–1916) in Depth*. 30 June.

9. Kifner, John (2017) *Armenian Genocide of 1915: An Overview*. The New York Times Archived Pages.
10. Akhmatova, Anna, 'Requiem', in Coffin, Lyn (1983) *Anna Akhmatova Poems*. New York: W.W. Norton. p 82.
11. Pembroke, Michael (2018) *Korea: Where the American Century Began*. Melbourne: Hardie Grant Books. p 171.
12. Pembroke, Michael (2018) *Korea: Where the American Century Began*. Melbourne: Hardie Grant Books. p 172.
13. Gilbert, Martin (1986) *The Holocaust: A History of the Jews of Europe during the Second World War*. New York: Holt, Rinehart and Winston. Hilberg, Raul, *The Destruction of the European Jews*. New York: Yale University Press.
14. Auden, W.H., 'Epitaph on a Tyrant', in Forché, Carolyn (ed) (1993) *Against Forgetting: Twentieth Century Poetry of Witness*. New York: W.W. Norton. pp 166–7.
15. Tharoor, Shashi (2017) *Inglorious Empire: What the British Did to India*. London: C. Hurst & Co.
16. Mukerjee, Madhusree (2010) *Churchill's Secret War*. New York: Basic Books.
17. Dikötter, Frank (2004) *Mao's Great Famine: The Story of China's Most Devastating Catastrophe*. London: Bloomsbury.
18. Anderson, David (2005) *Histories of the Hanged: Britain's Dirty War in Kenya*. London: Weidenfeld & Nicolson. Elkins, Caroline (2016) *Britain's Gulag: The Brutal End of Empire in Kenya*. London: Jonathan Cape.
19. McGreal, Chris (2006) 'Shameful legacy', *Guardian*. 13 October.
20. Adam, A.W. (2015) 'How Indonesia's 1965–66 anti-communist purge remade a nation and the world', *The Conversation*. 1 October.
21. Robinson, Geoffrey (2018) *The Killing Season*. Princeton, NJ: Princeton University Press.
22. Heuveline, P. (1998) '"Between one and three million": towards the demographic reconstruction of a decade of Cambodian history 1970–79', in *Population Studies*. London: Taylor & Francis. pp 49–65. Etcheson, Craig (2005) *After The Killing Fields: Lessons from the Cambodian Genocide*. Westport, CT: Greenwood Publishing Group.
23. Van Klinken, Gerry (2012) *Death by Deprivation in East Timor 1975–1980*. World Peace Foundation. 17 April. *ABC report 2006*. 'At least 102,000 killed in East Timor under Indonesian Rule', 19 January.
24. *The Economist* (2012) 'Iran, 1988, What Happened?', 21 June.

25. Robertson, Geoffrey (2011) *Report of an Inquiry: The Massacre of Political Prisoners in Iran, 1988*. London: The Abdorrahman Boroumand Foundation. pp 116–17.

26. Fenton, James, 'Tiananmen', in Forbes, Peter (ed) (1999) *Scanning the Century: The Penguin Book of the Twentieth Century in Poetry*. Bury St Edmunds: Viking. p 357.

27. BBC News (2011) 'Rwanda: how the genocide happened'. 17 May. Epstein, Helen (2017) 'America's secret role in the Rwandan genocide', *Guardian*. 12 September.

28. Engelberg, S. and Weiner, T. (1995) 'Massacre in Bosnia: Srebrenica, the days of slaughter', *New York Times*. 29 October.

29. Specia, Megan (2019) 'Sudan protesters met with tear gas on march to the Presidential Palace', *New York Times*. 17 January. Tchie, Andrew (2019) 'No easy end to stand-off between al-Bashir and Sudan's protesters', *The Conversation*. 1 March.

30. Rees, Stuart (2014) 'Thanks to Stéphane', in *A Will To Live*. Port Adelaide: Gininderra Press. p 199.

31. Hessel, Stéphane (2010) *Time for Outrage*. New York: Twelve, Hachette Book Group.

32. Kershner, Isabel (2018) 'Video shows Israeli forces shooting a Palestinian, then rejoicing', *New York Times*. 9 April. Al-Tarabeesh, Hamza Abu (2018) 'I came today to tell the Israeli sniper we are not afraid of him', *Mondoweiss*. 6 April.

33. Oren, Amir (2016) 'The truth about the Israel defence forces, "The World's Most Moral Army"', *Haaretz*. 3 April.

Chapter 2

1. Personal communication from Professor Chomsky, and see: Adams, Tim (2003) 'Question time', *Observer Books*. 30 November. https://www.theguardian.com/books/2003/nov/30/highereducation.internationaleducationnews.

2. Ray, Mohit K. (2004) *Studies on Rabindranath Tagore*. New Delhi: Atlantic Publishers. p 427.

3. Saviano, Roberto (2018) 'Italy's war on migrants makes me fear for my country's future', *Guardian Journal*. 19 June. pp 1–2. Perraudin, Frances (2018) 'Roma communities fear deportation in post-Brexit Britain', *Guardian*. 2 July. p 11.

4. Australian Human Rights and Equal Opportunity Commission (1997) *Bringing Them Home: The 'Stolen Children' Report*.

5. Reynolds, Henry (1990) *With the White People*. Ringwood, Victoria: Penguin. p 169.

6. van Krieken, Robert (1901) *Children and the State: Social Control and the Formation of Australian Child Welfare.* Sydney: Allen & Unwin. p 108.

7. Johnson, Eva (1988) 'Letter to My Mother', in Gilbert, Kevin (ed) (1989) *Inside Black Australia.* Ringwood, Victoria: Penguin. p 24.

8. *Royal Commission into Aboriginal Deaths in Custody.* Canberra: (1987–1991).

9. Bowcott, Owen (2010) 'Britain's child migrants lost their childhood to years of hard labour', *Guardian.* 25 February.

10. Chenery, Susan (2011) 'I can still hear the kids scream', *Sydney Morning Herald.* 12 June.

11. *National Apology for Forced Adoptions* (2013) Parliament House: Canberra. 21 March.

12. Howe, David, Sawbridge, Phillida and Hinings, Diana (1992) *Half a Million Women: Mothers Who Lose Their Children by Adoption.* London: Post Adoption Centre.

13. Roberts, Yvonne (2013) 'Forced adoption: the mothers fighting to find their lost children', *Guardian.* 27 October. Sherwood, Harriet (2018) 'MPs demand apology for unmarried mothers who gave up children', *Observer.* 10 June.

14. Refugee Council of Australia (2016) 'The true cost of Australia's refugee policies'. 26 September.

15. Rees, Stuart (2017) 'A symphony of life: rescuing refugees by recovering humanity', *New Matilda.* 8 July.

16. Polakow-Suransky, Sasha (2017) *Go Back to Where You Came From: The Backlash Against Immigration and the Fate of Western Democracy.* New York: Nation Books.

17. Timm, Trevor (2017) 'Ice agents are growing threat to civil rights', *Guardian Weekly.* 9 June. p 20.

18. Baca, Jimmy 'Immigrants in Our Own Land', in Forché, Carolyn (ed) (1993) *Against Forgetting: Twentieth Century Poetry of Witness.* New York: W.W. Norton. p 672.

19. Romo, R. (2012) 'Mexicans feeling persecuted flee US', *CNN Report.* 27 November.

20. *The Economist* (2019) 'Fewer rivers to cross: Mexico becomes a destination for migrants'. 27 July.

21. Nieves, Evelyn (2014) 'Laws targeting homelessness have increased dramatically across the country', *AlterNet.* 19 July.

22. Khlebnikov, Victor 'Suppose I Make a Timepiece of Humanity', in Forché, Carolyn (ed) (1993) *Against Forgetting: Twentieth Century Poetry of Witness.* New York: W.W. Norton. p 98.

23. McGreal, Chris (2006) 'Shameful legacy', *Guardian*. 13 October. Selva, Meera (2011) 'UK tortured in Kenya in 1950s', *News24 Archives*. 7 April.
24. McGreal, Chris (2006) 'Shameful legacy', *Guardian*. 13 October.
25. Dowden, Richard (2005) 'State of shame', *Guardian*. 5 February.
26. McVeigh, Karen (2017) 'Closure of Yemen's borders is "catastrophic", UN warns', *Guardian*. 8 November.
27. UNICEF (2017) Report: *Falling Through the Cracks: The Children of Yemen*. March.
28. Brull, Michael (2017) 'The war in Yemen is turning to genocide, and Australia is quietly supporting it', *New Matilda*. 19 March.
29. Naiman, Robert (2017) 'Congress, Amartya Sen and the Saudi-imposed famine in Yemen', *Huffington Post*. 26 June.
30. Schell, Jonathan (2017) 'Cruel America', *The Nation*. 28 September.
31. Rees, Stuart (2011) 'Vengeance is never sweet', *New Matilda*. 5 May.
32. Darwish, Mahmoud, 'Psalm 2', in Forché, Carolyn (ed) (1993) *Against Forgetting: Twentieth Century Poetry of Witness*. New York: W.W. Norton. p 564.
33. Sabawi, Abdul (2014) 'Home of Passion', in *Blood for Freedom*. Oiratzen: Basque Country, August.
34. Rees, Stuart (2015) 'We want the chance to prove we are human beings: inside a Beirut refugee camp', *New Matilda*. 2 October.
35. Karkar, Sonja (2012) 'The massacre at Sabra and Shatila, thirty years later', *Counterpunch*. 14 September.
36. Khalidi, Rashid (2017) 'The United States was responsible for the 1982 massacre of Palestinians in Beirut', *The Nation*. 16 September.
37. Booth, William and Balousha, Hazem (2015) 'Amnesty International: Hamas guilty of torture, summary executions', *Washington Post*. 27 May.
38. Millett, Kate (1995) *The Politics of Cruelty*. London: Penguin Books. p 110.
39. Fisk, Robert (2013) 'It took decades for truth to be revealed in Algeria. How long will it take Syria?', *Independent*. 20 October.
40. Hernández, Miguel, 'Waltz Poem of Those in Love and Inseparable Forever', in Forché, Carolyn (ed) (1993) *Against Forgetting: Twentieth Century Poetry of Witness*. New York: W.W. Norton. p 168.
41. Adonis (Ali Ahmad Sa'id), 'Elegy for the Time at Hand', in Forché, Carolyn (ed) (1993) *Against Forgetting: Twentieth Century Poetry of Witness*. New York: W.W. Norton. p 554.
42. Cockburn, Patrick, 'The war in five sieges', *London Review of Books*. Vol 40. No 14. 19 July.

43. Rahim, Najim and Nordland, Rod (2018) 'A family of 14 dies in an airstrike. U.S. officials deny they were civilians', *New York Times International*. 21 July.

44. Brecht, Bertolt, 'When evil-doing comes like falling rain', in Willett, J. and Manheim, R. (eds) (2000) *Bertolt Brecht: Poems 1913–1956*. London: Methuen.

45. MacKinnon, Mark (2016) 'The graffiti kids who sparked the Syrian war', *Globe and Mail*. 2 December.

46. Parry, Robert (2017) 'An apology and explanation', *Consortium News*. 31 December.

47. Brecht, Bertolt, 'To Those Born Later', in Willett, J. and Manheim, R. (eds) (2000) *Bertolt Brecht: Poems 1913–1956*. London: Methuen. p 318.

48. Beech, Hannah (2017) 'Across Myanmar, denial of ethnic cleansing and loathing of Rohingya', *New York Times*. 24 October.

49. Gettleman, Jeffrey (2017) 'Rohingya recount atrocities: "They threw my baby into a fire"', *New York Times*. 11 October.

50. Nichols, Michelle (2017) 'UN blacklists Saudi-led coalition for killing children in Yemen', *Reuters*. 5 October.

51. Al Jazeera English News Saudi Arabia (2017) 'Saudi rejects UN blacklisting over Yemen child deaths'. 7 October.

52. Potter, Mitch (2017) 'How an embedded photographer exposed torture at the hands of Iraqi "heroes"', *Toronto Star*. 25 May.

53. Reuters (2017) 'Iraq collectively punishing Islamic state families: rights group', 13 July.

54. Justice Michael Kirby and Commissioner Sonja Biserko of Serbia (2013) *UN Inquiry into Human Rights in the Democratic People's Republic of Korea (DPRK) North Korea*. 21 March.

55. Kirby, Michael (2017) 'Otto Warmbier's death underlines plight of thousands of North Koreans', in National Opinion, *Sydney Morning Herald*. 21 June.

56. Dassin, Joan (ed) (1986) *Torture in Brazil: A Report by the Archdiocese of Sao Paulo*. New York: Vintage. pp 28–32.

57. Skidmore, Thomas (2004) *Modern Latin America*. Oxford: Oxford University Press.

58. Dao, James (2002) 'US Releases 1980's files on repression in Argentina', *New York Times*. 21 August.

59. Timerman, Jacobo (1988) *Prisoner Without a Name, Cell Without a Number*. New York: Alfred Knopf. pp 37–41.

60. Malik, Nesrine (2018) 'Trump creates his caliphate and democracy has no defence', *Guardian*. 18 June. p 3.

61. Jones, Owen (2017) 'Chechen and anti-gay brutality will not win', *Guardian Weekly*. 21 April. p 21.

62. Varagur, Krithika (2017) 'The public flogging of two gay men and what it says about Indonesia's future', *Guardian*. 27 May.

63. England, C. (2016) 'Woman caned in Indonesia for "standing too close to her boyfriend"', *Independent*. 18 October.

64. *UCLA Law* (2016) 'Human rights in Iran: a conversation with Iranian human rights lawyer Mehrangiz Kar'. 10 March.

65. McTighe, Kristen (2012) 'Years of torture in Iran comes to light', *New York Times*. 21 November.

66. *Amnesty International News* (2017) 'Iran: shameful execution of man arrested at 15'. 10 August.

67. News-Iran News (2016) 'UN Human Rights condemns floggings in Iran'. 31 May.

68. Vasefi, Saba (2018) 'Asylum', in *Refuge*. Issue 93. https://www.wasafiri.org.

69. Haidar, Ensaf (2017) 'The first 50 lashes: a Saudi activist's wife endures her husband's brutal sentence', *Guardian*. 17 May. Brown, Andrew (2017) 'Ten years in jail and 1,000 lashes: why we must defend Saudi blogger Raif Badawi', *Guardian*. 18 June.

70. Sherwood, Harriet (2018) 'Asia Bibi and the violence of Pakistan's blasphemy laws', *Guardian Weekly*. 9 November. p 19.

71. Hesse, Josiah (2016) 'Apocalyptic upbringing: how I recovered from my terrifying evangelical childhood', *Guardian*. 5 April. McElwee, Sean (2013) 'Five things Christian fundamentalists just don't get', *Huffington Post*. 8 June.

72. Soyinka, Wole, 'Forest of Hate', in Forché, Carolyn (ed) (1993) *Against Forgetting: Twentieth Century Poetry of Witness*. New York: W.W. Norton. p 732.

73. Rees, Stuart and Dhizzala, James (2012) 'Why Kony is not the main game', *New Matilda*. 15 March.

74. Charlton, C. (2016) 'Kony's cannibals: commander "ordered his men to cook and eat captured civilians and use rape to train child fighters in Uganda"', *Mail Online*. 21 January.

75. Piotrowski, Daniel (2014) 'What ever happened to African warlord Joseph Kony?', *News.com.au*. 12 June.

Chapter 3

1. Wordsworth, William, 'Humanity', in (1994) *Collected Poems 1942–85*. Pymble: Angus and Robertson. pp 315–18.

2. Wright, Judith (1990) 'Two Dreamtimes', in *Collected Poems*. Sydney: Harper Collins. p 317. Available at http://ro.uou.edu.au/kuaapipi/vol26/iss2/12.

3. Benn, Tony (2005) *Dare to be a Daniel*. London: Arrow Books. Ch 6.

4. Arendt, Hannah (1963) *Eichmann in Jerusalem*. New York: Viking Press.

5. Szymborska, Wislawa (1990) 'Children of Our Age', in (2015) *Map: Collected and Last Poems*. New York: Houghton Mifflin.

6. Hersh, Seymour (2018) *Reporter: A Memoir*. New York: Knopf.

7. Éluard, Paul, 'Dawn Dissolves the Monsters', in Forché, Carolyn (ed) (1993) *Against Forgetting: Twentieth Century Poetry of Witness*. New York: W.W. Norton. p 203.

8. Phillips, Amber (2017) '10 things to know about Sen. Jeff Sessions, Donald Trump's pick for attorney general', *Washington Post*. 10 January.

9. Luckerson, Victor (2015) 'New report documents 4,000 lynchings in the Jim Crow South', *Time Magazine*. 10 February.

10. Bouie, Jamelle (2015) *Christian Soldiers*. Slates.com. 10 February.

11. Button, James (2018) 'Angels or arrogant gods', *The Monthly*. February p 29.

12. Manne, Robert (2016) 'How we came to be so cruel to asylum seekers', *The Conversation*. 26 October.

13. Manne, Robert (2018) 'How Australia came to be so inhumane', *Sun Herald*. 4 March. pp 28–9. Edited extract from Manne, Robert (2018) *On Borrowed Time*. Sydney: Black Inc.

14. Sarmiento, Bong S. (2017) 'Why Filipinos support Duterte's drug war', *Asian Times*. 23 August.

15. Ellis-Petersen, Hannah (2018) 'ICC launches crimes against humanity inquiry into Duterte's war on drugs', *Guardian*. 9 February.

16. Holmes, Oliver (2017) 'Human rights group slams Philippines President Duterte's threat to kill them', *Guardian*. 17 August.

17. Ellis-Petersen, Hannah (2018) 'ICC launches crimes against humanity inquiry into Duterte's war on drugs', *Guardian*. 9 February.

18. Vlazna, Vacy (2016) '"Banality of evil": Zionist and Nazi moral disengagement', *Palestine Chronicle*. 11 February. Vlanza, Vacy (2017) 'How do they sleep at night?', *Counterpunch*. 26 September.

19. Blumenthal, Max (2013) *Goliath: Life and Loathing in Greater Israel*. New York: Nation Books. p 13.

20. Blumenthal, Max (2013) 'Chapter 50, The Prophets', in *Goliath: Life and Loathing in Greater Israel*. New York: Nation Books. pp 265–8.

21. Havel, Václav (1978) *The Power of the Powerless*. London: St Martin's Press.

22. Younge, Gary (2018) 'Hounding Commonwealth citizens is no accident. It's cruelty by design', *Guardian*. 13 April.

23. Malik, Nesrine (2018) 'I felt a nausea of fury – how I faced the cruelty of Britain's immigration system', *Guardian*. 5 March.

24. Malik, Nesrine (2018) 'I felt a nausea of fury – how I faced the cruelty of Britain's immigration system', *Guardian*. 5 March.

25. MacNeice, Louis, 'Prayer Before Birth', in Longley, Michael (ed) (1990) *Louis MacNeice Selected Poems*. London: Faber & Faber. p 93.

26. Bochenek, Michael (2016) *Children behind Bars: The Global Overuse of Detention of Children*. Human Rights Watch.

27. Beckett, Lois and Dart, Ian (2018) 'Americans share blame for dividing families at the border says Democrat', *The World*. 18 June. p 26.

28. Bochenek, Michael (2016) 'Detention and incarceration in response to crime', in *Children Behind Bars: The Global Overuse of Detention of Children*. Human Rights Watch. p 3.

29. Cook, Catherine, Hanieh, Adam and Kay, Adah (2004) *Stolen Youth: The Politics of Israel's Detention of Palestinian Children*. London: Pluto Press.

30. Ofir, Jonathan (2017) '"We should exact a price" from Ahed Tamimi "in the dark," Israeli journalist says', *Mondoweiss*. 23 December.

31. Levy, Gideon (2017) 'And if Ahed Tamimi were your daughter?', *Haaretz*. 31 December.

32. Nelson, F. (2016) 'High Court ruling a blow to lawyers fighting offshore detention', *Lawyers Weekly*. 5 February.

33. Roethke, Theodore, 'Dolor', in Forbes, Peter (ed) (1999) *Scanning the Century: The Penguin Book of the Twentieth Century in Poetry*. London: Viking. p 268.

34. Barns, Greg and Newhouse, George (2015) 'Border Force Act: detention secrecy just got worse', *The Drum*. 28 May.

35. Goffman, Erving (1961) *Asylums: Essays on the Social Situation of Mental Patients and Other Inmates*. New York: Anchor Books.

36. Bennett, Caroline (2017) 'Violent politics and the disintegration of democracy in Cambodia', *The Conversation*. 11 September.

37. Keenan, Brian (1992) *An Evil Cradling*. London: Vintage. p 131.

38. Younge, Gary (2018) 'Why are nearly all mass killers male?', *Guardian Weekly*. 4 May. p 18.
39. Robertson, Geoffrey (2011) *Report of an Inquiry: The Massacre of Political Prisoners in Iran, 1988*. London: The Abdorrahman Boroumand Foundation.
40. *First Post* (2016) 'South Sudan civil war: death toll rising but nobody is counting'. 11 March.
41. Gitau, Lydia (2018) *Trauma-Sensitivity and Peacebuilding*. Berlin: Springer International Publishing.
42. Doran, Stuart (2015) 'New documents claim to prove Mugabe ordered Gukurahundi killings', *Guardian*. 19 May.
43. Cameron, Hazel (2017) 'British policy towards Zimbabwe during Matabeleland massacre', *The Conversation*. 17 September.
44. *Al Jazeera* (2016) 'Hissene Habre: trial of a dictator', 3 November.
45. Searcey, Dionne (2016) 'Hissène Habré, ex-president of Chad is convicted of war crimes', *New York Times*. 30 May.
46. Zotova, Anastasiya (2017) 'How to hide evidence of torture inside Russia's prison system', *Open Democracy*. 17 October.
47. Jannuzi, Frank (2013) '6 of President Vladimir Putin's most oppressive laws', *Huffington Post*. 9 September.
48. Walker, Shaun (2016) 'The murder that killed free media in Russia', *Guardian*. 5 October.
49. Harding, Luke (2009) 'Who shot Natalia Estemirova?', *Guardian*. 23 July.
50. Harding, Luke (2016) 'Alexander Litvinenko: the man who solved his own murder', *Guardian*. 19 January. Harding, Luke (2016) *A Very Expensive Poison*. London: Guardian Faber.
51. Nechepurenko, Ivan (2017) '5 Convicted in killing of Boris Nemtsov Russian opposition leader', *New York Times*. 29 June.
52. Russian-untouchables.com (2009) *Stop the Untouchables. Justice for Sergei Magnitsky*. 26 June.
53. Kramer, Andrew (2017) 'Turning tables in Magnitsky case, Russia accuses a nemesis of murder', *New York Times*. 22 October.
54. Browder, Bill (2016) *Red Notice: How I Became Putin's No. 1 Enemy*. London: Corgi Books.
55. Higgins, Andrew (2018) 'As authoritarianism spreads, Uzbekistan goes the other way', *New York Times*. 1 April.
56. Human Rights Watch (2018) 'You can't see them but they're always there – censorship or freedom in the media in Uzbekistan'. 28 March.
57. Cook, Jonathan (2017) 'Israel's ever more sadistic reprisals help shore up a sense of victimhood', *The National*. 11 July.

58. B'Tselem (2017) Israeli Information Centre for Human Rights in the Occupied Territories: *House Demolitions as Punishment.* 29 June.

59. Levy, Gideon (2017) 'Only Israelis, not Palestinians, Are Entitled to Mourn Their Dead', *Haaretz.* 24 June.

60. Middle East Monitor (2017) '6 Gaza cancer patients die after Israel denies them treatment'. 28 September.

61. Otterman, Michael (2007) *American Torture: From the Cold War to Abu Ghraib and Beyond.* Melbourne: Melbourne University Press.

62. Lewis, Anthony (2008) 'Official American sadism', *New York Review of Books.* 25 September.

63. Pierce, Charles (2014) 'The United States of Cruelty', *Esquire.* 25 June.

64. Krugman, Paul (2017) 'Health care in a time of sabotage', *New York Times.* 21 July.

65. Krugman, Paul (2017) 'Understanding Republican cruelty', *New York Times.* 30 June.

66. Krugman, Paul (2018) 'The G.O.P.'s war on the poor', *New York Times International Edition.* 18 July. p 8.

67. Stiglitz, Joseph (2013) *The Price of Inequality.* London: Penguin Books. p 258.

68. Krugman, Paul (2011) 'Oligarchy American style', *New York Times.* 4 November.

69. Machiavelli, Niccolò (1992) *The Prince.* New York: Dover Publications. In Chapter 17, 'Better to be feared than loved'.

70. Hobbes, Thomas (1951) *Leviathan.* Oxford: Blackwell. p 47.

71. Fromm, Erich (1994) *Escape from Freedom.* New York: Henry Holt & Company. p 156.

72. Neruda, Pablo, 'The Dictators', in Forché, Carolyn (ed) (1993) *Against Forgetting: Twentieth Century Poetry of Witness.* New York: W.W. Norton. p 574.

73. Human Rights Watch (1991) *Whatever Happened to the Iraqi Kurds?* New York. 11 March. Human Rights Watch (1993) *Genocide in Iraq: The Anfal Campaign against the Kurds.* New York. July.

74. Mizrahi, A. (2017) 'War crimes and open wounds: the physician who took on Israeli segregation', *+972 Magazine.* 12 September.

75. Levertov, Denise (2001) 'In Thai Binh (Peace) Province', in *Poems 1972–1982.* New York: New Directions. p 22.

76. Hersh, Seymour (2015) 'The scene of the crime: a reporter's journey to Mai Lai and the secrets of the past', *The New Yorker.* 23 March.

77. Levertov, Denise (2001) 'Weeping Woman', *Poems 1972–1982.* New York: New Directions. pp 17–18.

78. Mashal, Mujib and Sukhanyar, Jawad (2018) 'It's a massacre: blast in Kabul deepens toll of a long war', *New York Times*. 27 January.

79. Newman, Jonathan (2016) 'Why Colombia voted "no" to peace with FARC', *The Conversation*. 4 October.

80. Boesten, Jan (2017) 'Farc's steps towards peace in Colombia must not be met with another political genocide', *The Conversation*. 29 August.

81. Guillermoprieto, Alma (2018) 'After five decades of civil war, Colombia's healing begins', *National Geographic*. January.

82. Charles, Mathew (2018) 'Farc deal opens for Colombia's other rebels: "the future has to be about war"', *Guardian*. 7 January.

83. Havana Agencies (2015) 'Mediators urge de-escalation of conflict between Colombia and Farc rebels', *Guardian*. 7 July.

Chapter 4

1. Owen, Wilfred, 'Anthem for Doomed Youth', in (2018) *The War Poems of Wilfred Owen*. Melbourne: Penguin. And in Forché, Carolyn (ed) (1993) *Against Forgetting: Twentieth Century Poetry of Witness*. New York: W.W. Norton. pp 82–3.

2. Russell, Bertrand. It is uncertain whether this observation is attributable to the philosopher and disarmament campaigner, although it has long been used by pacifists and peace activists.

3. Annan, Kofi (2000) *The Age of Human Rights*. Project Syndicate. 26 September.

4. Brecht, Bertolt, first two verses from 'On Violence', in Willett, J. and Manheim, R. (eds) (2000) *Bertolt Brecht: Poems 1913–1956*. London: Methuen. p 276.

5. Millett, Kate (1995) *The Politics of Cruelty*. London: Penguin Books. pp 294–5.

6. Agerholm, Harriet (2017) 'Outcry as Saudi Arabia executes 6 people in one day to bring 2017 death penalty total to 44', *Independent*. 11 July.

7. Bachelard, Michael (2015) 'Chan and Sukumaran execution "illegal" but Indonesia ignores Australia again', *Sydney Morning Herald*. 2 May.

8. Lurie, Stephen (2015) 'The death penalty is cruel, but so is life without parole', *New Republic*. 16 June.

9. Lurie, Stephen (2015) 'The death penalty is cruel, but so is life without parole', *New Republic*. 16 June.

10. Bachelard, Michael (2015) 'Chan and Sukumaran execution "illegal" but Indonesia ignores Australia again', *Sydney Morning Herald*. 2 May.

11. Dehghan, Saeed (2016) 'Iran executes at least 10 Sunni prisoners despite unfair trial claims', *Guardian*. 3 August.

12. Browder, Bill (2015) *Red Notice: How I Became Putin's No.1 Enemy*. London: Corgi. pp 454–5.

13. Boochani, Behrouz (2017) 'Diary of a disaster: the last days inside Manus Island Detention Centre', *Guardian*. 30 October.

14. Karáth, Kata (2016) 'Hungary's Prime Minister says refugees should be rounded up and shipped out', *Quartz Magazine*. 23 September.

15. Wintour, Patrick (2017) 'Hungary submits plans to EU to detain all asylum seekers', *Guardian*. 7 February.

16. Culik, Jan (2015) 'Beyond Hungary, how the Czech Republic and Slovakia are responding to refugees', *The Conversation*. 7 September.

17. Malik, Kenan (2018) 'How we all colluded in Fortress Europe', *Observer*. 10 June. pp 49–51.

18. Freeman, Hadley (2018) 'Trump's child cruelty shocks but shouldn't surprise', *Guardian Opinion*. 20 June. p 4.

19. Reuters (2017) 'Record numbers of Palestinian homes destroyed by Israel in 2016 – rights group'. 17 February.

20. Human Rights Watch (2010) *Israel: Halt demolitions of Bedouin homes in Negev*. 1 August.

21. Rees, Stuart (2015) 'Will violence against Bedouins shift opinion on Israel?', *New Matilda*. 16 September.

22. PBS News Hour (2016) 'Saudi court sentences man to 10 years, 2,000 lashes for atheist tweets'. 27 February. https://www.pbs.org/newshour/rundown/saudi-court-sentences-man-to-10-years-2000-lashes-for-atheist-tweets.

23. Dangerfield, Katie (2017) 'North Korean prisons: UN reports torture, starvation and execution', *Global News*. 9 August.

24. Pembroke, Michael (2017) 'North Korea: there is only one acceptable endgame', *Sydney Morning Herald*. 5 July. Pembroke, Michael (2018) *Korea: Where the American Century Began*. Melbourne: Hardie Grant Books.

25. Pembroke, Michael (2018) *Korea: Where the American Century Began*. Melbourne: Hardie Grant Books. pp 193–4.

26. Walker, Kath (1970) first two verses from 'The Protectors', in *My People*. Milton, Queensland: The Jacaranda Press. p 28.

27. Barbash, Fred (2014) 'Decades-old mass graves of children of unwed mothers confirmed in Ireland', *Washington Post*. 4 March.

28. Hilliard, Mark (2017) 'Tuam reminds of unmarried mothers being "judged and rejected"', *Irish Times*. 8 March. And in Grierson, Jamie (2017) 'Mass graves of babies and children found at Tuam care home in Ireland', *Guardian*. 4 March.

29. McDonald, Henry (2013) 'Ireland finally admits state collusion in Magdalene Laundry system', *Guardian*. 6 February.
30. Singer, Peter (2009) *Animal Liberation: A New Ethics for Our Treatment of Animals*. London: Harper Collins.
31. Singer, Peter (2003) 'Some are more equal', *Guardian*. 19 May.
32. Siebert, Charles (2010) 'The animal cruelty syndrome', *New York Times Magazine*. 11 June.
33. Winter, Stuart (2016) 'The cruel, the bad and the sickening ... Britain's pet crime shame', *Daily Express*. 23 March; RSPCA, Facts and Figures, 2016.
34. Jensen, Derrick (2016) *The Myth of Human Supremacy*. New York: Seven Stories Press.
35. Thekaekara, Mari Marcel (2010) 'India's caste system is alive and kicking – and maiming and killing', *India Opinion, Guardian*. 16 August.
36. Gidla, Sujatha (2017) *Ants among Elephants*. New York: Farrar, Strauss and Giroux. p 4.
37. Dhillon, Amrit (2016) 'How India's caste system pushed a Dalit man to choose death', *Globe and Mail*. 1 February.
38. James, Clive (2008) first and last verses from 'Statement from the Secretary of Defense', in *Opal Sunset, Selected Poems, 1958–2008*. London: Picador. p 142.
39. Smith, Charles (1917) *Palestine and the Arab–Israeli Conflict 103*. (Final text) 31 October.
40. Regan, Bernard (2017) *The Balfour Declaration, Empire, the Mandate and Resistance in Palestine*. London: Verso. p 64.
41. Rees, Stuart (2017) 'The Balfour Declaration is another colonial distortion of history', *New Matilda*. 19 October.
42. Macintyre, Donald (2017) 'Could Priti Patel's secret meetings in Israel signal a shift in British foreign policy?', *Independent*. 7 November.
43. Beaumont, Peter (2017) 'What did Israel hope to gain from Priti Patel's secret meetings?', *Guardian*. 8 November. Woods, Ngaire (2017) 'Free market economics on trial – governments must pass a guilty verdict', *Guardian*. 16 October.
44. Woods, Ngaire (2017) 'Free market economics on trial – governments must pass a guilty verdict', *Guardian*. 8 November.
45. Greenfield, Patrick and Marsh, Sarah (2018) 'Hundreds of homeless people fined and imprisoned', *Guardian Weekly*. 25 May. p 16.
46. Sanders, Bernie (2011) 'Dear Mr President: the transcript of Bernie's 90 minute speech on the budget'. 28 June. https://www.sanders.senate.gov/newsroom/press-releases/dear-mr-president-the-transcript-of-bernies-90-minute-speech-on-the-budget.

47. Mann, Thomas and Ornstein, Norman (2017) 'How Republicans broke Congress', *New York Times*. 3 December.

48. Lusher, Adam and Rhodes, Anna (2017) 'Poverty, hunger and suicidal despair: whistle-blower exposes chaos at the heart of government's universal credit system', *Independent*. 13 October.

49. Butler, Patrick (2017) 'Welfare reform is not only cruel but chaotic, Theresa May must address this', *Guardian*. 2 May.

50. Lusher, Adam and Rhodes, Anna (2017) 'Poverty, hunger and suicidal despair', *Independent*. 13 October.

51. Wismayer, Henry (2017) 'Grenfell was no ordinary accident', *City Lab*. 17 August.

52. Hanley, Lynsey (2017) 'Look at Grenfell Tower and see the terrible price of Britain's inequality', *Guardian*. 16 June.

53. Ramdani, Nabila (2012) 'Fifty years after Algeria's independence, France still in denial', *Guardian*. 5 July. See also Evans, Martin (2012) *Algeria: France's Undeclared War*. New York: Oxford University Press.

54. Kevin, Tony (2004) *A Certain Maritime Incident: The Sinking of SIEV X*. Melbourne: Scribe.

55. *Sydney Morning Herald* (2003) 'SIEVX: Another Howard lie, another official cover-up'. 22 May.

56. Brull, Michael (2017) 'The cover-up of Australian arms sales to Saudi Arabia', *New Matilda*. 1 December.

57. Brull, Michael (2017) 'Revolting humanitarian fraud on Yemen: the cases of Julie Bishop and Lisa Singh', *New Matilda*. 25 November.

58. Rees, Stuart (2004) first two verses from 'Tell Me the Truth About War', in *Tell Me the Truth About War*. Canberra: Ginninderra Press. p 151.

59. Skidmore, Thomas (1988) *The Politics of Military Rule in Brazil 1964–85*. London: Oxford University Press.

60. Watts, Jonathan (2014) 'Brazil president weeps as she unveils report on military dictatorship abuses', *Guardian*. 11 December.

61. Dinges, John (2004) *The Condor Years: How Pinochet and His Allies brought Terrorism to Three Continents*. New York: The New Press.

62. Cameron, Hazel (2017) 'British policy towards Zimbabwe during Matabeleland massacre: licence to kill', *The Conversation*. 17 September.

63. Cameron, Hazel (2017) 'British policy towards Zimbabwe during Matabeleland massacre: licence to kill', *The Conversation*. 17 September.

64. *Al Jazeera* (2016) 'Hissene Habre trial of a dictator', 3 November.

65. *Al Jazeera* (2016) 'Hissene Habre trial of a dictator', 3 November.
66. Cobain, Ian, Bowcott, Owen, Crerar, Pippa and Shaheen, Kareem (2018) 'Britain apologises to Libyan dissident', *Guardian Weekly*. 18 May. p 16.
67. Hutton, Will (2018) 'In the Belhaj case, Britain set aside the rule of law and moral principles', *Guardian*. 13 May. p 21.
68. Cobain, Ian (2018) 'Analysis', *Guardian*. 29 June.
69. Cobain, Ian and MacAskill, Ewen (2018) 'Revealed: true scale of the UK role in torture and rendition after 9/11', *Guardian*. 29 June.
70. Murdoch, Lindsay and Koziol, Michael (2016) 'Australia's Cambodia refugee resettlement plan "a failure"', *Sydney Morning Herald*. 3 April.
71. Cochrane, Liam (2017) 'Australia remains committed to refugee resettlement in Cambodia despite "concern for democracy"', *ABC News*. 5 December.
72. Mohdin, Aamna (2015) 'The UK made a list of repressive regimes, then invited some of them to buy weapons', *Quartz Magazine*. 15 September.
73. Doward, Jamie (2017) 'British arms sales to repressive regimes soar to 5 billion pounds since election', *Observer*. 10 September.
74. Reuters (2017) 'Saudi Arabia agrees to $7 billion in precision munitions from US firms', *Fortune Magazine*. 23 November.
75. Mirovalev, Mansur (2016) 'Syria's war: a showroom for Russian arms sales', *Al Jazeera English*. 6 April.
76. Reuters (2016) 'US, Israel sign $38 billion military aid package', *Fortune Magazine*. 13 September.
77. Halper, Jeff (2015) *War Against the People*. London: Pluto Press.
78. Beit-Hallahmi, Benjamin (1987) *The Israel Connection*. New York: Pantheon. p xii.
79. Rees, Stuart (2015) 'Will violence against Bedouins shift opinion on Israel?', *New Matilda*. 15 September.
80. Ashrawi, Hanan (2017) 'Trump is making a huge mistake on Jerusalem', *New York Times*. 7 December.
81. Gonn, A. (2011) 'Israeli arms industry a major economic engine', in *Xinhuanet*. 2 June.
82. Halper, Jeff (2015) *War Against the People*. London: Pluto Press.
83. Beit-Hallahmi, Benjamin (1987) *The Israel Connection*. New York: Pantheon Books. pp 243–8.
84. Sachs, Jeffrey (2018) 'Ending America's war of choice in the Middle East'. *Horizons: Journal of International Relations and Sustainable Development*. Spring edition.

85. Sachs, Jeffrey (2018) *Killer Politicians*. Project Syndicate, 24 October. And in Sorokin, Pitirim and Lunden, Walter (1959) *Power and Morality: Who Shall Guard the Guardians?*, Boston, MA: Porter Serjeant Publishers.

86. Hersh, Seymour (2018) *Reporter: A Memoir*. New York: Knopf.

Chapter 5

1. Paine, Thomas (1796) 'The Age of Reason, ch 1', in Conway, Moncure Daniel (ed), *The Writings of Thomas Paine*. New York: G.P. Putnam's Sons.

2. Younge, Gary (2017) 'We should value people more than money', *Guardian Weekly*. 20 October. p 19.

3. Wordsworth, William, 'Humanity', in Rhys, Ernest (ed) (1913) *The Shorter Poems of William Wordsworth*. London: Dent & Sons. p 505.

4. Rees, Stuart (1991) *Achieving Power: Practice and Policy in Social Welfare*. Sydney: Allen & Unwin.

5. Solnit, Rebecca (2017) 'Weinstein's fall is a cue to rethink masculinity', *Guardian Weekly*. 20 October. p 18.

6. Stafford, William (1996) 'Poetry', in *Even In Quiet Places*. Idaho: Confluence Press. p 25.

7. Brecht, Bertolt 'The Bread of the People', in Willett, J. and Manheim, R. (eds) (2000) *Bertolt Brecht, Poems 1913–1956*. London: Methuen. p 435.

8. Rees, Stuart (1991) *Achieving Power: Practice and Policy in Social Welfare*. Sydney: Allen & Unwin.

9. Falk, Richard (2017) *Palestine's Horizon: Toward a Just Peace*. London: Pluto Press. p 37.

10. Donne, John 'No Man Is an Island', in Chernaik, J., Benson G. and Herbert, C. (eds) (2007) *Poems on the Underground*. London: Weidenfeld & Nicolson. p 288.

11. Walker, Kath (1981) *My People*. Milton, Queensland: Jacaranda Press.

12. Angelou, Maya (1994) *The Complete Collected Poems of Maya Angelou*. New York: Random House. pp 224–5.

13. Tutu, Desmond (1999) *No Future without Forgiveness*. London: Random House.

14. Klein, Naomi (2014) *This Changes Everything: Capitalism vs. the Climate*. London: Allen Lane. p 462.

15. In Reiman, Donald and Powers, Sharon (eds) (1997) *Shelley's Poetry and Prose*. New York: W.W. Norton. pp 301–10.

16. Rees, Stuart (2003) *Passion for Peace: Exercising Power Creatively*. Sydney: UNSW Press.

17. McCurry, Justin (2015) 'The man who survived Hiroshima', *Guardian*. 4 August.
18. Thakur, Ramesh (2017) 'Instead of congratulating ICAN on its Nobel Peace Prize, Australia is resisting efforts to ban the bomb', *The Conversation*. 14 December.
19. ICAN representatives. *The 2017 Nobel Lecture*. Nobel Institute: Oslo. December.
20. (a) Roger Waters, personal approval; (b) Roger Waters, personal communication.
21. Rees, Stuart (2017) 'A symphony of life: rescuing refugees by recovering our humanity', *New Matilda*. 8 July.
22. Seeger, Pete (1961), with approval December 2019 from Universal Music Publishing Group.
23. Millett, Kate (1995) *The Politics of Cruelty*. London: Penguin Books. pp 27–8.
24. Zuboff, Shoshana (2019) *The Age of Surveillance Capitalism*. London: Profile Books.
25. Brophy, David (2018) 'The book Xi Jinping wants you to read for all the wrong reasons', *Sydney Morning Herald*. 28 February. p 23.
26. Brophy, David (2018) 'China's Uyghur repression', *Jacobin*. 31 May.
27. Andrew-Gee, E. (2018) 'Your smart phone is making you stupid, anti-social and unhealthy, so why can't you put it down?', *Globe and Mail*. 6 January.
28. Harris, John (2018) 'Silicon valley is eating your soul', *Guardian Weekly*. 5 January.
29. Harris, John (2018) 'Silicon valley is eating your soul', *Guardian Weekly*. 5 January.
30. Lewis, Tim (2018) 'Arundhati Roy: "The point of the writer is to be unpopular"', *Observer Interview*. 17 June. pp 20–4.
31. Murray, Les (1987) 'Equanimity', in *New Oxford Book of Australian Verse*. Melbourne: Oxford University Press. pp 289–90.
32. Stafford, William (1996) 'You Reading This Stop', in *Even In Quiet Places*. Idaho: Confluence Press. p 100.
33. MacLean, Nancy (2017) *Democracy in Chains: The Deep History of the Radical Right's Stealth Plan for America*. New York: Random House.
34. Judt, Tony (2009) 'What is living and what is dead in social democracy?', *New York Review of Books*. 17 December. And in Judt, Tony (2010) *Ill Fares The Land*. New York: Penguin.
35. See Keynes, John Maynard (1931) 'The economic possibilities for our grandchildren', in Keynes, J.M. *Essays in Persuasion*. London: Macmillan. pp 358–73.

36. Spiritual Activism for a New Bottom Line, personal communication, Rabbi Michael Lerner, 24 December 2017. And in Lerner, Michael (2017) 'Trump's evil policies, Democrats aligning with the Deep State, and the Left in shaming and blaming', *Tikkun*. Vol 32. No 3. pp 4–7.

37. Mason, Paul (2015) *PostCapitalism: A Guide to Our Future*. London: Penguin. pp 563–4.

38. Marmot, Michael (2016) *Boyer Lectures: Fair Australia: Social Justice and the Health Gap*. Sydney: Australian Broadcasting Corporation.

39. Piketty, Thomas (2014) *Capital in the Twenty First Century*. Cambridge, MA: The Belknap Press of Harvard University Press. Piketty, Thomas (2016) 'What does it mean to be free?' and 'Spreading the democratic revolution to the rest of Europe', in Piketty, Thomas, *Chronicles on Our Troubled Times*. London: Viking. pp 127–30 and 152–5.

40. Galbraith, Kenneth (1984) *The Affluent Society*. New York: Houghton Mifflin. 4th edition revised.

41. Terrill, Ross (1973) *R.H. Tawney and His Times: Socialism as Fellowship*. New York: Harvard University Press.

42. MacIntyre, Alasdair (1984) *After Virtue: A Study in Moral Theory*. Indiana: University of Notre Dame Press.

43. Krieger, David (2017) 'True to Himself', in *Portraits, Peacemakers, Warmongers and People Between*. Santa Barbara, CA: Nuclear Age Peace Foundation. pp 62–3.

44. Menchu Tum, Rigoberta (2000) 'The role of Indigenous people in a democratic Guatemala', in Hopkins, J. (ed) *The Art of Peace*. New York: Snow Lion Publications. pp 78–86.

45. Muller, B. (2000) 'The international campaign to ban landmines', in Hopkins, J. (ed) *The Art of Peace*. New York: Snow Lion Publications. pp 177–87.

46. Williams, Betty (2000) 'Children's rights: the need to create havens for children of war', in Hopkins, J. (ed) *The Art of Peace*. New York: Snow Lion Publications. pp 51–60.

47. Foulcher, Keith (1978) *Taking Poetry to the People: Pamphlet Penyair Poet 1977*. Jakarta: Burung Merak Press.

48. Foulcher, Keith (1978) *Taking Poetry to the People: Pamphlet Penyair Poet 1977*. Jakarta: Burung Merak Press.

49. Piper, Suzan (2010) *Remembering Rendra*. Jakarta: Burung Merak Press.

50. See Phillips, Tom (2017) 'Liu Xiaobo, Nobel Laureate and political prisoner dies at 61 in Chinese custody', *Guardian*. 14 July.

51. Rees, Stuart (2014) 'The Empty Chair', in Rees, Stuart, *A Will To Live*. Port Adelaide: Ginninderra Press. p 198.

52. Baynes, Chris (2018) 'Iran says it has ended anti-government protests and blames US, Israel and Saudi Arabia for unrest', *Independent*. 7 January. Habibi, Nader (2018) 'Why Iran's protests matter this time', *The Conversation*. 8 January.

53. Centre for Human Rights in Iran. 5 January 2018 and 26 January 2018.

54. Free Tibet Website (2013) 24 December.

55. Details of the murder of Hevrin Xelef broadcast by ABC's Foreign Correspondent, 10 March 2020.

56. Wright, Judith (1994) 'The Flame Tree', in *Collected Poems*. Sydney: Angus & Robertson. p 9.

57. Milosz, Czeslaw (1995) 'This World', in *Facing the River*. Manchester: Carcanet Press. p 58.

Chapter 6

1. Zinn, Howard (1994) from the documentary film of the US historian's life, and in Zinn, Howard (1994) *You Can't Be Neutral on a Moving Train*. Boston, MA: Beacon Press. p 208.

2. Luther King, Martin Jr (1966) 'Non-violence: the only road to freedom', *Ebony*. pp 27–34.

3. Cornelius, Stella, personal message from the late peace campaigner and founder of Australia's Conflict Resolution Network.

4. Hussein, Zeid Ra'ad Al (2017) 'Is international human rights law under threat?', *Grotius Lecture*. Law Society: London. 26 June.

5. Clements, Kevin (2018) 'The politics of compassion in an age of ruthless power', *Global-E*. Vol 11. No 2. 9 January.

6. Friedersdorf, Conor (2012) 'Under Obama men killed by drones are presumed to be terrorists', *The Atlantic*. 29 May.

7. Ashrawi, Hanan (2018) 'PLO: Palestinian rights are not for sale', *Wafa*. 3 January.

8. Weiwei, Ai (2018) 'The refugee crisis isn't about refugees. It's about us', *Guardian*. 2 February. p 8.

9. Knight, Kelvin (ed) (1998) *The MacIntyre Reader*. London: Wiley. pp 227–36.

10. Loewenstein, Antony (2013) *Profits of Doom*. Melbourne: Melbourne University Press.

11. Loewenstein, Antony (2015) *Disaster Capitalism*. Melbourne: Melbourne University Press.

12. Jacobs, K., Perry, I. and MacGillvary, J. (2015) *The High Public Cost of Low Wages*. University of California Berkeley, Labor Centre. 12 April.

13. Meadway, James (2016) 'Taxpayers spend £11bn to top up low wages paid by UK companies', *Guardian*. 20 April.

14. Moulds, Josephine (2017) 'Child labour in the fashion supply chain', *Guardian*. 22 May.

15. Fair Wear Foundation (2015) *Country Study of Bangladesh*, and (2016) *Country Study of India*.

16. Phillpott, Siôn (2016) '10 companies that still use child labour', *Company Culture*. 10 October.

17. Phillpott, Siôn (2016) '10 companies that still use child labour', *Company Culture*. 10 October.

18. UNICEF (2014) *Hidden in Plain Sight: A Statistical Analysis of Violence Against Children*.

19. Report from the Commission to the European Parliament and the Council (2016) *First Report of the Progress Made in the Fight Against Trafficking in Human Beings*.

20. Markey, P. (2016) 'In Iraq, Nigeria and now Turkey, child bombers strike', *Reuters World News*. 22 August. Al Jazeera English (2017) *UNICEF* 'Boko Haram use of child bombers soars'. 23 August.

21. UNHCR (2018) *Children on the Run*.

22. Hartung, William (2016) 'There's no business like the arms business', *Huffington Post*. 26 July.

23. Calio, Vince and Hess, Alexander (2014) 'Here are the 5 companies making a killing off wars around the world', *Time Magazine*. 14 March.

24. Chan, Gabrielle (2017) 'Pyne wants Australia to be major arms dealer but vows not to export weapons "willy nilly"', *Guardian*. 17 July.

25. Calio, Vince and Hess, Alexander (2014) 'Here are the 5 companies making a killing off wars around the world', *Time Magazine*. 14 March.

26. Whyte, David (2007) 'The crimes of neoliberal rule in occupied Iraq', *British Journal of Criminology*. Vol 47. No 2. 1 March.

27. Animals International (2017) 'For a kinder world'.

28. Animals International (2017) 'For a kinder world'.

29. Press Association (2015) 'Cruelty to pets is rising and disturbingly inventive'. 22 April.

30. Agerholm, Harriet (2017) 'RSPCA reports a 340% increase in animal cruelty on Snapchat', *Independent*. 14 October.

31. Animalaid.org.uk (2016) *The Trouble with Horse Racing*. September.

32. Barnett, Antony (2006) 'The slaughtered horses that shame our racing', *Guardian*. 2 October.

33. *Animals Australia* (2016) 'Animal liberation Queensland investigation'. 10 August.

34. Campbell, M.L.H. (2013) Editorial. *Equine Veterinary Education*. 10 November. pp 489–92.

35. Keane, Bernard (2014) 'Yes I hate the Cup – and for damn good reason', *Crikey*. 4 November.

36. Schipp, Debbie (2018) 'This is bulls★★t': horror footage shows cruel sheep export deaths, sparks inquiry', *News.com.au*. 6 April.

37. Wahlquist, Calla (2018) 'Live exports could be dramatically reduced if animal cruelty case succeeds', *Guardian*. 17 April.

38. Cameron, James (2018) 'Putin just bragged about Russia's nuclear weapons. Here's the real story', *Washington Post*. 5 March.

39. Kube, Courtney, Welker, Kristen, Lee, Carol E. and Guthrie, Savannah (2017) 'Trump wanted tenfold increase in nuclear arsenal, surprising military', *NBC News*. 11 October. Mizokami, Kyle (2017) 'A tenfold increase in nukes would be a $15 trillion waste of time', *Popular Mechanics*. 11 October.

40. Kaplan, S. (2018) 'Trump floats idea of a "space force"', *Washington Post*. 13 March.

41. Borger, Julian (2018) 'US and Russian nuclear arsenals set to be unchecked for first time since 1972', *Guardian*. 18 April.

42. White, R.S. (2008) *Pacifism in English Literature: Minstrels of Peace*. London: Palgrave Macmillan. p 215. From Tolstoy, Leo (1930) *What Is Art?*, trans. Aylmer Maude. London: Oxford University Press.

43. Yeats, W.B., 'Letter to a Friend Whose Work Has Come to Nothing', in Poetry Foundation (1989) *The Collected Poems of W.B. Yeats*.

44. Yeats, W.B., 'Meditations in a Time of Civil War', *Yeats Annual No 18*; and in Burt, S. (2016) 'Reading Yeats in the age of Trump', *Boston Review*. 29 November.

45. White, R.S. (2008) *Pacifism in English Literature: Minstrels of Peace*. London: Palgrave Macmillan. pp 254–5.

46. Angelou, Maya (1995) *A Brave and Startling Truth*. New York: Random House.

47. Sabawi, Samah (2019) personal note converting prose into a poem 'We Will Cultivate Hope'.

48. *The Saturday Paper* (2018) Editorial: 'Waving the white flag'. 17 March. p 14.

49. Levertov, Denise (1987) *Breathing the Water*. New York: New Directions. p 40.
50. Webb, Daniel, cited in Human Rights Law Centre (2018) 'Turnbull government promises United Nations to respect all human rights findings', *News*. 9 March.
51. Levertov, Denise (2001) 'What It Could Be', in *Poems 1972–1982*. New York: New Directions. pp 248–9.
52. MacIntyre, Alasdair (1984) *After Virtue: A Study in Moral Theory*. Indiana: University of Notre Dame Press. p 191.
53. Gitau, Lydia (2018) *Trauma-Sensitivity and Peacebuilding*. Berlin: Springer International Publishing. p 91.
54. Moore, Marianne (1994) 'Blessed Is the Man', in *Complete Poems*. London: Penguin Books. p 175.
55. Levertov, Denise (2001) 'About Political Action in Which Each Individual Acts from the Heart', in *Poems 1972–1982*. New York: New Directions. p 247.
56. von Meding, Jason (2017) 'Agent Orange, exposed: how US chemical warfare in Vietnam unleashed a slow-moving disaster', *The Conversation*. 4 October.
57. Heard, Linda (2018) 'Israel sniggers at a cowardly world', *Gulf News*. 2 April.
58. Pasternak, Boris, 'The Nobel Prize', in (2008) *Selected Poetry of Boris Pasternak*. Amazon sources.

Chapter 7
1. Levi, Primo, 'Almanac', in Forbes, Peter (ed) (1999) *Scanning the Century: The Penguin Book of the Twentieth Century in Poetry*. Bury St Edmunds: Viking. p 252.
2. Ife, Jim (2019) personal observation from the author of several books on human rights.

Chapter 8
1. Snowden, Edward (2019) *Permanent Record*. London: Macmillan. p 296.
2. Arendt, Hannah (2004) *The Origins of Totalitarianism*. New York: Schocken.
3. Temelkuran, Ece (2019) *How to Lose A Country. Seven Steps from Democracy to Dictatorship*. London: Fourth Estate. p 10.
4. Yeats, W.B., 'The Second Coming', in Forbes, Peter (ed) (2019) *Scanning the Century: The Penguin Book of the Twentieth Century in Poetry*. Bury St Edmunds: Viking. pp 54–5.
5. Mason, Paul (2019) *Clear Bright Future*. London: Penguin. p 257.

6. Zuboff, Shoshana (2019) *The Age of Surveillance Capitalism: The Fight for a Human Future at the New Frontier of Power*. London: Profile Books. pp 388–94.

7. Camilleri, Joseph (2019) 'China policy drowning in empty rhetoric – time for an informed public debate', in *Pearls and Irritations*. 20 August.

8. Darwish, Mahmoud (2009) 'If We Want To', in *A River Dies of Thirst*. New York: Archipelago.

9. (a) Falk, Richard (2013) *Re-Imagining Humane Global Governance*. London: Routledge. (b) Falk, Richard (1995) *On Humane Governance*. Pittsburgh: University of Pennsylvania Press.

10. Zuboff, Shoshana (2019) *The Age of Surveillance Capitalism: The Fight for a Human Future at the New Frontier of Power*. London: Profile Books. p 387.

11. Herro, Annie (2014) *UN Emergency Peace Service and the Responsibility to Protect*. London: Routledge.

12. Rees, Stuart (2019) 'Australia's authoritarian future? CPAC and the High Court', *Pearls and Irritations*. 16 August.

13. Fernandes, Clinton (2019) *What Uncle Sam Wants*. Sydney: Palgrave Macmillan.

14. Rees, Stuart and Rodley, Gordon (eds) (1995) *The Human Costs of Managerialism Advocating the Recovery of Humanity*. Sydney: Pluto Press.

15. Connell, Raewyn (2019) *The Good University*. Melbourne: Monash University Publishing.

16. These Shakespearean insights are provided by Bob White, Professor of Literature, University of Western Australia.

17. Lyons, Kate (2019) 'Former Tuvalu PM says he was "stunned" by Scott Morrison's behaviour at Pacific Islands Forum', *Guardian*. 23 October.

18. Zinn, Howard (2003) *A People's History of the United States*. New York: Harper and Row.

19. Lichtenstein, Alfred (1913) 'Prophecy', in Forbes, Peter (ed) (1999) *Scanning the Century: The Penguin Book of the Twentieth Century in Poetry*. Bury St Edmunds: Viking. p 11.

20. Auden, W.H., 'September 1, 1939', in Forbes, Peter (ed) (1999) *Scanning the Century: The Penguin Book of the Twentieth Century in Poetry*. Bury St Edmunds: Viking. p 76.

21. Rees, Stuart (2014) 'Ninety Plus Campaigner', in *A Will To Live*. Canberra: Ginninderra Press. p 38.

Select bibliography

Al Jazeera English (2017) 'Boko Haram use of child bombers soars', 23 August.

Amnesty International (2009) *Troubled Waters: Palestinians Denied Fair Access to Water*. London: Amnesty International Publications.

Anderson, David (2005) *Histories of the Hanged: Britain's Dirty War in Kenya*. London: Weidenfeld & Nicolson.

Angelou, Maya (1994) *The Complete Collected Poems of Maya Angelou*. New York: Random House.

Arendt, Hannah (1963) *Eichmann in Jerusalem*. New York: Viking Press.

Arendt, Hannah (2017) *The Origins of Totalitarianism*. London: Penguin Books.

Ashrawi, Hanan (1995) *This Side of Peace*. London: Simon & Schuster.

Ashrawi, Hanan (2014) 'Is a boycott of Israel just?', *New York Times*. 18 February.

Ashrawi, Hanan (2017) 'Trump is making a huge mistake on Jerusalem', *New York Times*. 7 December.

Barns, Greg (2019) *Rise of the Right*. Sydney: Hardie Grant.

Beech, Hannah (2017) 'Across Myanmar, denial of ethnic cleansing and loathing of Rohingya', *New York Times*. 24 October.

Beit-Hallahmi, Benjamin (1987) *The Israel Connection*. New York: Pantheon Books.

Bennett, Caroline (2017) 'Violent politics and the disintegration of democracy in Cambodia', *The Conversation*. 11 September.

Blanchard, Lynda-ann and Middleton, Hanna (eds) (2015) *Conversations in Peace*. University of Sydney Press.

Blumenthal, Max (2013) *Goliath: Life and Loathing in Greater Israel*. New York: Nation Books.

Blumenthal, Max (2015) *The 51 Day War: Ruin and Resistance in Gaza*. New York: Verso.

Brecht, Bertolt (2000) *Bertolt Brecht: Poems 1913–1956*. Edited by Willett, J. and Manheim, R. London: Methuen.

Brophy, David (2016) *Uyghur Nation, Reform and Revolution on the Russia/China Frontier*. Cambridge, MA: Harvard University Press.

Browder, Bill (2016) *Red Notice: How I Became Putin's No 1 Enemy*. London: Corgi Books.

Brull, Michael (2017) 'The war in Yemen is turning to genocide, and Australia is quietly supporting it', *New Matilda*, 19 March.

Brull, Michael (2017) 'The cover up of arms sales to Saudi Arabia', *New Matilda*, 1 December.

Brull, Michael (2018) 'The Left got it right on Iraq, but that's pretty small comfort', *New Matilda*, 26 March.

B'Tselem (2014) *Human Rights in the Occupied Territories: 2014 Annual Report*. Jerusalem, January.

B'Tselem (2017) *House Demolitions as Punishment*. Jerusalem: Israeli Information Centre for Human Rights in Occupied Territories, 29 June.

Burke, Anthony (2001) *In Fear of Security: Australia's Invasion Anxiety*. Sydney: Pluto Press Australia.

Button, James (2018) 'Angels or arrogant gods: Dutton, immigration and the triumph of border protection', *The Monthly*. February.

Cahill, Damien, Edwards, Lindy and Stilwell, Frank (eds) (2012) *Neoliberalism: Beyond the Free Market*. Gloucester, UK: Edward Elgar.

Camilleri, Joseph and Falk, Jim (1992) *The End of Sovereignty? The Politics of a Shrinking and Fragmenting World*. Cheltenham: Edward Elgar.

Camilleri, Joseph and Falk, Jim (2009) *Worlds in Transition: Evolving Governance Across a Stressed Planet*. Cheltenham: Edward Elgar.

Caputi, Ross, Hil, Richard and Mulhearn, Donna (2019) *The Sacking of Fallujah, A People's History*. Amherst and Boston: University of Massachusetts Press.

Chomsky, Noam (1967) 'The responsibility of intellectuals', in *American Power and the New Mandarins*. New York: Random House.

Chomsky, Noam (2001) *9/11 Was there an Alternative?*, Perth: UWA Press.

Chomsky, Noam (2010) *Hope and Prospects*. Victoria Australia: Hamish Hamilton.

Clements, Kevin (2018) 'Politics of compassion in an age of ruthless power', *Public Imagination*. Vol 11. No 2. 9 January.

Cockburn, Patrick (2018) 'The war in five sieges', *London Review of Books*. Vol 40. No 14. 19 July.

Collier, Paul (2009) *Wars, Guns and Votes*. London: The Bodley Head.

Connell, Raewyn (2019) *The Good University*. Melbourne: Monash University Press.

Cook, Catherine, Hanieh, Adam and Kay, Adah (2004) *Stolen Youth, The Politics of Israel's Detention of Palestinian Children*. London: Pluto Press.

Darweish, Marwan and Rigby, Andrew (2015) *Popular Protest in Palestine: The Uncertain Future of Unarmed Resistance*. London: Pluto Press.

Dikötter, Frank (2004) *Mao's Great Famine: The Story of China's Most Devastating Catastrophe*. London: Bloomsbury.

Elkins, Caroline (2016) *Britain's Gulag: The Brutal End of Empire in Kenya*. London: Jonathan Cape.

Elliott, Liz (2017) *A New Way Now: How We Can Afford a Happier Future and Can't Afford Not To*. Mullumbimby: Liz Elliott: newaynow.com.au.

Etcheson, Craig (2005) *After The Killing Fields: Lessons from the Cambodian Genocide*. New York, Greenwood.

Falk, Richard (1995) *On Humane Governance*. Pittsburgh, PA: University of Pennsylvania Press.

Falk, Richard (2013) *Re-Imagining Humane Global Governance*. London: Routledge.

Falk, Richard (2014) *Palestine: The Legitimacy of Hope*. Washington, DC: Just World Books.

Falk, Richard (2017) *Palestine's Horizon: Toward a Just Peace*. London: Pluto Press.

Fernandes, Clinton (ed) (2012) *Peace with Justice: Noam Chomsky in Australia*. Clayton, Victoria: Monash University Press.

Fernandes, Clinton (2018) *Island Off the Coast of Australia: Instruments of Statecraft in Australian Foreign Policy*. Melbourne: Monash University Press.

Fernandes, Clinton (2019) *What Uncle Sam Wants: U.S. Foreign Policy Objectives in Australia and Beyond*. Sydney: Palgrave Macmillan.

Forbes, Peter (ed) (1999) *Scanning the Century: The Penguin Book of the Twentieth Century in Poetry*. Bury St Edmunds: Viking.

Forché, Carolyn (ed) (1993) *Against Forgetting: Twentieth Century Poetry of Witness*. New York: W.W. Norton & Company.

Fromm, Erich (1994) *Escape from Freedom*. New York: Henry Holt and Company.

Gidla, Sujatha (2017) *Ants Among Elephants: An Untouchable Family and the Making of Modern India*. New York: Farrar, Straus and Giroux.

Gilbert, Kevin (1988) *Inside Black Australia*. Ringwood: Penguin Books.

Gitau, Lydia (2018) *Trauma-Sensitivity and Peace Building*. Berlin: Springer International Publishing.

Halper, Jeff (2015) *War Against the People*. London: Pluto Press.

Hamilton, Clive (2018) *Silent Invasion: China's Influence in Australia*. Sydney: Hardie Grant.

Hanley, Lynsey (2017) 'Look at Grenfell tower and see the terrible price of Britain's inequality', *Guardian*. 16 June.

Harari, Yuval (2018) *Sapiens, A Brief History of Humankind*. New York: Harper Collins.

Harding, Luke (2016) *A Very Expensive Poison*. London: Faber.

Havel, Václav (1979) *The Power of the Powerless*. London: St Martin's Press.

Herro, Annie (2014) *United Nations Peace Service and the Responsibility to Protect*. London: Routledge.

Hersh, Seymour (2015) 'The scene of the crime: a reporter's journey to Mai Lai and the secrets of the past', *New Yorker*. 20 March.

Hersh, Seymour (2018) *Reporter: A Memoir*. New York: Knopf.

Hessel, Stéphane (2011) *Be Outraged*. New York: Hachette Book Group.

Heywood-Smith, Paul (2014) *The Case for Palestine*. Adelaide: Wakefield Press.

Hicks, Celeste (2018) *The Trial of Hissène Habré*. London: Zed Books.

Hil, Richard (1995) *Selling Students Short*. Sydney: Allen & Unwin.

Hobbes, Thomas (1951) *Leviathan*. Oxford: Blackwell.

Human Rights Watch (1991) *Whatever Happened to Iraqi Kurds?* 11 March.

Human Rights Watch (1993) *Genocide in Iraq: The Anfal Campaign against the Kurds*. New York. July.

Human Rights Watch (2016) *Children Behind Bars: The Global Use of Detention of Children*.

Hussein, Zeid Ra'ad Al (2017) 'Is international human rights law under threat?', *Grotius Lecture*. London: Law Society. 4 September.

Ife, Jim (2001) *Human Rights and Social Work: Towards Rights Based Practice*. Cambridge: Cambridge University Press.

Ife, Jim (2009) *Human Rights from Below: Achieving Rights through Community Development*. Cambridge: Cambridge University Press.

Ikeda, Daisaku (2018) *Toward an Era of Human Rights: Building a People's Movement*. Tokyo: SGI International.

Ikeda, Daisaku and Inoue, Yasushi (1980) *Letters of Four Seasons*. Tokyo: Kodansha International.

Jensen, Derrick (2016) *The Myth of Human Supremacy*. New York: Seven Stories Press.

Johnson, Lissa (2018) 'Sick of dying: why the Skripal poisoning, foreign interference legislation and legality of US interventions are the business of health professionals', *New Matilda*. 20 April.

Judt, Tony (2009) 'What is living and what is dead in social democracy?', *New York Review of Books*. 17 December.

Judt, Tony (2010) *Ill Fares the Land*. New York: Penguin.

Keenan, Brian (1993) *An Evil Cradling*. London: Vintage.

Kevin, Tony (2004) *A Certain Maritime Incident: The Sinking of SIEV X*. Melbourne: Scribe.

Khalidi, Rashid (2014) *Brokers of Deceit: How the US has Undermined Peace in the Middle East*. Boston, MA: Beacon Press.

Khalidi, Rashid (2017) 'The United States was responsible for the 1982 massacre of Palestinians in Beirut', *The Nation*. 16 September.

Kirby, Michael and Biserko, Sonja (2013) *UN Inquiry into Human Rights in the Democratic People's Republic of Korea (DPRK)*. New York: United Nations. 21 March.

Klein, Naomi (2008) *The Shock Doctrine*. London: Penguin Books.

Klein, Naomi (2014) *This Changes Everything: Capitalism vs. the Climate*. London: Allen Lane.

Klein, Naomi (2017) *No Is Not Enough: Resisting Trump's Shock Politics and Winning the World We Need*. London: Allen Lane.

Klein, Naomi (2019) *On Fire: The (Burning) Case for a Green New Deal*. Melbourne: Penguin Books Australia.

Krugman, Paul (2009) 'How did economists get it so wrong?', *New York Times*. 6 September.

Krugman, Paul (2011) 'Oligarchy American style', *New York Times*. 4 November.

Levertov, Denise (2001) *Poems 1972–1982*. New York: New Directions.

Levy, Gideon (2010) 'The Jewish Republic of Israel', *Haaretz*. 10 October.

Levy, Gideon (2017) 'Only Israelis, not Palestinians are entitled to mourn their dead', *Haaretz*. 24 June.

Levy, Gideon (2017) 'And if Ahed Tamimi were your daughter', *Haaretz*. 31 December.

Levy, Gideon (2018) 'The Israel massacre forces', *Haaretz*. 1 April.

Lewis, Anthony (2008) 'Official American sadism', *New York Review of Books*. 25 September.

Loewenstein, Antony (2004) *My Israel Question*. Melbourne: Melbourne University Press.

Loewenstein, Antony (2013) *Profits of Doom: How Vulture Capitalism Is Swallowing the World*. Melbourne: Melbourne University Press.

Loewenstein, Antony (2015) *Disaster Capitalism*. Melbourne: Melbourne University Press.

Lynch, Jake and McGoldrick, Annabel (2005) *Peace Journalism*. Stroud, UK: Hawthorn Press.

Machiavelli, Niccolò (1992) *The Prince*. New York: Dover Publications.

MacIntyre, Alasdair (1984) *After Virtue: A Study in Moral Theory*. Notre Dame, IN: University of Notre Dame Press.

MacLean, Nancy (2017) *Democracy in Chains: The Deep History of the Radical Right's Stealth Plan for America*. New York: Penguin Putnam.

Manne, Robert (2016) 'How we came to be so cruel to asylum seekers', *The Conversation*. 26 October.

Manne, Robert (2018) *On Borrowed Time*. Melbourne: Black Inc.

Manning, Peter (2019) *Representing Palestine: Media and Journalism in Australia since World War I*. London: I.B. Tauris.

Mason, Paul (2015) *Post Capitalism: A Guide to Our Future*. London: Penguin.

Mason, Paul (2019) *Clear Bright Future: A Radical Defence of the Human Being*. London: Penguin.

Mayroz, Eyal (2019) *Reluctant Interveners: America's Failed Responses to Genocide, from Bosnia to Darfur*. New Brunswick: Rutgers University Press.

McCoy, David (2015) 'Re-engaging the health community around peace', *Lancet*. 31 October.

Milgram, Stanley (1974) *Obedience and Authority*. London: Tavistock.

Millett, Kate (1995) *The Politics of Cruelty*. London: Penguin Books.

Mitchell, Alex (2011) *Come the Revolution, A Memoir*. Sydney: New South Books.

Moore, Marianne (1994) *Complete Poems*. London: Penguin Books.

Mukerjee, Madhusree (2010) *Churchill's Secret War*. New York: Basic Books.

Nussbaum, Martha (2004) *Hiding from Humanity*. Princeton, NJ: Princeton University Press.

Nussbaum, Martha and Sen, Amartya (eds) (1993) *The Quality of Life*. New York: Oxford University Press.

Ondawame, Otto (2010) *One People, One Soul*. Adelaide: Crawford House Publishing.

Otterman, Michael (2007) *American Torture: From the Cold War to Abu Ghraib and Beyond*. Melbourne: Melbourne University Press.

Pappe, Ilan (2003) *The Ethnic Cleansing of Palestine*. Oxford: One World.

Pappe, Ilan (2010) *Out of the Frame: The Struggle for Academic Freedom in Israel*. London: Pluto Press.

Paul, Erik (2019) *Australia in the Expanding Global Crisis*. Melbourne: Palgrave Macmillan.

Pembroke, Michael (2018) *Korea: Where the American Century Began*. Melbourne: Hardie Grant Books.

Pierce, Charles (2014) 'The United States of Cruelty', *Esquire*. 25 June.

Piketty, Thomas (2014) *Capital in the Twenty-First Century*. Cambridge, MA: Harvard University Press.

Piketty, Thomas (2016) *Chronicles on Our Troubled Times*. London: Viking.

Pilger, John (1998) *Hidden Agendas*. London: Vintage.

Pilger, John (2016) *The New Rulers of the World*. London: Random House.

Polakow-Suransky, Sasha (2017) *Go Back to Where You Came From: The Backlash Against Immigration and the Fate of Western Democracy*. New York: Nation Books.

Rees, Stuart (1986) *A Brutal Game: Patients and the Doctors' Dispute*. Sydney: Angus and Robertson.

Rees, Stuart (1991) *Achieving Power: Practice and Policy in Social Welfare*. Sydney: Allen & Unwin.

Rees, Stuart (2003) *Passion for Peace: Exercising Power Creatively*. Sydney: UNSW Press.

Rees, Stuart (2004) *Tell Me the Truth about War*. Canberra: Ginninderra Press.

Rees, Stuart (2014) *A Will to Live*. Port Adelaide: Ginninderra Press.

Refugee Council of Australia (2016) *At What Cost? The True Cost of Australia's Refugee Policies*. 26 September.

Regan, Bernard (2017) *The Balfour Declaration, Empire, the Mandate and Resistance in Palestine*. London: Verso.

Report from the Commission to the European Parliament and the Council (2016) *Report on the Progress Made in the Fight against Trafficking in Human Beings*.

Reynolds, Henry (1990) *With the White People*. Ringwood: Penguin.

Reynolds, Henry (2016) *Unnecessary Wars*. Sydney: New South Books.

Rigby, Andrew (2001) *Justice and Reconciliation*. Boulder, CO: Lynne Rienner.

Rigby, Andrew (2010) *Palestinian Resistance and Nonviolence*. East Jerusalem: Passia.

Robertson, Geoffrey (2011) *Report of an Inquiry: The Massacre of Political Prisoners in Iran, 1988*. London: the Abdorrahman Boroumand Foundation.

Roy, Arundhati (2001) *The Algebra of Infinite Justice*. London: Flamingo.

Roy, Arundhati (2004) *Public Power in the Age of Empire*. New York: Seven Stories Press.

Roy, Sara (2007) *Failing Peace: Gaza and the Palestinian–Israeli Conflict*. London: Pluto Press.

Royal Commission into Aboriginal Deaths in Custody, 1987–1991. Canberra.

Said, Edward (1978) *Orientalism*. New York: Pantheon.

Said, Edward (2001) *Power, Politics and Culture*. New York: Pantheon.

Sand, Shlomo (2009) *The Invention of the Jewish People*. London: Verso.

Schell, Jonathan (2011) 'Cruel America', *The Nation*. 28 September.

Shiva, Vandana (2009) *Soil Not Oil: Climate Change, Peak Oil and Food Insecurity*. Melbourne: Spinifex Press.

Sharp, Gene (2005) *Waging Nonviolent Struggle: 20th Century Practice and 21st Century Potential*. Boston: Porter Sargent.

Singer, Peter (2009) *Animal Liberation: A New Ethics for Our Treatment of Animals*. London: Harper Collins.

Skidmore, Thomas (1988) *The Politics of Military Rule in Brazil, 1964–85*. London: Oxford University Press.

Snowden, Edward (2019) *Permanent Record*. London: Macmillan.

Solzhenitsyn, Alexander (1974) *The Gulag Archipelago*. London: Collins Fontana.

Stiglitz, Joseph (2010) *Freefall: America, Free Markets, and the Sinking of the World Economy*. New York: Norton.

Stiglitz, Joseph (2013) *The Price of Inequality*. London: Penguin Books.

Stilwell, Frank (2000) *Changing Track: A New Political Economic Direction for Australia*. Sydney: Pluto Press.

Stilwell, Frank (2019) *The Political Economy of Inequality*. Cambridge: Polity Press.

Temelkuram, Ece (2019) *How to Lose a Country: Seven Steps from Democracy to Dictatorship*. London: Basic Books.

Thakur, Ramesh (2017) 'Instead of congratulating ICAN on its Nobel Peace Prize, Australia is resisting efforts to ban the bomb', *The Conversation*. January.

Tharoor, Shashi (2017) *Inglorious Empire: What the British Did to India*. London: C. Hurst & Co.

The Economist (2017) 'Fewer Rivers to Cross: Mexico Becomes a Destination for Migrants'. 27 July.

Timerman, Jacobo (1981) *Prisoner Without a Name, Cell Without a Number*. New York: Alfred Knopf.

Tutu, Desmond (1999) *No Future Without Forgiveness*. London: Random House.

UNICEF Report (2014) *Hidden in Plain Sight: Statistical Analysis of Violence Against Children*. 4 September.

UNICEF Report (2017) *Falling through the Cracks: The Children of Yemen*. March.

Urbain, Olivier (2010) *Daisaku Ikeda's Philosophy of Peace, Dialogue, Transformation and Global Citizenship*. New York: I.B. Tauris.

Van Krieken, Robert (1991) *Children and the State: Social Control and the Formation of Australian Child Welfare*. Sydney: Allen & Unwin.

Walker, Kath (1970) *My People*. Milton, Queensland: The Jacaranda Press.

Welby, Justin (2018) *Reimagining Britain: Foundations for Hope*. London: Bloomsbury.

White, R.S. (2008) *Pacifism in English Literature: Minstrels of Peace*. New York: Palgrave Macmillan.

Zinn, Howard (2003) *A People's History of the United States*. New York: Harper and Row.

Zuboff, Shoshana (2019) *The Age of Surveillance Capitalism*. London: Profile Books.

Index

A

Abdullaev, Bobomurod 70
Aboriginal people 24–6, 90
    Garma Festival, Arnhemland 113
    incarceration 25, 147
    Mabo decision 96
    Stolen Generation 24–6
About Political Action in Which Each
    Individual Acts From the Heart
    148
Abu Ghraib 75, 89
abusive power 74–7, 111
Adonis (Ali Ahmad Sa'id) 37
adoptions, forced 27–8
Afghanistan
    drone strikes 132
    Taliban 38, 76, 89, 127, 132
    US bombing raids 38
Africa
    cruelty by collusion 100–101
    dictatorships 46, 66–7, 152
    sadism in 64–7
    ubuntu 113–14
Ai Weiwei 133
Akhmatova, Anna 15
Algeria 36–7, 98, 153
Ali, Muhammad 124
All One Race 113
Alleg, Henri 36
Amnesty International 35–6, 39–40, 53,
    83, 87, 103, 158
Angelou, Maya 113, 145
animals, cruelty to 91–3, 114, 139–41
Annan, Kofi 81
Apple 136
Arendt, Hannah 50, 163
Arkady, Ali 40
Armenian genocide 14
arms trade 99, 103–104, 105, 153–4
    corporations and 138–9
artificial intelligence (AI) 119–20
al-Assad, Bashar 39, 51, 158

Assange, Julian 169
Asylum 44
asylum seekers
    attitudes in Australia to 12, 28–9,
        52–4, 61–2, 99
    in Europe 86–7
    Manus Island detention centre 12,
        28, 62, 85–6, 147
    Nauru detention centre 12, 28, 54,
        61, 72, 85, 86, 103, 147
    security companies capturing and
        guarding 156
    see also immigration policies; refugees
Auden, W.H. 16, 172
Australia
    Aboriginal deaths in custody 25
    arms exports 99, 138
    attitudes to asylum seekers 12, 28–9,
        52–4, 61–2, 99
    Border Force Act 2015 62
    British children sent to 26–7, 91
    forced adoptions 27
    Garma Festival, Arnhemland 113
    High Court 41, 61, 96, 168
    horse-racing industry 140
    Mabo decision 96
    Manus Island detention centre 12,
        28, 62, 85–6, 147
    media criticism of Minister for
        Immigration 146
    Nauru detention centre 12, 28, 54,
        61, 72, 85, 86, 103, 147
    seat on UN Human Rights Council
        147
    settlement of refugees in Cambodia
        103
    stigmatizing of Aboriginal people
        24–6
    Stolen Generation 25–6
Australian Broadcasting Company (ABC)
    39
automaton behaviour 57–63

B

Badawi, Raif 12, 44
Balfour Declaration 94–5
banality of evil 31–2, 45, 49, 50–7
Banerji, Michaela 168
Bangladesh 12, 47, 136
al-Bashir, Omar 20
Bedouin people 88, 105
Beethoven, Ludwig van 117
Beit-Hallahmi, Benjamin 105
Belhaj, Abdel Hakim 101–102
belonging, interdependence and 112–14
Benn, Tony 49
Bibi, Asia 45
bin Laden, Osama 32–3
biological warfare 15
Blair, Tony 22, 102
blasphemy laws 45
Blessed Is the Man 148
Blumenthal, Max 56
Boko Haram 47, 137
Bon Secours Mother and Baby Home 90
Bosnia 19, 51
Boudchar, Fatima 101–102
Bouie, Jamelle 52
Bourj el-Barajneh refugee camp 34
A Brave and Startling Truth 145
Brazil 41, 100
Bread of the People 111
Breaking the Silence 75, 95
Brecht, Bertolt 38, 39, 82, 111
Browder, Bill 69, 84–5
Brown, Gordon 27, 32
B'Tselem 70–1, 88
bureaucracies, automaton behaviour of 57–63
Bush, George W. 32, 72

C

Cambodia 17, 55, 63, 103
Camilleri, Joseph 164
capital punishment 83
    see also execution
capitalism 118, 121
    inequity and 122, 166

privatization and 6, 122, 134–5, 155–6
    see also neoliberal economic policies
Catholic Church 26
Chad 66–7, 101
Chechnya 43, 68
child labour 135–6
    vulnerability to 136–7
children
    abuse in Iran 43–4
    Convention on the Rights of the Child 2
    crisis in Central America 137
    death penalty for 43–4, 60
    forced adoptions 27–8
    imprisonment of 59–61
    LRA abuse of 46
    poverty cycles 136–7
    removal of Aboriginal 25, 26, 85
    sent to Commonwealth countries from Britain 26–7, 91
    separated from parents at US border 12–13, 42, 59, 87
    street 83
    as suicide bombers 158
    torture in Syria 38–9
    trafficked into armed conflict 46, 137
    Yemeni 40, 99
Children of Our Age 50
Chile 41–2, 100
China
    animal cruelty 139
    Great Leap Forward 1, 16–17
    Liu Xiaobo 126
    rule in Tibet 127
    state executions 83
    surveillance and control 156, 163–4
    Tiananmen Square massacre 18–19
    Uighurs 118–19
Chomsky, Noam 23, 154
Christianity 31, 52
Christians
    fundamentalist 46, 52
    persecution of 14, 45, 152, 158
Churchill, Winston 16
climate change 163, 165, 170–1

collusion 99–106
Colombia 77–9
colonialism
    Balfour Declaration 94–5
    Mau Mau rebellions 17, 31–2
common denominator for cruelties
    156–9
compassion 114, 122, 123, 131, 143–4
concealment of cruelties 6–7, 99, 107,
    134, 149
    Katyn Forest murders 21, 22, 67, 69
    Potemkin 21, 22, 67
conditioned behaviour 57–63
Convention against Torture and other
    Cruel, Inhuman or Degrading
    Treatment or Punishment 2, 84
Cornelius, Stella 129
corporations 134–9
    arms trade 138–9
    child labour 135–6
    contracting out of state to huge 118
    paying poverty wages 135
courage to challenge cruelties 123–7,
    148, 149–50
Czech Republic 86
Czechoslovakia 57, 126, 166–7

D

Dalits 93–4
Darfur 19–20, 64
Darwish, Mahmoud 4, 33, 145, 164
Dawn Dissolves the Monsters 51
death penalty *see* execution
deception 94–9, 104, 107, 132
deliberate cruelty policies 82–90
democracy
    free-market ideology and erosion of
        73–4, 121
    humane governance and 165
    local, in action 161
denial 6–7, 21–2, 24, 99, 149, 157
    wars and 36–41
deregulation 73
The Dictators 74
discrimination 44, 58, 93–4, 98
    see also stigmatization

Disney 136
Doctors Without Borders 38
Dolor 62
Donne, John 112–13
Duterte, Rodrigo 55–6
Dutton, Peter 26, 28, 52, 54

E

Each Small Candle 116
East Timor 17–18
economic policies, free-market 6, 72–4,
    82, 97, 98, 121, 122, 130, 155–6
economy, an alternative 121–3
educational priorities 130, 145–50
efficiency 5–6, 154–5, 155–6
    automaton behaviour 57
    and civil war in Colombia 77–9
    managerialism and 169
    Universal Credit 97–8
Eichmann, Adolf 50
Elegy for the Time at Hand 37
Éluard, Paul 51
The Empty Chair 126
enabling cruelty, policies of 90–4
environmentalism 162, 163, 166, 171
Epitaph on a Tyrant 16
Equanimity 120
Estemirova, Natalia 68
ethnic cleansing 19, 38
    of Palestinians 88
    of Rohingyas 12, 39–40
European Court of Human Rights 2
European Union
    immigration policies 86–7, 117
    national anthem 117
    policy towards Israel and Palestinians
        34, 105
    silence on Yemen 149
    UK leaving 24, 58, 117, 133
execution 83–4
    children sentenced to 43–4, 60
    delays in 84
    by Hamas 35
    in Cambodia 17
    in Chile 41
    in Indonesia 152

execution (continued)
  in Iran 18, 43, 64, 84, 149
  in Iraq 75, 149
  in Myanmar 40
  in Russia 68
  in Saudi Arabia 83
  in Syria 156
  in US 32, 84
  under international law 83
  by ISIS 40
Extinction Rebellion 163

F

Falk, Richard 112, 165
FARC rebels 77, 78, 79
fascism 163, 164
  see also Nazi Germany
fear 6, 30, 35, 40, 64, 69, 74, 85, 141,
  163
  conquering 125, 149
  of the other 28, 29, 86, 87, 153
Fenton, James 18–19
The Flame Tree 127
floggings 43, 44, 60, 89
Forgotten Australians 26–7
France
  collusion with Habré 66, 101
  immigration and asylum laws 86
  North Africans in 98
  war in Algeria 36, 98, 153
Fromm, Erich 74
fundamentalism
  Christian 46, 52
  Islamic 18, 23, 43–5, 63, 64, 89

G

Galbraith, J.K. 6, 123
Gandhi, Mahatma 1, 115
GAP 136
Gardner, Joy 11
Garma Festival, Arnhemland 113
Gaza
  2009 invasion of 56
  British aid to 95
  Hamas rule in 35–6
  hope in 145, 165

March of Return protests 22, 149,
  157–8, 165
  normality 60
  Palestinian identity 164–5
  refugee camps for people fleeing
    34–5, 51
  siege of 12, 33–4, 88
Geneva Conventions 14, 131, 132
genocide 14–20
  Holocaust 15–16, 39, 50
  in Cambodia 55
  in Uganda 46
  of Iraqi Kurds 75
  of Rohingyas 12, 21, 39–40, 47,
    134, 144, 157, 159
Germany, Nazi 15–16, 39, 50, 71
Gettleman, Jeffrey 12, 40
Gillard, Julia 13, 27
global warming 170–1
governance, humane 165–7
Greece 86
Grenfell Tower 98
greyhound racing 140
Guantanamo Bay 71–2, 102
Guardian 27, 29, 43, 45, 102, 140
  Sustainability Report 135
Guatemala 83, 137
Guevara, Che 77
Gukurahundi massacre 65–6
Guterres, Antonio 129, 171

H

Habré, Hissène 66–7, 101
Haley, Nikki 132, 158
Hamas 35–6, 158
Harvest of Hate 46
Havel, Václav 57, 166–7
health 30, 71, 122, 126, 156
  Obamacare 72, 97
Hernández, Miguel 37
Hersh, Seymour 51, 76, 106
Hessel, Stéphane 21
Hibakusha 115, 142
Holland, Sekai 65
Holocaust 15–16, 39, 50
homeless people 30, 57, 88, 97

homophobia 42–3
horse-racing industry 140
Housman, A.E. 4
Human Family 113
human rights
    abuses in North Korea 41
    B'Tselem reporting on 70–1, 88
    of children in Iran 43–4
    education 130, 145–50
    erosion of 131–4
    redefining 167–8
    suing British government for abuses
        of 31
    terrorism and suppression of 42,
        131
    Universal Declaration of Human
        Rights 2, 21, 109, 131
Human Rights Law Centre 147
Human Rights Watch 35, 55, 59, 60,
    70, 75
humane governance 165–7
humanitarian alternatives to cruelties
    20–1, 109–128, 167–8, 171
    courage to challenge cruelties 123–7
    creative, non-destructive power
        110–12
    a different economy 121–3
    interdependence and belonging
        112–14
    non-violence 114–18
    technology 118–21
humanitarian law, rejections of 55–6,
    129–30, 132
Humanity 110
humanity, redefining 162–4
humour 169–70
Hungary 86
Hussein, Saddam 75

I

I Write This Pamphlet 125
ICAN (International Campaign to
    Abolish Nuclear Weapons) 116,
    141
identity, questions of 164–5
If I Had a Hammer 117–18

Ife, Jim 151
Immigrants in Our Own Land 29–30
immigration policies
    in Australia 12, 28–9, 52–4, 99
    in Europe 86–7, 117
    in UK 57–8
    in US 12–13, 29–30, 42, 59, 87
In Thai Binh (Peace) Province 75–6
India 16, 138, 155
    caste system 93–4
Indonesia
    bombing of Christian churches 158
    executions 83, 84
    floggings for sexual misconduct 43
    occupation of East Timor 17–18
    Rendra's poetry readings 125–6
    on the run from Kopassus 11–12
    treatment of Communist Party
        members 17
inequality
    government policies' contributing to
        5–6, 97–8
    reducing 121–3
interdependence and belonging 112–14
International Campaign to Abolish
        Nuclear Weapons (ICAN) 116,
        141
International Covenant on Civil and
        Political Rights 2, 83
International Criminal Court (ICC) 20,
        46, 55–6, 132
International Labor Organization (ILO)
        135–6
international law
    capital punishment under 83
    Duterte's view of 55–6
    flouting of 12, 18, 21, 28, 60, 70, 83
    Geneva Conventions 14, 131, 132
    International Criminal Court 20, 46,
        55–6, 132
    'legality' claims while breaking 60
    Responsibility to Protect rooted in
        166
    Special African Tribunal 66
    US disregard for 105, 132
internationalization, promotion of 171
Iran 18, 43–4, 64

courage of protesters in 126–7
executions 18, 43, 64, 84, 149
Iraq
    2003 invasion 22, 139
    Abu Ghraib 75, 89
    atrocities by ISIS and Iraqi forces
        40–1
    executions 75, 149
    Kurds in 43, 75
    trafficking of children into armed
        conflict 137
Ireland 90–1
ISIS 22, 37, 40, 89, 127, 137, 152–3
Islam
    extremism 22, 37, 40, 46, 152–3,
        158
    see also ISIS; Taliban
    fundamentalism 18, 23, 43–5, 63,
        64, 89
    see also Muslims
Islamophobia 29, 98
Israel
    2009 invasion of Gaza 56
    alliance with US 33, 88, 104, 105,
        132–3, 157–8
    arms sales 104, 105
    Breaking the Silence 75, 95
    collective punishments 70–1, 88
    destruction of Bedouin communities
        88, 105
    killings in Sabra and Shatila refugee
        camps 34–5, 51
    'legal' imprisonment of children 60–1
    Naqba 96
    opening of US embassy in Jerusalem
        157
    Palestinian prisoners' hunger strike
        13
    Patel's secret meetings in 95
    rejection of humanitarian law 56
    shooting of March of Return
        protesters 22, 149, 157–8, 165
    siege of Gaza 12, 33–4, 88
    West Bank occupation 33, 60, 88
    Western collusion with 104–105
Italy 24, 86

J

Jahalin Bedouin community 88, 105
James, Clive 94
Jandali, Malek 117
Japan 15, 115, 142
Johnson, Boris 95
Johnson, Eva 25
Jones, Alan 13
Judt, Tony 121
justice
    Australian High Court 41, 61, 96, 168
    'bread' of the people 111, 112
    courage and activism for 123–7
    in China 126
    in Iran 18, 43–4, 84
    in Philippines 55
    in Saudi Arabia 12, 44, 83, 89
    peace with 115, 117–18, 124, 167
    US administering of 29, 30, 33, 52,
        73, 84
    see also humanitarian law, rejections
        of; international law

K

Katyn Forest murders 21, 22, 67, 69
Keenan, Brian 63–4
Kenya
    Kakuma refugee camp 65, 148
    Mau Mau rebellions 17, 31–2
Keynes, John Maynard 121
Khashoggi, Jamal 12
Khlebnikov, Velimir 30
Killington, Jill 27–8
King, Martin Luther, Jr. 115, 125, 129
Klein, Naomi 114
Koje-do 89
Kony, Joseph 46–7
Korean war 15, 89–90
Krieger, David 124
Krugman, Paul 72–3, 73–4
Kurds 43, 75, 84, 127

L

language for humanity 161–72
    humane governance 165–7
    questions of identity 164–5

redefining human rights 167–8
redefining humanity 162–4
redefining politics 168–72
Lebanon 35, 51, 63
Leibowitz, Yeshayahu 56
Lerner, Michael 121–2
Lesbos 86
A Letter to My Mother 25
Levertov, Denise 75–6, 146, 147, 148
Levi, Primo 151
Levy, Gideon 61, 71
Libya 87, 101–102
Lichtenstein, Alfred 171
Litvinenko, Alexander 68–9
Liu Xiaobo 126
live-animal export trade 140–1
Loewenstein, Antony 134
Lord's Resistance Army (LRA) 46–7
lynchings of black Americans 52

M

Machiavelli, Niccolò 74
MacIntyre, Alasdair 123–4, 134, 148
MacLean, Nancy 121, 123
MacNeice, Louis 4, 58–9
Magdalene Laundry system 90–1
Magnitsky Act 2012 69
Magnitsky, Sergei 69, 84–5
Makanga, Espon 31
Makaratta 113
Making Peace 146
Malik, Kenan 87
Malik, Nesrine 42, 58
management consultant firms 156
managerialism 169
Mandelshtam, Osip 1
Manne, Robert 54
Manus Island 12, 28, 62, 85–6, 147
maras gangs 137
March of Return protests 22, 149,
    157–8, 165
Marmot, Sir Michael 122
Marton, Ruchama 75
The Mask of Anarchy 114–15
Mason, Paul 122, 163
mass murders 14–20

in Chad 66
in Philippines 55–6
in Zimbabwe 65–6
Mau Mau rebellions 30–1
by Syrian government 158
see also genocide
Mau Mau 17, 31–2
May, Theresa 58, 86, 97, 102
media 105–106, 146, 156, 165, 169, 170
medical treatment, refusal of 71, 126
Meditations in Time of Civil War 144
mental health 30, 85, 122, 156, 166
Mexican Americans 30
Mexico
    /US border 12–13, 29, 42, 59, 87,
        133
    refugee crisis 137
militarism 36, 37, 41, 60, 104, 143
military dictatorships 23, 41–2, 100, 152
Millennium Summit 167
Millett, Kate 83, 118
Milosz, Czeslaw 127–8
Mnangagwa, Emmerson 65, 66
Montaigne, Michel de 7
Moore, Marianne 148
mothers, unmarried 27–8, 90–1
Mugabe, Robert 65–6
Murray, Les 120
musical expression of non-violence
    116–18
Muslims
    Bosnian 19
    Rohingya 12, 21, 39–40, 47, 134,
        157, 159
    Sunni 40, 43, 84, 152–3
    see also Islam
MV Tampa 116
My Lai massacre 75–6
Myanmar 12, 21, 39–40, 47, 134, 157,
    159

N

nationalism 24, 42, 133, 158, 170
Nauru 12, 28, 54, 61, 72, 85, 86, 103,
    147
Navalny, Alexei 149–50

Nazi Germany 15–16, 39, 50, 71
Nemtsov, Boris 69
neoliberal economic policies 6, 72–4,
    82, 97, 98, 121, 122, 130, 155–6
Neruda, Pablo 74
New Matilda 28–9, 32, 105
New York Times 12, 38, 40, 72, 106
Nigeria 46, 64, 87, 137
    abduction of schoolgirls 47
Ninety Plus Campaigner 172
No Man Is an Island 112–13
Nobel Peace Prize 116, 124–5, 126,
    141–2, 150, 167
non-violence 114–18
North Korea 41, 65, 83, 89–90
Nuclear Non-Proliferation Treaty 1970
    115
nuclear weapons 115–16, 141–3
Nunucaal, Oodgeroo 90, 113

O

Obama, Barack 38, 132
Observer 27, 87
Ode to Joy 117
O'Hara, Ken 172
Ondawame, Otto 11–12
Owen, Wilfred 81

P

Pachamama 114
Paine, Tom 109
Pakistan 45
Palestine
    Balfour Declaration 94–5
    Bourj el-Barajneh refugee camp 34
    Hamas 35–6, 158
    Naqba 96
    Sabra and Shatila refugee camps
        34–5, 51
    West Bank occupation 33, 60, 88
    see also Gaza
Pasternak, Boris 150
Patel, Priti 95
Paz, Octavio 11
peace with justice 115, 117–18, 124, 167
Pembroke, Michael 15, 89–90

Philippines 55–6
Pianos for Peace 117
Pierce, Charles 72, 155
Piketty, Thomas 122–3
Pinochet, Augustus 41–2
poetry 1, 3, 130, 143–5
    see also individual poets/poems
Poetry 111
Poland 86
    Katyn Forest murders 21, 22, 67, 69
policy, cruelty as 81–108
    collusion 99–106
    deception 94–9
    deliberate cruelty 82–90
    enabling cruelty 90–4
    spawning of agendas 107–108
politics, redefining 168–72
Politkovskaya, Anna 68
populism 58, 163
Potemkin, Grigory 21, 22, 67
poverty
    Americans in 73
    corporate contributions to 135
    cycles 136–7
    in Colombia 78
    in UK 97–8
    inequalities and 5–6, 121–3
power
    abusive 74–7, 111
    multi-dimensional 110, 112
    non-destructive 110–12
    one-dimensional 45, 111
Prayer Before Birth 59
prisoners
    Aboriginal 25, 147
    of Abu Ghraib 75
    Argentinian 42
    awaiting death penalty 84
    biological warfare experiments on 15
    children 59–61
    hunger strike 13
    in Chad 66–7
    in Korean War 89–90
    torture and murder in Iran 18, 43,
        64, 84
    treatment in Russia 67–8
    US torture of 32, 71–2, 75, 102

Prophecy 171
The Protectors 90
Psalm 2 33
punishments
    collective 70–1, 88
    in response to religious rules 43, 44,
        45, 52, 60, 89
    international rules on use of 2
    see also capital punishment; execution;
        floggings; torture
Pussy Riot 68
Putin, Vladimir 67–8, 142

R

racism 15, 16, 52, 87, 95, 149
refugee camps 34–5, 51, 65, 88, 148,
    157
refugees 137, 153
    Cambodia paid to take 103
    children 137
    Palestinian 34–5, 51
    resilience of 148
    Syrian 34, 37
    see also asylum seekers; immigration
        policies
religious justifications for cruelty 23,
    42–7, 52, 60, 89
rendition 101–102
Rendra, W.S. 125–6
Republican Party 72–3, 97
Requiem 15
Responsibility to Protect 166
Robertson, Geoffrey 18
Roethke, Theodore 62
Rohingyas 12, 21, 39–40, 47, 134, 157,
    159
Roma people 24
Roy, Arundhati 119–20
Royal Society for the Prevention of
    Cruelty to Animals (RSPCA)
    92
Rudd, Kevin 26, 27
Ruddock, Philip 52–4
Russell, Bertrand 81, 149
Russia
    arms sales 104

    bombing of Syria 38–9
    homophobia 43
    nuclear weapons 142
    Potemkin 21, 22
    suppression of dissent 67–9, 84–5
    see also Soviet Union
Rwanda 19

S

Sabawi, Abdul 33
Sabawi, Samah 145
Sabra and Shatila refugee camps 34–5, 51
Sachs, Jeffrey 106
sadism 63–74
Santiago Baca, Jimmy 29–30
satire 162, 163, 169
Saturday Paper 146
Saudi Arabia
    deliberate cruelties 12, 44–5, 89
    election to UN bodies 96
    executions 83
    export of Australian arms to 99
    floggings 44, 60, 89
    -led coalition in Yemen 32, 40, 88,
        104
    treatment of women 23, 60, 96
Schell, Jonathan 32
Schiller, Friedrich 117
The Second Coming 163
security
    arguments and erosion of rights 42,
        60, 131, 133, 162–3
    companies 156
    humane interpretation of 166
Seeger, Pete 117–18
September 1, 1939 172
Sessions, Jeff 42, 51–2
sexual
    conduct 42–3
    motives for violence 24, 41
Shakespeare, William 169–70
Sharon, Ariel 35
Shelley, Percy Bysshe 114–15
Shostakovich, Dmitri 117
silence 20–1, 149
    breaking the 75, 148

Singer, Peter 91–2, 93
smartphones 119
Smith, Adam 121
Smith, Veronica 28
Snowden, Edward 162
social policies 72–3, 97–8, 154–5
    language of 155–6
Solnit, Rebecca 111
South Korea 89, 164
South Sudan 65, 148
Soviet Union
    forced famines 14–15
    former republics of 69–70
    Katyn Forest murders 21, 22, 67, 69
    secret police 21, 69, 75
    see also Russia
Soyinka, Wole 46
Special African Tribunal 66
Srebrenica 19, 51
Sri Lanka 152
Stafford, William 111, 120–1
Stalin, Joseph 14–15, 21
Statement from the Secretary of Defense 94
Statue of Liberty, New York 96–7
Stiglitz, Joseph 73
stigmatization 23, 24–8, 31, 152–3
Stockholm International Peace Research
    Institute (SIPRI) 138–9
Stolen Generation 25–6
Strategic Arms Reduction Treaty
    (START) 143
street children 83
Sudan 19–20, 64
Suppose I Make a Timepiece of Humanity 30
surveillance capitalism 118
Suu Kyi, Aung San 21, 157
Syrian civil war 37–8, 38–9, 153, 158
    refugees 34, 37
    siege of Ghouta 129–30
Szymborska, Wislawa 50

T

Tagore, Rabindranath 23, 166
Taliban 38, 76, 89, 127, 132
tam 2
Tamimi, Ahed 61

technology 118–21
Tell Me the Truth About War 99–100
terrorists
    Boko Haram 47, 137
    erosion of rights in war against 42,
        60, 131, 133, 162–3
    ISIS 22, 37, 40, 89, 127, 137, 152–3
    Taliban 38, 76, 89, 127, 132
    torture of suspected 24, 32, 71–2,
        102
Thailand 101, 134
Thanks to Stéphane 21
theory 4–7
This World 127–8
Thunberg, Greta 171
Thurlow, Setsuko 142
Tiananmen 18–19
Tibet 127
time frame, cruelty within a 151–2
To a Friend Whose Work Has Come to
        Nothing 144
To Those Born Later 39
torture
    collusion in 100, 102
    by Hamas 35–6
    in Algerian War 36
    in Argentina 42
    in Chad 66, 101
    in Chile 41
    in Gaza 35–6
    in Iran 18, 43, 64, 84
    in North Korea 89
    in Saudi Arabia 12, 44, 89
    in South American dictatorships 41,
        42
    in Syrian civil war 38–9
    by ISIS and Iraqi forces 40–1
    of Mau Mau 31
    psychological 46
    public approval of 55
    of terrorist suspects 24, 32, 71–2, 102
    of women in Brazil 41
Treaty on the Prohibition of Nuclear
        Weapons 115–16, 141
True to Himself 124
Trump, Donald 29, 30, 64, 87, 104,
        105, 117, 132, 133, 142–3

Turkey 14, 95, 129, 133, 158, 163
Tutu, Archbishop Desmond 113–14

U

ubuntu 113–14
Uganda 46–7
Uighurs 118–19
UNICEF 32, 59, 99, 136
United Kingdom (UK)
    adoptions of illegitimate children 27–8
    arms sales 103
    Balfour Declaration 94–5
    Brexit 24, 58, 117, 133
    brutalities in Kenya 17, 31–2
    children sent to Commonwealth
        countries 26–7, 91
    collusion in Gukurahundi massacres
        101
    collusion in torture and rendition
        101–103
    deportations 11, 58
    Grenfell Tower 98
    homeless people 97
    horse-racing industry 140
    Indian famine 16
    Intelligence and Security Committee
        (ISC) 102
    Investigative Powers Act 2016 131
    poverty wages 135
    Roma people 24
    Universal Credit 97–8
    Windrush scandal 57–8
United Nations (UN)
    Children's Human Rights
        Committee 43
    collusion with Israel 104–105
    Commission on the Status of Women
        96
    Committee Against Torture 89
    Convention against Torture and other
        Cruel, Inhuman or Degrading
        Treatment or Punishment 2, 84
    Convention on the Rights of the
        Child 2
    Emergency Peace Service (UNEPS)
        167

High Commission for Refugees
    (UNHCR) 137
High Commissioner for Human
    Rights 119, 131
Human Rights Council 24, 93, 96,
    132, 147
International Covenant on Civil and
    Political Rights 2
North Korea report 41
peace-building responsibilities 166–7
peace-keeping missions 167
Responsibility to Protect 166
Secretary General Guterres 129, 171
Security Council 105, 157, 166
Treaty on the Prohibition of Nuclear
    Weapons 115–16, 141
UNICEF 32, 59, 99, 136
Universal Declaration of Human
    Rights 2, 21, 109, 131
Yemen report 40
United States of America (US)
    Abu Ghraib 75
    administering of justice 29, 30, 33,
        52, 73, 84
    alliance with Israel 33, 88, 104, 105,
        132–3, 157–8
    arms sales 104, 138
    biological warfare 15
    bombing of Afghanistan 38
    collusion with Habré 101
    cooperation with Saudi Arabia in
        Yemen war 88, 104
    Department of Justice 29, 52
    disregard for international law 105,
        132
    Emergency Immigration Act 1921 87
    execution delays 84
    free-market ideology 97
    Guantanamo Bay 71–2, 102
    homeless people 30
    Humane Society 92
    Immigration Customs Enforcement
        (ICE) 29, 87
    immigration policies 12–13, 29–30,
        42, 59, 87
United States of America (US) (contd.)
    imprisonment of children 59

intervention in Colombia 78
Johnson-Reed Act 1924 87
killing of Bin Laden 32–3
lynchings of black Americans 52
Magnitsky Act 2012 69
My Lai massacre 75–6
nuclear policy under Trump
    142–3
Obamacare 72, 97
opening of embassy in Jerusalem
    157
Republican Party social policies
    72–3, 97
separating children and parents at
    Mexican border 12–13, 42, 59,
    87
Statue of Liberty 96–7
subsidy of low wages 135
Supreme Court 30
tax cuts 72, 73, 97, 135
torture of terrorist suspects 32, 71–2,
    75, 102
UK collusion on torture and
    rendition with 102–103
violence of government policies
    32–3
Universal Credit 97–8
Universal Declaration of Human Rights
    2, 21, 109, 131
University of California Berkeley 18,
    135
unmarried mothers 27–8, 90–1
untouchables 93–4
Uzbekistan 70

V

Vasefi, Saba 44
Vemula, Rohith 94
victims of cruelty 152–3
Vietnam 75–6, 139, 149
violence
    fascination with 23, 30–6
    non- 114–18
    sexual motives for 24, 41
    state-organized 65–6
    against women as legitimate 43

Violence 82

W

wages, low 135
walls 5, 133
    looking beyond 109, 170
    Trump's 29, 117, 133
Walmart 136
*Waltz Poem of Those in Love and
    Inseparable Forever* 37
war
    denial and 24, 36–41
    different types of 153–5
Waters, Roger 116–17
Weeping Woman 76
West Bank 33, 60, 88
West Papua 11–12, 13
What It Could Be 147
When Evil-Doing Comes Like Falling Rain
    38
WikiLeaks 169
Wilde, Oscar 109
Windrush scandal 57–8
Wordsworth, William 49, 110
Wright, Judith 49, 127

X

Xelef, Hevrin 127

Y

Yeats, W.B. 144, 163
Yemen war 32, 40, 88, 99, 103–104, 149
You Reading This Stop 120–1
Younge, Gary 64, 109
Yushenkov, Sergei 68

Z

Zimbabwe
    Gukurahundi massacres 101
    state-organized violence 65–6
Zinn, Howard 129, 171
Zionism 95, 96
Zuboff, Shoshana 118, 163, 165